Berkshire Stories

History • Nature • People • Conservation

Berkshire Stories

History • Nature • People • Conservation

Morgan Bulkeley, Sr.

Drawings by Morgan Bulkeley, Jr.

LINDISFARNE BOOKS

Text © 2004 Morgan Bulkeley, Sr.
Drawings © 2004 Morgan Bulkeley, Jr.

Published by Lindisfarne Books
400 Main Street, Great Barrington, MA 01230
www.lindisfarne.org

Library of Congress Data in Publication Data is available

10 9 8 7 6 5 4 3 2 1

Printed in the United States of America

Contents

Acknowledgements

I must thank Pete Miller, past editor of *The Berkshire Eagle,*
for giving me the opportunity to write the "About the Berkshires" column. I also wish to express my gratitude to its current editor, David Scribner, for granting permission to reprint
these essays, and to the following individuals: Jon Swan, who
had the original idea for this book and selected and arranged
the essays; Marianne Swan, who designed the preliminary layout; Keith Emerling who provided the photograph of the cover painting; Christopher Bamford for his editorial wisdom
and enthusiasm; Mary Giddens for typographic design and
final layout; and Eleanor Tillinghast, my daughter-in-law, for
the final proofreading and the photograph of my son and me.
I am particularly grateful to my son, Morgan, who provided all
the artwork and oversaw the production of this book. And
always to my wife, Barbara, who made our gardens bloom.

Foreword

LIFE WAS MAGICAL when I was a boy. I didn't know that having Poobah, our pet red fox, jumping from chair to couch chasing Cheerios was an unusual experience. People were always bringing small animals, and birds which had fallen out of nests, injured or orphaned, to my parents for treatment, for doll-bottle feedings or chopped mouse tartar until they could re-enter their wild world.

Boswell arrived at our house looking for all the world like a four-inch oblong of cotton with two raisins glued into the top. A neighbor had cut down a dead oak and found three barred owl chicks in a rotted hole. My dad would hold a dead mouse in front of the inscrutable fluff, whereupon a larger than expected pacman-like beak would yawn open and accept the mouse head. Silence. Calm. Then a sudden contortion of the cotton, like a seasoned "bar hand" tossing back a shot; a second toss, and all that was left was a stringy tail. One more lurch, and back to the pure white ball—no inkling left of the event. After two or three days, Bos would cough up a grape-sized ball of fur and bones, quite dry, the only sign of an extraordinarily efficient digestive system, necessary for a bird so small that it couldn't butcher its lunch.

Amelia and Orville generally sat on the valence at the north end of our living room. Flying squirrels always like to sprint to the highest place so they can increase their flight options, since they can only glide. One day, a friend entered the door at the south end of the room, in a summery, light dress. I'm not sure if her legs suggested trees to whichever squirrel, but after the rapid side-to-side head bobs to triangulate and judge the distance and a quick flight, our astonished—no, terrified—

friend began shrieking and clutching her dress to her thighs as the small, white-bellied offender scampered upward with tiny toenails.

Much of life in those days was a glowing green warmth of shucking peas and small farm tasks: chopping, splitting and stacking wood, cutting brush, throwing stones out of new-ploughed fields, hoeing, weeding, quartering and drying potatoes for seed, fixing fences, feeding the pigs and sheep, collecting chicken eggs, plucking and dressing turkeys, mowing, pruning, harvesting, and the startlingly frigid job of collecting maple sap on early days in March.

My mother's family, the Spoors (later changed to Spurr) were Dutch farmers who moved up onto the Taconic plateau (presently Mount Washington in Massachusetts) to escape the landlord's taxes in the Hudson Valley, in 1692.

My father, from a prominent political family in Connecticut, decided after college to spend a year living in a Thoreau-like cabin in the tiny town of Mount Washington. His winter baths were taken in holes chopped through the ice of Plantain Pond. At the time, the early 1940s, there were 32 residents in the town.

One day, walking with a sprained ankle and cane, my father happened to meet my mother riding her horse on a path near his cabin. Several years afterward, they were married in front of the big gilt mirror hanging at Pennyroyal Arms, the old Spurr farm and boarding house still standing on East Street in Mount Washington.

My parents lived with nature. They were curious and exact about its details, always excited about some newly noted pattern or oddity, always ready for a new season. A friend of mine was shocked one day at lunch when he mumbled "there's a hawk"—forks dropped, and the table cleared in a second, everyone rushing out for an ID.

Our food was almost exclusively what they raised, harvested, butchered, pickled, froze, or canned. I recall a day when I was four that my father was hiving a wild swarm of honey bees; he had worked with bees for so long that he no longer bothered to put on the usual head-net hat. The job required cutting a branch with a basketball-sized cluster of bees while standing on a ladder, then dropping the swarm onto a sheet with an empty adjacent hive. The branch broke, swung, hit the tree, exploded into an angry cloud which enveloped him. At the hospital, they found his pulse virtually stopped, but adrenaline brought him back.

Usually my father sat quietly at his desk in our little living room where my sister and I would be involved in some noisy game. He wrote with stoic focus. The essays included here are some of the more than 750 articles that he wrote for the *Berkshire Eagle* from 1960 to 1973.

After he became blind from glaucoma in the early 1970s, I had a hard time accepting that he couldn't continue to share his intimate wealth of knowledge, perception, and the philosophy earned from earth-bird life. The world seemed to be quickly moving in a different direction from his self-sufficient vision, toward the instant gratification of TV dinners, TV ads, disposable everything, speed, a world where observation and contemplation were overwhelmed by extraneous noise, external and internal. I pestered him to use a dictaphone. He quietly asserted that he loved to see the pencil lines move across the page, to study them, to erase and tweak them, to get the idea right. It sounded like a flower growing.

Today, some people accuse environmentalists of being anti-progress. One pundit recently asserted that "all ex-commies are now radical enviros," and that environmental decisions should be made on a "cost-effective" basis. This is, of course, exactly the kind of thinking that fills the Housatonic River with PCBs, the bald eagles with DDT, and human beings with thalidomide, asbestos, nicotine, etc. If one believes in a future for humanity, one could hardly do better than strive to pass on a world of natural beauty and health to our children: breathable air, fertile soil, and unpolluted water. How can anyone argue that these are not worth struggling to save?

This book talks about a world where the fate of nature, community, and humanity are inextricably interwoven, where there is respect for all life, and the earth's gifts are treasured because they are the very ground of our existence.

Morgan Bulkeley, Jr.
June 5, 2004

By Way of Introduction

MY FIRST ACQUAINTANCE with the Berkshires came at the age of fourteen in 1928, when small groups of Hotchkiss School boys, occasionally freed by surprise holidays, would take off in all directions like so
many hatching turtles.

The first of these days was a golden fall one and a group of us
stumbled on the inviting, curving road leading from Salisbury up to
Forge Pond, thence northward to Bear Mountain and Mount Everett. We added our initials to the old log watering tub, ate our sandwiches too early on top of the tumbling blast furnace, took a dip in
Forge Pond, and headed up the road with its grassy middle into the
unknown hills, eventually winding up on the stone pyramid marking Connecticut's highest point. From there we could survey the
mountains, valleys, and lakes that were to be scenes of future esca-
pades, the Bash Bish cut for cliff-climbing, Race and Mount Everett
for distance challenge, Twin Lakes for spring swimming, and the
Housatonic for some disastrous canoeing. The Berkshires had cut
their initials into us.

My next extended stay in the same hills came after college, where
I had made a term study of Emerson and Thoreau, which induced
me to live a postgraduate year in a small cabin on the wild shores of
Plantain Pond in the township of Mount Washington.

There I stayed the four seasons without spending more than a
hundred dollars; I incurred no bills, there being no electricity, running water, automobile, radio, nor even a clock. Necessity quickly
taught me such basic trades as wood chopping, carpentry, laundering,

cooking, and vegetable raising, and fringe benefits from willow basket weaving to lining bee trees.

Sometimes I would enjoy such neighborly pursuits as town meetings, ice cutting, sap gathering, haying, potato digging, or square dancing. Often my days were taken up with walking Berkshire back roads, woods, and fields up to 36 miles in a day, with no particular destination.

The realm of nature was mine. The wildcat left his round footprint in the snow outside my window. The sound of flying squirrels playing over my roof was like rain in the night. The drumming of the partridge was my sunrise gun. The minstrelsy of the hermit thrush sounded along the laurelled pond shores. And on a still, frosty night I could drift on the pond over the reflected stars, listening to the weird conversations of the owls. These memories stay along with many others. Then there ensued a few years of the insurance business which were enough to show I belonged on the farm.

At this time marriage brought me to the Berkshires for a stay that has lasted. Our family keeps a small farm in the town of Mount Washington among good neighbors. Here we have raised chickens, turkeys, and potatoes between the stones, with various writing projects for by-products. We have produced and preserved a good part of our food. In this day of mass-production farming we have witnessed with many others the dwindling numbers of subsistence farms that for generations were the foundation of our country.

We are glad to be part of that vestige; for where else can one see growing children swinging from birch tops, hesitant little fingers dipping into a hot sap pan, or a wife picking blueberries against a great white cloud on a mountain top? Here in spring the rich brown earth curls fall away behind the plow; in summer lush green rows of plants are combed by the cultivator, and in autumn potatoes string endlessly off the digger. Then all is buried in snow, and the fields are marked only by the tracks of deer, fox, and ski. The cycle is regular, yet never the same. It constantly invites the family to be a part of it.

So it is from this kind of base we shall write on "Our Berkshires" from time to time, taking subjects where they come, from Greylock to Mount Everett, from the Indians to spacemen (if the county produces any), from literary lights to kerosene lights, from natural history to plain history, and from strict fact to a higher truth, sometimes, if we are lucky.

Anyone have a farm to swap a little nearer town?

Morgan Bulkeley, Sr.

PART 1

Berkshire History

Two Calendars

Two days before New Year's a new fall of snow blanketed this little mountain town as though all old tracks, trees and landmarks were purposefully obliterated by a white brush and the whitened canvas was prepared for a new beginning. It was easy to visualize the deer moving silently or lying quietly in the deep woods, their coats flecked with the first, great, goose-feather flakes, making them once again spotted fawns, also ready for a new beginning.

It seems part of nature's method to disguise familiar permanence with slow or sudden renovation. This may be as gradual as the greening of a Berkshire spring, or it may be as sudden as awakening to a snowy world.

There was a time in the history of our hills 500 million years ago when the renovation took some 100 million years. It was the longest Berkshire blizzard on record and it piled up the white rock drift that is presently Monument Mountain and laid down crusts beneath the county that were never fully plumbed by a well-drilling attempt in Sheffield abandoned at 1,200 feet.

This great snowstorm took place during the Cambrian and Ordovician periods beneath a vast inland sea extending from Labrador to Central America. For eons little flakes of marine organisms, limey distillates, settled to the ocean floor. This accumulation of sediment thousands of feet deep became gradually cemented into thick layers of limestone. How ephemeral and Lilliputian our snowstorms by comparison! As we tear off another calendar page, all of nature's present manifestations seem thin as paper by comparison with these rocky documents thousands of feet thick.

The next layers upon the limestone were thick layers of mud washed out into shallow seas by slow rivers bearing away the eroding continent. Where layers of sandstone occur below and interspersed with the limestone, it is presumed the rivers were much faster and the continent much higher. In this manner the construction materials of our county were laid down.

Today's topography was elevated by a great crustal upheaval known as the Taconic Disturbance, occurring 400 million years ago on the geological calendar. This too may have taken eons, and the heat and pressure of the folding were sufficient to metamorphose the sedimentary rock, obliterating all fossil traces. Sandstones became quartzite, mud shales became the common Berkshire schist, and limestone became the much-quarried Berkshire marble. The latter has been commonly used within the county for dams, abutments, and foundations, as well as for grindstones, doorsteps, hearthstones, and gravestones. West Stockbridge furnished the marble for the New York City Hall; Lanesboro, the marble for the old Albany Capitol; and Lee, the marble for the extension to the nation's Capitol. Like Eskimos we have quarried our edifices from ancient snows.

The next great folding was the Appalachian Revolution, occurring some 200 million years ago as we flip another geological page. This convulsion disturbed the eroded remains of the Taconics and upheaved the towering Appalachians. Our hills are the rounded remains of both cataclysms.

As if this were not show enough, nature staged a further episode that ridiculously dwarfs our snowstorms. Four times in the last million years, great ice sheets several thousands of feet thick overrode parts of North America. One spectacular evidence of their steamrolling, bulldozing power may still be seen in the Richmond area. There seven boulder trains are strewn in a southerly direction from the ridges of their origin, the longest being nine miles with a maximum width of 500 feet. The boulders vary in size from 125 feet in circumference and 30 feet in height down to small fragments that nearly cover the ground in places.

The time element and the slow gigantic forces involved in the great geological calendar are almost as hard to comprehend as spatial time and distance in an expanding universe. Somehow it is more humanly comforting to throw away last year's calendar, put up the new calendar, and then go out and shovel the latest snowfall.

The new stratum of snow lay light as a down puff upon lawn, leafmold, earth, and rock. Under gray sky we shoveled our little paths and driveway, which would not leave as much mark upon the next summer as a worm left upon antediluvian shale.

All day it remained darkly overcast, perfectly setting the scene for what was to come. The painter had not tried all his ideas yet. The last color was still to be brushed, the shade to impart meaning, the lightest touch of all. Anyone indoors would have missed it entirely.

With nose in a snowbank we were suddenly aware of having quarried into rose quartz. The white clapboard house was the color of pink marble. The dark woods were invested with soft, glowing, red brilliance, and overhead the tinted clouds arched like a great abalone shell.

The pearl pink that unified everything lasted only a few moments, but it was a page as meaningful as the calendar of all the millennia.

Beaver Traders in Berkshire

Major Talcot's massacre and rout of 200 Indians at the fordway of the "Ausotunnoog River in the middle way betwixt Westfield and the Dutch river and Fort Albany" in August of 1616 is commonly taken as the beginning of white man's history in Berkshire County. As a matter of fact, it is far more likely that the first white men to set foot in the wilderness within the mountains were on peaceable trading terms with the Indians, that they were seeking to extend their trade in beaver skins, and that they were first French, second Dutch, and finally English. The early history of Albany and of Springfield leads to these conclusions.

Jean Allefonsce's fur traders from Saint Ange, France, coming south from the St. Lawrence, settled at Chescodonta in 1540 and began a stone chateau on Castle Island opposite the site of Albany. This was swept away by flood before completion, which may have prompted them to seek a more docile stream, for that same year, accompanied by a Jesuit father, they explored a long way up the Hoosic River, where the priest was said to have built Saint Antoine's chapel overlooking the valley, thus establishing the Catholic banner 80 years before the Pilgrims landed.

Whether this little band of fur traders, following the river in search of peltry, crossed the corner of what was to be Vermont and set foot in Williamstown remains pure speculation. It would have been a short step after all their travels. Certainly they had the time, since they remained in the Hoosac Valley for two years.

The first claims embracing Berkshire were more sweeping, if equally intangible. The English claim based on the offshore sailing of Cabot in 1497-8 between the 40th and 48th parallels of latitude resulted in the great patent of James I in 1606 and was extended to the Plymouth company within the same parallels "throughout the main land from sea to sea, provided the same or any part be not actually possessed or inhabited by any other Christian prince or state." The opposing Dutch claim was based on the sailing of Hudson in 1609 from the Delaware River to and up the Hudson, extended by Block a few years later to and up the Connecticut and along the Massachusetts coast to Nahant.

These original claims caused much wrangling, which in the case of the western Massachusetts boundary line was not finally settled until 1787, when Berkshire County was defined on the west and measured at 50 miles, 41 chains, and 79 links.

Meanwhile, the business of taking possession and extinguishing Indian claims commenced. In 1614 Fort Nassau, a fortified trading post, was built on the Hudson near the site of Albany. Jacob Eelkins, the Dutch commandant, established a lucrative fur trade and his scouting parties explored widely, cultivating friendly relations with the Indians. They may well have followed the Indian trails into Berkshire. In 1623 the Dutch West India Company built Fort Orange on the present site of Albany, and by 1630 patroon Van Rensselaer made the first purchase from the Indians of lands that eventually became a feudal manor extending 24 miles east of the Hudson into Berkshire. The quitrent for this entire tract, which by 1649 comprised 870,000 acres, was "50 bushels of good winter wheat." Settlement on the manor progressed, and before 1656 there was a community at Kinderhook. Shortly thereafter, Abraham Staats built his stone house that still stands at the mouth of Stockport creek. A 1657 record shows that he sent 4,200 beaver skins to New Amsterdam that year, and that at the same time he had "a considerable bowery."

The English also were eager about beavers. In 1635 William Pynchon and a few stouthearted followers established a "plantation at and over against Agaam," where the Westfield River joins the Connecticut at Springfield. He made the beaver trade of the upper Connecticut Valley his monopoly, trading textile and manufactured goods, sugar, molasses, and rum for furs, meat, grain, and wampum. Also he dealt in theology, which proved his undoing when the Puritan fathers detected "horrid heresies" in his book and badgered him back to England in 1651.

His son, Capt. John Pynchon, carried on the business some 50 years, branching westward into the hills for "wildcat, martin, woodshaws (fishers), and moose." He probably served as guide to the exploring party sent by the General Court of the Province of Massachusetts Bay in 1659 to investigate the western lands to the very shores of the Hudson. This first recorded probing of Berkshire initiated the long boundary dispute.

The biography of Henry Knox by Prof. North Callahan states without sources that in 1662 John Pynchon was said to be traveling from Springfield to Albany transporting trading goods to and from his partner in Albany, a Maj. Hawthorne, reportedly an ancestor of Nathaniel. Interestingly enough, Nathaniel, writing *The House of the Seven Gables* in the Berkshires almost 200 years later, chose the name Pynchon for the family name in his romance. Could he, with his deep genealogical interest, have known that these partners were two of the first white men to set foot in the county where he was writing the book?

Livingston Manor

In what we think of as a land of freedom, it is interesting to remember that the southwest townships of Berkshire were for nearly a century partly claimed and ruled by old-world feudalism, or settled by those avoiding it. The medieval history transposed to the Hudson Valley influenced our own. The feudal estates of Rensselaerwyk and Livingston Manor determined Berkshire's western boundary, and at the cost of a few lives.

Robert Livingston was born in Ancram, Scotland, the son of a clergyman who was driven to Holland by religious persecution. Well-schooled in English and Dutch, the young man set out in 1674 to find a fortune in the new world. He was soon conversing in gutterals with the Indians. Within a year, though only age twenty, he was made town clerk of Albany and secretary of Indian affairs, which office he held nearly fifty years. Other duties soon added were collector of excise and quit rents, clerk of the peace, and clerk of the Court of Common Pleas.

His obvious ability was rewarded by Governor Andros in 1683 with a grant of 2,000 acres on the east bank of the Hudson extending up the Roeliff Jansen Kill. This included "flatts, kills, creeks, woods, vlys, and cripple bushes with all fishing, hawking, hunting and fowling priviledges," for which he paid the Indians "300 guilders, 8 blankets and 2 child's blankets, 25 duffels, 4 garments of strouds, 10 large and 10 small shirts and ditto of stockings, 6 guns, 50 pounds of powder, 50 staves of lead, 4 caps, 10 kettles, 10 axes, 10 adzes, 2 pounds of paint, 20 little scissors, 20 little looking glasses, 100 fish hooks, 100 each of awls and nails, 4 rolls of tobacco, 100 pipes, 10 bottles, 3 kegs of rum, one barrel of strong beer, 20 knives, 4 coats and 4 tin kettles." Hoodwinked by such a plenty in thousands of similar trades, the Indians lost all their lands.

After a view and survey, Livingston declared his land "contraire to expectation, very little being fitt to be improved," whereupon he petitioned for and received Tahkanick, alleged to be "two or three hundred acres" extending vaguely eastward to certain Indian stone piles. He carefully marked the trees at his bounds with an L.

At the same time, he allied himself to two of the most powerful families in America by marrying Alida Schuyler, widow of his friend Nicholas van Rensselaer.

A survey map dated 1714, which may be the earliest depiction of any part of Berkshire, shows that the canny Scot had hoodwinked the English as well as the Indians. He was paying an annual quit-rent of 28 shillings for what proved to be 160,240 acres. The map shows that the baronial manor embraced the present Clermont, Germantown, Livingston, Gallatin, Taghkanic, Ancram, Copake, part of Hillsdale and Egremont, half of Mount Washington, Boston Corners, and the northwest corner of Connecticut.

It is plain that feudalism retarded the settlement of the manor while fostering independent farms along the Berkshire edge as early as 1692. Livingston built his own manor house and mill at the mouth of Roeliff Jansen Kill in 1699, and two years later the Earl of Bellamont wrote the Board of Trade in London: "Mr. Livingston has on his great grant of 16 miles long and 24 broad, but 4 or 5 cottages as I am told, men that live in vassalage under him and work for him and are too poor to be farmers having not wherewithal to buy cattle."

The map thirteen years later still showed only five houses, a few furlongs cleared along the Hudson, a wagon path leading south, and "the King's hie way" dotted forlornly eastward through a maze of carefully drawn trees ending abruptly before haystacks of Berkshire hills.

Patroon Livingston in 1710 at Queen Anne's behest sold his Germantown tract of land to the Crown for the settlement of expatriated German Palatines. The land was represented to be rich enough in pines to supply the entire English navy with masts, tar, pitch, and turpentine. The German workers were to make New York the "Emporarium of the Continent." Livingston supplied all food at a contracted minimum of one-third of a loaf of bread and one quart of beer per day per adult, to "content his cupidity."

The experiment was a failure for all. In three years fewer than 200 barrels of tar were made; a thousand Germans, previously forbidden to flee, were cast adrift in three-foot snows and obliged to seek relief from Indians to the west.

Livingston did not languish. He was voted a member of the General Assembly in Albany by the handful of families on his manor and by the few Palatines who remained. In 1721 he resigned all his Albany offices in favor of his son Philip, staying on in the Assembly, sometimes as speaker, until two years before his death in 1728. His was one of the largest and most enduring patrimonies in America.

Few ever outmaneuvered the shrewd Scot. One who did was Captain William Kidd. In 1695, while in England promoting various claims against the Crown, Livingston hatched a scheme to equip a privateer "to fight with and subdue pyrates" and to share in the spoils. Lord Bellamont, governor of New York and Massachusetts, furnished the money and Captain Kidd the necessary nautical skill and fighting qualities.

Kidd deceived his partner Livingston by absconding with the galley and joining the bloody fraternity. The difference between the two was that Livingston worked on land and kept his acquisitions respectable under the guise of feudalism.

Sheriff's War

The clash that determined the west boundary of Massachusetts still remains untold in history and unsung in the historical novel. It was a dramatic confrontation of old-world feudalism, introduced by the Dutch and carried on after 1664 by the English in New York, versus the newly emerging, democratic town governments of the Bay Colony. The anti-rent squabbles might be called the Sheriffs' War since they were waged by local petitions, counter-petitions, posses, and incarcerations in the Albany and Springfield jails.

The feudal lands extending vaguely eastward from the Hudson were the 205,000 acres of Adolph Philipse on the south, Robert Livingston's manor from Roeliff-Jansen Kill to Stockport Creek embracing lands for thirty miles along southern Berkshire, and the vast Rensselaerswyck encroaching on northern Berkshire. Title was held as much by possession as by law, and Indian claims were never completely extinguished. Indeed, the canny Scot, Livingston, parlayed his holdings from the original 2,500-acre grant to 175,000 acres by veiling land limits in the unwritten, ambiguous, and misspelled Indian language. He had already materially advanced his cause by marriage to Mrs. Nicholas Van Rensselaer (née Alida Schuyler), which liaison joined him with two of the richest, most powerful landowning families on the Hudson.

The feudal lords demanded of their tenants land improvement within six years' time, a specified number of days' labor, payment of one-third of receipts for any sale of improvements, rents to be collected in wheat or other produce, and an annual quitrent of 7 pounds, 10 shillings. The hardworking tenants grew more restive as they mingled increasingly along the indefinite border with Yankees who held their grants in fee simple.

The long-simmering differences frequently referred by the Colonial governors to the king himself flared into active revolt in 1751 when twenty "Mountain Men," as the men of Mount Washington were called, joined with twenty-five from Sheffield in a petition to the Massachusetts governor and General Court for protection and privileges under that government. Robert Livingston, Jr., grandson of the original patentee, thereupon doubled efforts to hold his line.

A full moon shone upon the Berkshires 210 years ago as it does tonight, and on April 15 there was murder in Mount Washington. A letter to Lieutenant Governor Phips relates: "A considerable number of men armed with guns and swords broke open the house of Jonathan Darby living on the province land and there in a vilent and tumultuous manner assaulted Josiah Loomis carried him away to Albany gaol...appeared at the house of Joseph Gillet, broke open his house knocked down his wife and took him prisoner ... proceeded to the house of Jacob Bacon broke open his house and threatened the life of his wife who was sick in bed, robed the house of sundry things then proceeded to the house of Robert Noble broke it open, stole and carried away sundry valuable things."

"The next morning about brake of day they assaulted the house of William Race broke it open and as sd William Race was attempting to escape they shot him Dead with a charge of Buck shot. May it please your Honors the case of the poor people living on sd lands is most distressing. They daily expect repeated assaults from Livingston and Ranslaus Banditti which consists of abandoned irishmen and negroes. If your honors do not appear for their relief they are finally dumed."

Another account tells how William Race, firing in self-defense, was shot from his own ridgepole by John Van Rensselaer's posse. Phips demanded the "taking up and securing" of those who had committed this "Barbarous murther."

To encourage frontier settlement, Massachusetts sold lands at twopence an acre or gave it away. Livingston soon found sixty more families on his land. He retaliated by burning houses and imprisoning farmers who had held their lands for many years. Joseph Pain and his wife, both over eighty, pleaded to Phips for relief from the Albany gaol where, in three years, they had "become Like Skilitons." Jacob Spoor in peaceable travel on the Kings Road in "Taghnack" (Mount Washington) was accosted: "Dam you and struck on the head with his sword and cut through my hat and cap and cut my head so that the blood came out and sd Connor said he could cut off my Ears."

Later, two more men were killed in Mount Washington. Many such records and petitions are to be discovered in the Albany and Massachusetts archives, attesting to the boundary war that repeatedly flared as far as "Dutch Hoosick" and beyond into Vermont.

In 1757 The Lords of Trade in London passed on a line twenty miles east of the Hudson, but it was not surveyed and subsequent commissions could not agree upon it. Ten years later, a convention at New Haven agreed on the south terminus but concluded a mile apart on the north. In 1773 another set of commissioners at Hartford settled on the precise boundary recommended by the king's commissioners ninety-nine years before, but this could not be applied to the rugged, mountainous terrain because the compass varied westerly as the transit and sight-stakes proceeded north. Then, for a short time, the larger war of independence held up the local war over boundary.

In 1784 a new joint commission attempted to run the line but could not agree on the allowance to be made for change in declination of the magnetic needle since 1773. After arguing for ten days in the woods of Mount Washington, the surveyors abandoned the job.

At last, a federal commission began a survey July 19, 1787, from the "old corner," and after much precipitous travail reached the Williamstown corner August 4. This ended the feud between Yankees and Yorkers, but did not end feudalism nor finally define the state line. These matters went beyond the middle of the next century, requiring a constitutional change on the part of New York to end feudalism and a cession of Boston Corners on the part of Massachusetts to settle the line after an altercation of 196 years.

Pioneer Frontier

The process of settling the 950 square miles of "thick and almost impenetrable forests" that comprised the vague mountain-beleaguered county took more than 100 years. The first census of 1791 showed a county population of 30,291; yet as late as 1758, Pittsfield was but twenty log cabins in the wilderness.

Some of these wild, unappropriated lands of the Bay Colony along the disputed western border were first cleared and settled by the Dutch under Livingston land grants, or without them. The normal procedure for English settlers was by petition to the General Court in Boston of groups within the colony or from Connecticut and Rhode Island, who wished to move westward.

Some townships like Cheshire were bought by wealthy persons for speculation with or without intent to settle; Governor Bernard himself purchased one-third of Peru. Some were granted to individuals, as Pittsfield to Col. Stoddard "in consideration of his great sufferings in and for the public"—meaning journeys to Canada, Albany, and eastern parts to pacify the Indians or to war with them. Savoy was a gift outright to the heirs of Capt. Gallop for his gallantry in King William's War. After survey, some towns like Richmond were sold at auction. Others like Sandisfield were divided into lots to "be put into a hat and be drawn by an indifferent person"; drawing lots had intrinsic meaning.

In accordance with the General Laws of the province, townships were commonly laid out "in a compact and defensible form" six miles square and divided into 63 lots, one for the first settled minister, another for the second, and one "for the use and support of schools in the town forever." It was required that within five years there be 60 settled residents "who shall have a dwelling house 24 feet long, 18 feet wide, and 7 feet studd and have 7 acres of land well cleared and fenced and brought to English grass or plowed; and also settle a learned Protestant minister." Usually the settlers gave 20 to 40 pounds security guaranteeing performance of conditions. So much for the basic mechanics, which varied in each township as much as the terrain.

It took men, however, to implement all this; and their implement was the axe. Matthew Noble came from Westfield to Sheffield in the autumn of 1725 and, according to family tradition, spent the winter in a wigwam when he was not girdling or felling trees. In the spring he returned for his sixteen-year-old daughter, Hannah; other settlers came soon after.

Benjamin Wheeler spent "the memorable hard winter" of 1739-40 in New Marlborough "and continued to fell the forest." The

Indians forbade him the use of a gun lest he kill all the deer. At long intervals some snowshoer from Sheffield ten miles away called on him. At Richmond in 1760 it was not quite so sociable. The Mudge and Wood families, only three miles apart, never saw each other during the entire first winter. Pittsfield (Pontoosack) received an alphabetical start in the summer of 1749 when Ashley, Bush, Cadwell, Deming, Ensign, Fairfield, Gunn, Habbard, and a few others labored clearing the land and erecting log cabins for their families, this in the lull between the two French and Indian Wars. Most of the first settlers hailed from Westfield and Wethersfield. From the latter town in the summer of 1752 came Solomon Deming with his wife, Sarah, on a pillion behind him. Fairfield and Stiles brought their wives that same summer; and Charles Goodrich, after cutting his way for miles through the forest and over the eastern barrier, drove the first cart and team into the fledgling community, which within a few years needed three forts to preserve its very existence.

Adventurers once went from Boston to Boston Corners; now travel is in the other direction, and spirit is submerged in sophistication. One story 200 years old shows the difference. Hancock was receiving its first settlers in 1765. It was said to be a long, ungainly town, so badly located that the inhabitants of one end could not reach the other end without going out of the town, and mostly out of the county and state. It was hemmed in by mountains so steep that "one could not climb out without spoiling the knees of his pantaloons, or go back without spoiling their seat."

In this town Theodore Townsend, age seventeen, saw red-haired Susannah Allen walking the dirt road barefoot, carrying her shoes to save wear. He was so impressed with her virtues that he made the fourteen-year-old girl his bride. First meals together in their humble home were spread on the head of a barrel. She bore him sixteen children, dying with the birth of the last at age forty. O pioneers!

His next four wives gave him a total of two children.

Happy Birthday, Berkshire!

We do not mean to be over-precise in the matter of birthdays. Being husband, we might forget our wife's; and being husbandman, we might forget Berkshire's. But we have seen the birth certificate of the county in the archives division of the Boston State House, where a carefully guarded room holds the precious original documents of the Commonwealth, many signed by Indians back in the first days of the Massachusetts Bay Colony. The contents of this room will soon be moved underground for protection from fire to quarters being built beneath the front lawn of the State House. Then anyone willing to do a little digging can unearth the fact that Berkshire County was born April 21, 1761. The church bells will ring all through the county at 8 a.m. tomorrow in celebration. We will be ringing one of them.

This birthday is doubly interesting because it seems to involve twins, but that is not quite precise since Berkshire separated from Hampshire like Eve from Adam, while five days later Pittsfield was born, the son of Poontoosuck Plantation. Col. William Williams was sponsor of both. He was the son of the Weston minister and nephew of Col. John Stoddard, one of the three original proprietors of the plantation. In 1748 his uncle presented young Williams with a 100-acre lot on the Square. The Indian country was a challenge to this pioneer, and he built a home with heavy wooden ramparts and walls of four-inch white ash planks, and named it Fort Anson. In 1758 he raised a regiment of 906 men in Poontoosuck, and fought in two assaults on Fort Ticonderoga. The next year the British victory at Quebec ended the French and Indian threat in Western Massachusetts and settlement could proceed safely.

By January 1760, Poontoosuck was surveyed and divided into some 70 parcels of land for the proprietors. There was an annoying limitation of corporate powers and duties under the plantation regime; accordingly, Col.Williams as agent of the several towns and plantations was sent to the General Court in Boston to petition for the division of Hampshire County, the western third of the colony incorporated in 1662. At the same time, he was to seek the incorporation of Pittsfield.

The General Court was composed of two bodies, the House being the immediate representative of the people, and His Majesty's Council. Bills had to pass both and then be approved by the governor. Col. Williams brought the county bill to the House April 18. It was read three times, passed to be engrossed, and sent to the Council, where it was passed April 20. The governor, Sir Francis Bernard, signed it April 21, 1761, and Berkshire was born. The Pittsfield bill was introduced in the House, where it passed April 13; the Council approved April 16, and the governor signed April 26. The county was five days older than the town.

The county charter is on a large piece of parchment, capped by the seal of the Province of Massachusetts Bay. It is in a graceful but rather faded script. The towns of Sheffield, Stockbridge, Egremont, and New Marlborough, the plantations of Poontoosuc, New Framingham (Lanesboro), and West Hoosuck, and the Districts Nos. 1, 3, and 4 are enumerated in the act, plus "all lands within" certain described limits. Sheffield was declared to be "for the present, the shire or county town" (meaning its North Parish, which soon became Great Barrington). Court was to be held alternately there and in Pittsfield. At the end is the large signature, "Fra Bernard."

Sir Francis Bernard was born in the valley of the Thames, Berkshire County, England. He was exercising gubernatorial prerogative and probably some nostalgia in conferring the name Berkshire on a region he had never seen. Somehow 200 years later the name seems indigenous and proper. The baby has acquired the necessary character. The governor usually consulted those interested in such matters, and it is highly probable his friend Col. Williams was influential in the naming of Pittsfield. Prime Minister William Pitt was much esteemed throughout New England for his vigorous conduct of the war against France, and Williams' very home was an outpost in that war.

Col. Williams could never forget these two birthdays. Like an expectant father, he walked the State House corridors for two weeks. This excerpt from a letter to his brother-in-law in 1767 shows how he felt about the infants: "Since my removal to this place, I challenge any man in the government, that has not had the half Feateague, to compare with me for Health or freedom from pain. All my Doctors Bill has been a gallopot or two of Unguent for the Itch ... No man or woman of but common Understanding, that ever came and got settled among us wished themselves back. The air sufted them, they felt frisk, and alert, or ... something indeared their Scituation to them; this with regard to the women. The men perceived soon the difference of the soil, and put what you would upon it, it would yeald beyond what they were acquainted with. ..."

The Last Innocent Mahican

What were the Indians like when the first settlers came into the Berkshire Hills? How many were there? Where did they live and how? What were their manners and beliefs before they were persuaded to rum and swindled of their pelts by the Dutch, then persuaded to Christianity and bilked of their lands by the well-meaning English?

From the light scattering of artifacts between Williamstown and Weatogue, it may be assumed that Indian population was always very low in the upper Hoosic and upper Housatonic river valleys. Such camp and village sites as there were at rock shelters, springs, lakes, and riversides seem to have been occupied back to postglacial times by small, nomadic bands of hunters and seasonally resident family groups.

On October 12, 1734, when youthful Yale teacher John Sergeant first arrived at Housatunnuk (Great Barrington) to plan for an Indian mission, he found only four or five families led by Umpachenee at Skatekook (Sheffield) and the same number with Kunkapot at Wnahktukgok (Stockbridge). These fringe families of Hudson River Mahicans, fewer than fifty individuals, along with several Dutch families settled since 1692, formed the entire population of the present county.

The Dutch regarded the Indians as barbarians to be taken advantage of, while the English looked upon them as uncultured heathens to be civilized and Christianized. In reality, they were children of nature adapted to a rugged environment by some 7,000 years of prehistory. Until Sergeant wrote down and translated their strange, guttural language, their only records were in "wampum," which served the double purpose of money and as bond and remembrance of treaties and agreements. Without this black or white shellfish beadwork, messages between tribes were "empty words," unheeded in the present and unknown to posterity.

The Indians lived in wigwams or longhouses covered with sheets of bark fastened upon a framework of withes affixed to pairs of arched saplings. Fires were built on the earthen floors, the smoke escaping at roof apertures. The women performed all the tasks of daily living, including the back-breaking husbandry of corn and beans, while the men were hunting, fishing, traveling, powwowing, pipe smoking, and, even occasionally, indolent.

Of the marriage relationship, Rev. Sergeant reported: "It us'd rarely happen that a married couple live together till they are old. And as they use but little ceremony in the business of marriage, so they make a less thing of parting. In such a case 'tis their law that the children and all the household stuff belong to the woman; and indeed everything else but the Gun, for that is the man's livelihood."

From the same account it is very clear that these Indians were stoics. They endured great irregularity of diet, often going several days without food. In sickness: "So long as the sick person can stand and walk he goes out of doors upon all occasions, be it rain or snow or whatever the weather is."

What did these laconic stoics believe? Rev. Sergeant learned from his interpreter, Ebenezer: "Some he had known were Atheists ... others believed the Sun to be God, or at least the Body or residence of the Deity; but that now they generally believed the existence of one supreme, invisible Being, the Maker of all things."

Their traditional beliefs, like their lives, were at all points interlocked with nature. The stars of Ursa Major were "so many men hunting a bear; they begin the chase in the Spring and hold it all Summer; by the Fall they have wounded it and the blood turns the leaves red; by the Winter they have killed it and the snow is made of its fat, which being melted by the heat of the Summer, makes the sap of trees."

They had received it from their fathers "that there once lived a Man among them who was seen to come down from Heaven with snow-shoes on (which was the original of snowshoes), that he lived in great reputation among them, was esteemed a Hero and a Prophet.... He married a wife among them and had two children by her, and when they offered a deer he acted as their priest. ... On one occasion he began to pray with his two children upon his knees, and was in a wonderful manner raised from the ground, rising gradually as he continued praying; but when he had got just to the top of the wigwam they called to him to leave one of his children, at least, behind him—and letting one down, he was carried up out of their sight."

These happy, innocent, unlettered Indians believed as firmly in their ancient traditions as the Rev. Sergeant did in the Bible. Now the white man was the serpent in Eden.

The Great Road

Since Berkshire had neither entity nor unity before 1700, the first traveled way across it was the east-west, single-file, Indian footpath known to Dutch traders from the Hudson Valley as the New England Path and to the English in the Connecticut Valley as the New Connecticut Path or Albany Road.

Hawthorne wrote: "The forest track trodden by the hobnailed shoes of these sturdy and ponderous Englishmen has now a distinctness which it never could have acquired from the light tread of a hundred times as many moccasins. It goes onward from one clearing to another, here plunging into a shadowy strip of woods, there open to the sunshine, but everywhere showing a decided line along which human interests have begun to hold their career."

So began one of the oldest and most historically colorful public ways in the realizing of America. The Great Road was literally tramped out by explorers and adventurers, first settlers and Indian fighters, missionaries and pioneers west; it was improved rod by rod by local citizenry; it was hacked wider by Gen. Amherst's five regiments; it was compacted by horses, oxen, cattle, and sheep; by cart, pung, and dray; by stage coach and post chaise; it was dragged and leveled by the tonnage of Ticonderoga cannons travailed to Boston by Henry Knox to midwife an infant country; it was cursed by Burgoyne and pounded by the feet of his beaten Convention Army; it was the course of farm boys to the Civil War and runaway slaves from it; it was the way of the tin peddler and the Shaker seed salesman; it was shivered to a washboard by the rattling, early-model, horseless carriage; it was the one-way road of many a World War draftee. It was the romance that only an open road can be.

When the Rev. Benjamin Wadsworth, later president of Harvard College, took this road to Albany in 1694, he recorded of the Berkshire section: "Ye road which we traveled this day was very woody, rocky, mountainous, swampy; extreme bad riding it was. I never yet saw so bad traveling as this was." These were times when His Excellency, the governor of Massachusetts, was carried across a fordway on the older Bay Path pickaback by his Indian guide.

In 1736 the General Court granted a petition for a tract of 6,000 acres between Westfield and Blandford, "provided they do forthwith, or as soon as may be, open and constantly keep in repair hereafter, a good and safe cart-way over the premises in the road that leads from Westfield to Husatonock, commonly called the Albany Road." This may have officially opened the middle stretch of the Great Road that

came in from two directions like the borings of the Hoosac Tunnel;
but up to 1750 it was still sometimes impassable, as it proved for two
men who "sank down and expired on their way to Great Barrington."

Before Berkshire's incorporation in 1761, many roads ramified
from this original artery. They were first blazed as mere passages
from farm to farm, then laid out to suit the convenience of the
growing towns, then surveyed to join townships, and only last fitted
into the pattern of surrounding states. Interestingly enough, the
exceptions to the Topsy-type growth seem to have been the Great
Road, the Mohawk Trail, and the Massachusetts Turnpike, all of
which knew where they were going before they started.

Though the Great Road was a long Indian vision, it still had to be
maintained locally, as may be guessed from the many names applied to
short stretches in Revolutionary times such as "the Tunock Road" or
"the High Way from Blandford Street to ye Green woods road."

By 1800, chartered stock companies were forming throughout
New England to lay and grade turnpikes and build bridges. These
were, in general, good investments widely demanded in speculation. Rival roads were sometimes laid out, and fortunes were made
and lost. Tolls were charged, the word turnpike deriving from the
gate constructed of two crossed pikes sharpened at the outer ends,
turning on a centered post.

In 1827 the Massachusetts legislature passed an act allowing
these companies to surrender their charters whenever the county or
town would receive them. They gradually became unprofitable, and
the last toll in Berkshire County was probably collected about 1845
on the twelfth Massachusetts turnpike at the little red house hugging the road north of Ashley Falls. The Great Road by its very
antiquity seems to have escaped ever becoming a toll road.

Nevertheless, antiquity has been unable to preserve the road's
entity. Between Boston and Albany it is marked by a score of differ-
ing route numbers. Stretches of difficult terrain have been abandoned entirely or bypassed, as where the road enters and leaves
Berkshire. In places it is dirt road, wood road, or once again the forest mold that was trod by moccasined feet. In places it is marked by

the vanishing cellar holes of hospitable old taverns. In other places it bears the commerce of today.

The difference between this Great Road and the Massachusetts Turnpike is not simply the difference between leaf mold and cement, nor the difference between a pickaback governor and a pickaback trailer-truck. The difference is between modern convenience and the free, romantic, open highway of history.

Old Wood Road

Old wood roads have a way of getting lost. They wander off invitingly into the hills from the back of the farm property, then disappear as unobtrusively as they began, in a blackberry jungle, in a tangle of undergrowth, in a crisscross of fallen chestnut poles, or in a rocky, brushy gully that was once a roadbed. Everything conspires to obliterate them: spring runoff, summer growth, smother of autumn leaves, and winter's wreckage of iced branches and windfall trees. Often it is easier to walk through the woods beside them than it is to trace their very track.

The Appalachian Club member, the Boy Scout, the birdwatcher, botanist, hiker, horseback rider, hunter, snowshoer, and skier know the invitation of these old roads, and a few enjoy clearing them.

Such a road we opened lately, as time permitted, with the help of tractor, chain saw, and occasional work parties. This road at its closest approach to the sky was in real danger of being lost altogether, like the staircase in a long abandoned house leading to no second floor at all.

Such decrepit estate was not surprising in view of the fact that this was one of the earliest roads in the county. One old map of obscure date shows it as a faint, dotted line labeled "Indian Trail" leading up through the Bash Bish cut, over the Mount Washington plateau, through the pass between Sunrise Rock and Undine Mountain, and down the eastern slope past Black Rock into the Housatonic Valley.

Proof of Indian travel is offered by an arrowhead, a long ceremonial point, and a flint knife found along the course of the trail.

A map of 1841 calls the trail, by then a cartway, the Old Spurr Road. It was the link joining two brothers, one of whom chose to farm the mountain, the other the valley a thousand feet below. That was in 1762. Some decades later it served as a public way and narrow town road out of Mount Washington, known as the Old Sheffield Road. It was traversed by farm wagons, high-sided charcoal carts, sleighs, cutters, buggies, and surreys, but never by an automobile, for the woods closed in on it about 1900.

The woodman can determine this date easily by counting the annular rings of trees sprung up in the very wheel track. Birches especially seem to capture an old road, the lovely white and the aromatic yellow and black. In places these three woodland graces of white, golden, and black skin filed in lines as straight and parallel as two railroad tracks.

Laurel, too, had appropriated the road here and there. Stems an inch thick grew from the depressed bed while at the sides mother thickets leaned out gnarled trunks up to three inches in diameter. At one place in the middle of the road a black-throated blue warbler, the one bird of laurel devotion, had lodged its small russet nest of stripped laurel bark lined with black rootlets in a fork of laurel. Where wagons creaked and harness bells once spoke, like faint echoes the fledglings peeped beneath June masses of pink and white blossom and learned their own songs in the glistening laurel in the middle of the road.

Now light snow was on the ground to aid in delineating the obscure course, which was marvelously straight in pursuing its way through hills and dells, skirting ledges and gullies, finding always the gradual climb and level ground where there seemed so little.

Occasionally the road passed directly through the charmed circle of an old charcoal pit, a twenty-to-thirty foot leveled area where the sweetness of ashy soil still repelled all laurel and all but a few seedling trees. Toward its highest point the road passed a sod rectangle with a heap of stones at one end which we took to be the remains of a charcoal burner's hut, the mound indicating crumbled sod walls, and the stones, the fireplace and chimney.

Unraveling this highest, most remote stretch of old wood road was like riffling through pages of history and natural history. One half-expected to encounter a stalwart Indian or a grimy charcoal burner, or at least the farm wagon jouncing down with a load of cranberries from the lofty bog. Now the road was open for them. But deer, fox, and wildcat imprinted it as proxy.

The Monument

Like prospective parents the residents of Great Barrington, Stockbridge, and West Stockbridge are beginning to think of names for the new school that will stand in Monument Valley under the beetling brow of Monument Mountain. One name as obvious as the mother mountain is Monument Mountain Regional.

A better name, not simply for brevity but because more meaningful, more historical, and more individual, would be Monument Regional, naming the school, as mountain and valley were named, for man's earliest creation in that richly storied area. This would be using the father name.

The monument was a sizable cairn of small stones erected through time immemorial by passing Indians on the high point of their trail on the divide between Housatunnuk (Great Barrington) and Wnahtukook (Stockbridge). This was on the southeast slope of Mas-wa-se-hi or Maus-wau-se-ki, meaning "the standing-up nest" or "fisher's nest," now Monument Mountain.

The first white man to write of the monument was John Sergeant, missionary and first schoolmaster in the Housatonic Valley. He rode past it with his Indian interpreter, Ebenezer Poo-poo-nuck, and recorded on November 3, 1734: "There is a large heap of stones, I suppose 10 cartloads, in the Way to Wnahtukook, which the Indians have thrown together as they have pass'd by the place; 'for it us'd to be their custom, every time any one pass'd by, to throw a stone upon it. But what was the end of it they cannot tell; only they say their fathers us'd to do so, and they do it because it was the custom of their fathers. But Ebenezer says he supposes it was design'd to be as an expression of their gratitude to the Supreme Being, that he had preserv'd them to see the place again."

Two days later Berkshire's first schoolmaster began teaching in the schoolhouse the Indians had built for him, and within a week he had twenty-two pupils.

Other early explanations of the monument by the variously named Muhekunnucks, Mahicans, Housatunnuks, Stockbridge, or River Indians were that it marked the grave of their first sachem in the region or that it commemorated the great ambush and defeat of an enemy tribe. Captain, Chief, and Selectman Konkapot said it was a boundary marker by treaty with the Mohawks, his people having hunting rights within one day's journey in every direction. But the Indians were always reluctant to talk about the monument.

The Rev. Gideon Hawley, Stockbridge schoolmaster under Jonathan Edwards in 1752, concluded from wide travels among the Indians that such monuments were unspoken acknowledgment of an invisible being, the unknown god whom this people worship. He added, "The largest heap I ever observed is that large collection of small stones on the mountain between Stockbridge and Great Barrington."

The Rev. Jonathan Edwards, Stockbridge author of *Freedom of Will*, the earliest important, influential book written in America, must often have seen the monument by the roadway in his comings and goings, as did every passerby. A little research in the still-unpublished notebooks that he carried in his pockets to record names, accounts, Indian remedies, cranberry bogs, *ad variorum*, would probably reveal that he had written about it.

William Cullen Bryant next gave the monument the immortality that only America's first poet of stature could confer. At the time, he was town clerk of Great Barrington and, among his other offices, committee man for examining schoolmasters. In 1824 he visited the cairn with Ralph Taylor and soon after wrote "Monument Mountain," giving the monument legendary significance for the Indian maid said to have leapt from the cliff for forbidden love: "There was scooped upon the mountain's southern slope, a grave; and there they laid her. ... The tribe built up a simple monument, a cone of small loose stones. Thenceforward all who passed, hunter, and dame, and virgin, laid a stone in silence on the pile. It stands there yet. ... The mountain where the hapless maiden died is called the Mountain of the Monument."

The great educator, Mark Hopkins, and his brothers knew the monument and the mountain well from youthful expeditions from Cherry Cottage, the family farm, in pursuit of squirrels, whortleberries, chestnuts, and bee trees. Shortly before taking his seat upon the log at Williams College, he burned a piece of stone from the mountain in his stove and declared it "bituminous shale which usually accompanies coal."

On August 5, 1850, there was a memorable picnic of literati on the mountain. Henry Sedgwick was the only man present who had not written a book. Hawthorne, then writing *The House of the Seven Gables*, first met and formed a lasting friendship with Melville, who at the time was writing *Moby Dick*. On the cliffs Oliver Wendell Holmes opened champagne for all, while Cornelius Mathews read Bryant's "Monument Mountain," whereupon "a long life to the dear old poet" was toasted.

So in the 1600s the Indians knew the monument beside the footpath of their forefathers. In the 1700s Sergeant wrote of it along his bridle path, and Edwards saw it by the widening cartway. In the 1800s Bryant mused beside it, and Hopkins passed it on the first county road leading north. Hawthorne, Melville, and Holmes knew of it.

In the 1900s can those so rich in history afford to neglect Berkshire's oldest shrine, still standing five rods from Route 7 and less than a mile from the proposed school? May the unbuilt institution stand as long and bear the name Monument Regional School!

Indian, Negro, and White

Just 240 years ago the first English grant of land in Berkshire County was given to Joseph Parsons, Thomas Nash, and their pioneer followers from Westfield and Northampton. The resident Mohican Indians were given a pittance of 460 pounds and a pacifier of three barrels of cider and thirty quarts of rum. From the very beginning race problems were upon the county. Even earlier they were upon the country, when a year before the Pilgrims landed, a Dutch ship sold twenty African slaves to the colonists at Jamestown. Ever since, we have been learning that it is far easier to give freedom and mouth equality than it is to live them. As schools reopen this fall, those in Alabama, Mississippi, and South Carolina are still segregated at all grade levels; one Virginia county has closed all schools to Negroes for the last three years. Three Negro churches in Georgia have recently been burned. All through the South the franchise has been restricted by intimidation, and recently by shooting. Nor do we live equality in everyday affairs in the North, as witness housing and job opportunities.

Berkshire history speaks to us eloquently on racial matters, and not without showing both sides of the coin. We need look no further than the Stockbridge Cemetery for testimony of tolerance; the very tombstones talk. First Selectman Konkapot is buried near his well-meaning benefactor, missionary John Sergeant, whose poetic epitaph was written by an Indian; and Mumbet, said to be the first slave freed in America, is buried close to her defender, the Hon. Theodore Sedgwick, and beside her devoted mistress, Catharine Sedgwick, whose brother penned the tender lines on her stone. Could this happen today?

Dr. Samuel Hopkins, first minister in Great Barrington, from 1743 till removal to Newport in 1769, was one of the earliest and most effective spokesmen for human rights. He repeatedly spoke on behalf of the slave, urging masters to free their bondmen, and published a dialogue against slavery dedicated to the Continental Congress, which had widespread effect on public opinion, so that in 1776 Congress itself resolved without opposition that "no slave be imported into any of the 13 colonies."

The constitution of Massachusetts was adopted in 1780, its Bill of Rights declaring that "all men are born free and equal, and have certain natural, essential, and inalienable rights; among which may be reckoned the right of enjoying and defending their lives and liberties."

Such words had been discussed in the Colonel Ashley House since 1773, when a Sheffield town meeting had formulated some of the actual words that later went into the Declaration of Independence. Slave Mumbet was armed with these words on the day that she warded off the blow of a hot fire iron directed at her younger sister. She immediately went to Col. Theodore Sedgwick four miles away. Being an astute lawyer, he saw that the very words that freed Americans from British control also freed slaves from their masters. The memorable test case was tried in the Great Barrington courthouse in September 1781. A month later Cornwall surrendered at Yorktown, and all Americans achieved the freedom that Theodore Sedgwick had just won for Massachusetts slaves.

On the other side of the coin is the irony of the Indian head. In these very years of progress in race relations the much-preached-to Mohicans were first squeezed into the Stockbridge meadows and then bilked out of them.

After many had enlisted as Revolutionary Minutemen, Chief Uhhaunhauwaumut summed up the tribe's position: "Brothers, you remember when you first came over the great water I was great and you was little, very small. I then took you in for a friend and kept you in my arms so no one would injure you. Since then we have been friends. There has never been any quarrel between us, but now our conditions are changed. You have become great and tall, you reach to the clouds and you are seeing all around the world, and I am very small, very little, I am not so high as your heel. Now you take care of me and I look to you for protection."

The Provincial Congress had voted each Indian a blanket and some ribbons as an inducement to enlist. After Yorktown, for their sacrifice in a struggle they could not fully comprehend, such stragglers as got back to Stockbridge might have been returned some of their land that had been sold for debt. Instead, by order of George Washington, they received an ox and "supply" of whiskey for a barbecue that was held on Laurel Hill. In 1784-5, over 200 of them emigrated to the Oneida reservation in New York, leaving only a few aged paupers in the valley of their birth.

If there is any lesson to be learned from these ironies of history, it must be the knowledge that human nature does not change, that justice and injustice persist. And when we read that a Georgia county sheriff says, "We want our colored people to go on living like they have for the last hundred years," and when we see on television, as a few nights ago, the governor of Mississippi saying proudly: "The schools will not be integrated while I am your governor," let us be proud of the marble stone of "Elizabeth Freeman known by the name of Mumbet" close beside the ivied cross of Catherine Sedgwick in our Berkshire Hills.

Place Names and Ghost Towns

From Alandar to Zip Thunder, from Amoldsville to Zylonite, from Bethlehem and Jerusalem to Hades and Hell's Kitchen, from Jacob's Dream to Skunk's Misery, from New Providence to Podunk, from Sand Spring to In the Sands, Berkshire place names have their tales to tell, tales filled with history and romance.

What better summer pastime than to take to Berkshire back roads armed with an old map or gazetteer to discover long-lost communities like Beartown, a straggling string of disappearing cellar holes along a lofty, forested mountain ridge, where the inhabitants in the 1700s were said by an itinerant preacher to be as impossible to convert "as for a shad to climb an apple tree, yea, tail foremost."

Or to investigate and reconstruct in the mind's eye at the other extreme the nearby, saintly and celibate-doomed Shaker community at Fernside in the lovely Tyringham Valley, commenced in 1792 and ended in 1874 in a little overgrown cemetery with ninety-nine stones. The men busied themselves too much about the vegetable seed business whilst the spinsters spun. Today three houses, the community dining room and kitchen, and the great cattle barn flank that byway of history, mute witnesses to former industry and other-worldliness.

In the same Hop Brook valley and the hills about it may be found Hades, Sodom, Jerusalem, and one of Berkshire's three Jerichos, reminding us of our strong Calvinist and Puritan traditions. The early settlers, by assuming damnation or its opposite, seem to have placed themselves at all stages along the road to glory. Sister to Sodom is the little hamlet of Gomorrah, still showing on some maps just north of Clayton on the Connecticut line. Another Jericho surrounded by mountain walls became Hancock in 1776, as interest shifted from the Bible to patriotism. Similarly, Bethlehem became part of Otis in 1810.

The third Jericho three miles east of Dalton is no more than the overgrown foundation of a three-story, stone woolen mill that flourished in Civil War times, requiring tenements for its many workers; it burned in the 1890s, and the walls came tumbling down. Jacob's Pillow, always a ghost town in winter where wind and snow perform the ballet, seems likely to be the last Berkshire community of Biblical name, Jacob's Dream and Jacob's Well being broken rungs on the Ladder. Communities come and communities go; only where Bible names have been applied to the hills themselves have they remained.

Indian names quite naturally came into Berkshire early and have remained on many natural features, but only on four communities—the mill town of Housatonic and the hamlets of Konkapot, Seekonk (Indian for wild goose), and Hoosac Tunnel (once East Portal Camp), each a river name, reminding us how closely the Indians stuck to larger waters while the earliest settlers favored the Bible-named hills and the smaller brooks.

Indian names gave way to English ones in a wave of loyalty at incorporation time, as Housatunnuk to Sheffield, Podunk to Alford, Indiantown to Stockbridge, Yokuntown and Mount Ephraim to Richmond and Lenox, Pontoosuc to Pittsfield, New Seekonk to Savoy, East and West Hoosuck to Adams, North Adams, and Williamstown.

Somewhere south of the Great Wigwam site at Great Barrington is the Indian ghost town of Skatekook or Schaghticoke, meaning, "where the small stream meets the large one and corn lands adjoin." This confluence near the Great Barrington-Sheffield line, once known as Umpachene's Point, remains mysterious since both streams have changed course materially, the meandering Housatonic appropriating much of the Green River bed. The settlement may have been more than a quarter mile south of the present confluence. But this is a matter for the arrowhead and artifact hunter.

The West Sheffield section of Bow Wow, also a ghost town as shown by its large cemetery with oldest stone dated 1766, may, in the manner of Schliemann's Troy, rest upon earlier Indian villages, since the unique name is presumed to be a corruption of the word "powwow." Ghost towns are discovered by such nebulous clues.

The Dutch names that linger on Berkshire's southwestern landscape are a clue to the first white settlers in the county. These early Dutch traders and settlers gave their Dutch sobriquets to certain Indians such as John Van Guilder, the guilder being a Dutch coin and the word also meaning "to work in a gulch"; this particular individual seems to have hacked out a clearing in Guilder Hollow where Jug End Barn is, to have owned extensive lands thereabouts, and to have bequeathed his name to the Mount Everett pond. Another Indian dubbed by the Dutch was Konkapot, whose name may have derived from a word for coffee pot.

Hollenbeck's, a mile south of Van Deusenville, had a house as early as 1735 and later was a stage stop with a post office, as were the communities of Van Deusen and Van Deusenville.

Census on the Mountain

"Lies, damn lies, and statistics," Mark Twain once said, to put tables of figures in their proper place. But sometimes there is a story or even a history under the table. So it is with the census figures of the Town of Mount Washington, smallest town in the Commonwealth, and the home of the first white settlers in Berkshire County.

In the dimness of Colonial history, stroke of ax preceded stroke of pen; survival was more vital than statistics. The earliest table of any kind in the Massachusetts Archives regarding Mount Washington is dated 1752. This lists by name forty-four men owning thirty-two houses, having 966 acres fenced, 772 acres improved, and making forty-nine barrels of "syder." The last column is headed, "years cultivated by any person." Christopher and Henry Brazee, John Hallenbeeck and son, Abraham and Richard Spoor all testify that their lands had been worked for sixty years, or as early as 1692.

Thus, this early record indicates the Dutch from the Hudson Valley were settled in the Berkshires some thirty-three years before Matthew Noble brought his daughter and her feather bed from Westfield to Sheffield. But if the English couldn't beat the Dutch to Mount Washington, by 1752 they had joined them, for the list is half English and half Dutch names. This early period was one of land clearing and subsistence farming, with some Indian hostility and considerable tyranny by New York landlord Livingston and his heirs.

The population of the town in 1776 was 259, and by the first official U.S. census in 1790 it was 261. By 1810 it reached its residential peak of 474 people. Behind these figures is the growth of a young country flexing its muscles. There were three schools, two post offices, and a town meeting house, "to be free for all religious sects not intruding upon each others appointments." The Methodists, Presbyterians, Universalists, and Baptists must have stood or kneeled, because there were no seats until 1818.

For industry there were several saw mills and grist mills, a tannery, blacksmith shop, and the Joyce forge and trip hammer employing twenty men in the manufacture and repair of all kinds of agricultural implements, harpoons for Hudson whalers, heavy chain and iron wheels for hauling Berkshire marble, and axes to tame the forest. Much of the population was employed in charcoaling, to fuel the Salisbury and Copake Iron Works.

As these industries dwindled or moved, so also did the population. By state census in 1865 the number was 237, exactly half that of 1810. By 1910 it had been halved again. This post-Civil-War period saw the town reach comfortable middle age. The natural beauties of the countryside drew many summer boarders, and many returned to build summer homes. The summer population began to double as residents departed.

Three cemeteries, countless apple trees lost in the woods, and stone walls rambling half up the mountains bear witness to the life behind the peak statistics, as do the numerous cellar holes with their clumps of lilacs or mats of day lilies. There is a story with each. At one site down the Old Plantain Pond Road lived an old woodchopper who is reported to have said in the face of winter: "I have one barrel of salted skunks and another of fat woodchucks; and if I don't live better this winter than last, I just as soon go to hell as to heaven."

It was symbolic when the 1960 census takers got stuck in the March mud trying to drive into an empty house. It seemed nearest to them to get help from another town, rather than to try to find anyone in Mount Washington. Eventually they found twenty-nine residents in twelve houses to complete their statistics. Yet the summer population in about fifty-five houses and three summer camps approximates that of 1810.

Now we have the anomalous situation of a community that in its youth sought the mother protection of the Commonwealth, perhaps having, in its old age, to fight the same mother for its very existence, there being some talk in late years of making the mountain area a state park or reservation. If this comes to pass, it seems likely the last twenty residents will put up as good a fight for a town as the first did 250 years ago.

Tyringham History

It takes time for history to unfold enough to write about it. While it is unfolding, there is constant danger that facts will be lost in the living. It took 200 years of incorporated existence for Berkshire County to generate a historical society; it may take another 200 for that society to collect and evaluate all the pertinent facts of those first two centuries.

The best history of the early and middle years of Berkshire's thirty-two towns is contained in the 1,400-page compendium edited by J. E. A. Smith of Pittsfield and published by the Beers Co., in 1885. Now thirty of the towns need updated, individual, hardcover, definitive histories patterned on an admixture of Taylor's *History of Great Barrington* (1928), which accents research, and Sedgwick and Marquand's *Stockbridge* (1939), accenting evaluation.

A Hinterland Settlement, written by Eloise Stedman Myers, is a ninety-five-page book relating and updating the history of the only Tyringham on earth. It may be ordered for $3.50 at England Brothers or from the Rev. Franklin Couch in Tyringham.

How often we hear it said that the memories of our eldest citizens should be recorded! The Berkshire County Historical Society has begun a series of tapes to realize this end. Mrs. Myers' history does this in print. Her book is a fusion of research, town records, letters, and memories of many residents. Being a native of Tyringham and once for two years head of the longest-established rake industry in the United States, she is well grounded to be historian for this lovely valley where three descendants of early settlers still farm and where rakes are still manufactured.

The book makes no pretense of being the definitive history. An editor might have guided it that way. Unfortunately, there are no maps in the book to pinpoint the old roads and homesteads or to juxtapose Jericho, Sodom, and Jerusalem, or the saintly Shaker community and Hades. An appendix and index would have given the book increased reference value. The many folksy tales included do not always reach the level of color, which is their raison d'etre; yet it is a strength of this history that so many do. Of the sixteen chapters, only the one on houses and inhabitants seems drawn out; the rest the historically-minded reader would wish longer.

Now for the first time is revealed the true origin of the town name, Tyringham, 201 years after incorporation. A native of the Tyringham Estates in England emigrated to Massachusetts and brought the name to the valley while prospecting for iron. Before that time, the region's history was bound up with that of Monterey as "No. 1 of the Housatonic Townships." The town's records are unique in being complete and bound from the first meeting of proprietors, October 6, 1737. First settlers built in the high hill country; and it was not until 1762 that Deacon Thomas Orton ventured northward down into the tangled forest and morass of Hop Brook, which settling and farming slowly transformed into the meadowed Tyringham valley celebrated by poet-editor Richard Watson Gilder.

Mrs. Myers has assembled and preserved fascinating lore of this Berkshire byway. The first settled minister was Adonijah Bidwell, who served the community thirty-four years. His sermons in his own indecipherable system of shorthand are in the Pittsfield Athenaeum. There also, among the vital records he kept, are listed: "Twins of Thomas Robbins Jr., the 14th pair of twins—more than one twin to 25 single births since 1750"; and among deaths, he wrote: "Polly Harris, 20th wife of Amos Rice." It may sometimes have been a gentle gesture on the part of the men to build a room with no windows in the middle of the house, as Deacon Williams Hale did in 1747, "where the women folk could gather during thunderstorms."

We are given the interesting building contract for the still-standing Capt. Ezekiel Hearick house "to be 32 feet by 26 feet on the ground one story and a half or the posts 12 feet ... the cellar to be under the whole building with a kitchen room, fireplace and oven in the same," the house to be entirely painted, plastered, and one room paneled. The cost in 1808? $350—$100 paid in warranted obligations upon other men, $100 in neat cattle, and the remainder in two years in current money of the time.

One of the most interesting chapters is on old roads like the Boston to Albany Great Road, opened for oxcarts in 1737. Gen. Knox passing over this in 1776 wrote: "Reached No. I after having climbed mountains from which we might almost have seen all the Kingdoms of the Earth." Another was the mistakenly named Royal Hemlock Road, opened in 1743. In Colonial days the finest trees were marked with an R for "royal," reserving them for His Majesty's ships. One traveler passing in his oxcart saw the RH for Road to Hopbrook carved on a giant hemlock; he took this to mean Royal Hemlock, which ever after clung.

Industries are among the many subjects well treated in this history. Isolated hill towns had to be self-sufficient and this little town, which numbered 1,712 souls at its peak in 1800, before division from Monterey, at one time or another turned out flour and meal, lumber, bricks, lime, cider and brandy, wood products from high chairs to coffins, shoes, cotton goods, spools, and tubs, rakes galore, paper, wallpaper, and the first watermarked paper in the country.

We believe this history has put us on the track of a relative or ancestor, one Abraham Collins, who carved cross-eyed angels on tombstones which are still to be seen in the oldest cemetery. Many Berkshire people will find forebears in this book.

Not the least of its accomplishments may be its stimulus to others to write the other town histories that are needed before too much disappears in the dimness of the past.

The Sheffield Declaration

Berkshire County ties to the American Revolution are fairly numerous and may be discovered in the history of every town; but no significant tie is earlier than the Sheffield Resolutions drawn up for town meeting and passed unanimously exactly 200 years ago tomorrow.

In their introductory preamble, the drafting committee carefully avoid treason by professing "the most emicolable regard and attachment to our most graicous Sovereign...and respect due to the Country on which we are and always hope to be dependent."

Then the fireworks blew off in fourteen clarion indictments of British rule that have commonly been called the "Sheffield Declaration of Independence," and with serendipitous justice because it was so suggestive of the language and grievances in Jefferson's Declaration three and a half years later. For example, they began: "Resolved that Mankind in a state of nature are equal, free and independent of each Other, and have a right to the undisturbed Enjoyment of their Lives, their Liberty and Property."

How, we might ask, did such prescient and defiant resolves get written and voted "Nemini contradicentes," way out on the Massachusetts frontier? Probably because only at that safe distance from Boston did citizens with quill in hand feel so audacious.

At this late date it may be impossible to prove who was the Jefferson of the piece, although many circumstances seem to point conclusively to Col. John Ashley. At a preliminary meeting January 5, 1773, at which he was moderator (as he usually was in Sheffield over a period of forty-three years), a committee of eleven was chosen, in view of grievances, "to make a Draught of Such Proceedings as they think are necessary for this Town." Those nominated and chosen were Theodore Sedgwick, Deacon Silas Kellogg, Col. Ashley, Doctor Lemuel Bernard, Mr. Aaron Root, Maj. John Fellows, Mr. Philip Callender, Capt. William Day, Deacon Ebenezer Smith, Capt. Nathaniel Austin, and Capt. Stephen Dewey. The resolves were signed by Theodore Sedgwick, possibly as clerk, or to attest the copy, but it is by no means clear that he was the chairman who read the report.

It must be remembered that at this time Col. Ashley, age sixty-four, was a revered first settler and longtime selectman of the town, whose citizens forty years earlier had voted him a gift of 200 acres of land for his efforts in behalf of the town. In addition to his many town and county offices held, over the years, he was a respected judge and their repeatedly elected representative to the General Court in Boston, where he had opportunity to hear such ardent patriots as Hancock and Adams (whose words Jefferson later heard in the Continental Congress). Col. and Hon. John Ashley was usually placed in leadership positions as, for example, in the following year when he was named chairman of the Stockbridge Congress of nineteen Berkshire towns that effectively banned British goods from the county. Incidentally, Theodore Sedgwick served that assemblage as clerk.

At this time, Sedgwick, who much later went on to become president of the U.S. Senate, speaker of the House and justice of the Massachusetts Supreme Court, was a twenty-seven-year-old newcomer and neophyte lawyer in Sheffield. Though he and Ashley became lifelong friends, the relationship at first must have been more like that of a justice and apprentice. The Dictionary of American Biography makes the interesting statement that: "As late as May 1776 Theodore Sedgwick was opposed to Independence."

It is easy to picture those eleven Sheffield men in the early days of January just 200 years ago, in the commodious upstairs paneled study (that is envied by the Metropolitan Museum) gathered around a table before the glowing fireplace, busily framing the town's grievances against Britain, just short of treason.

This Colonial home, the oldest standing in Berkshire County, is our humble equivalent of Monticello and Independence Hall. On this and on several other counts, it will be considered for the National Register of Historic Places.

The three-year campaign for its preservation, with six months to go, is over 80 percent of goal, with $30,000 still needed by the Trustees of Reservation for land acquisition, repairs, and permanent operation. If you have not yet joined the honor roll of more than 1,000 donors, your tax-deductible contribution of any size to the Cobble-Ashley House Fund will be gratefully received at 515 Holmes Road, Pittsfield, Mass. 01201.

The Minutemen

By the rude bridge that arched the flood,
Their flag to April's breeze unfurled,
Here once the embattled farmers stood
And fired the shot heard round the world.

So sang poet Emerson in 1837. George Bancroft devoted two chapters and a total of sixteen pages to April 19, 1775, in his *History of the United States*. Gradually historians since then have given less and less attention to that memorable day until some are now down to a single paragraph.

Today, made obsolete by later and greater wars, the fateful skirmish at Lexington Green that killed eight and wounded ten patriots and the aftermath at Concord that triggered the American Revolution seem as slight as a flintlock beside a ballistic missile.

Recently, on the radio from Connecticut, the land where Israel Putnam cast aside his plow to answer the Lexington call, we heard the master of ceremonies speculating with guests about Patriots Day. They concluded that the day was "some kind of a Massachusetts holiday on April 15." This year Massachusetts did officially down-grade it to April 16 for the sake of a long weekend, as Samuel Adams turned in his grave.

The events leading up to the Revolution have a mounting, con-trapuntal, symphonic grandness of oppression and resistance about them: the Sugar Act of 1764 that James Otis said "set the people a-thinking in six months, more than they had done in their whole lives before"; the Stamp Acts in 1765 that led to a congress and open resistance to taxation without representation; the Townshend Acts of 1767 that resulted in the mob violence of the Boston Tea Party; the closing of the cod fishery and of Boston harbor and the suppres-sion of town meetings, followed by the Boston Massacre; the Coer-cive Acts of 1774, termed by the colonials the "Intolerable Acts" that brought forth the First Continental Congress; and finally "the shot heard round the world."

Whether we remember or forget, the Minutemen were the heroes of this symphony. It is interesting to note that their sobriquet originated in western Massachusetts. A petition to the Provincial Congress on November 24, 1774, came from "the officers of the minute men in the northwest part of Worcester County."

Until then, throughout the province, local militia companies had been training in perfunctory fashion, though their "Alarm Lists" were subject to immediate call. By January 1775, they were more commonly called Minutemen and more actively drilled, although for obvious legal reasons they were considered "civilians" under the control of the Committee of Safety.

Although it was geographically the tail of the Boston kite, Berk-shire was only a little behind in pre-Revolutionary activities, as may be seen from numerous town records after 1770. The various Com-mittees of Correspondence pledged aid and comfort to Boston. Local Tories were suppressed as the Berkshire Constitutionalists arose.

The Sheffield Declaration, the Stockbridge Convention, and the Great Barrington Court closing were defiant challenges; and Pittsfield's Parson Thomas Allen earned the reputation of being "the most dangerous character to the king's cause in the western part of the colony."

Berkshire Minutemen were being enlisted as early as in autumn of 1774. Col. (later Brig. Gen.) John Fellows of Sheffield commanded a regiment from south county towns, and Col. (later Maj.Gen.) John Paterson of Lenox, a regiment from central and northern Berkshire. Pittsfield voted to pay each Minuteman one shilling, six pence a day provided he equip himself completely, but Capt. David Noble sold family farm property in order to arm his company.

The news of Lexington and Concord reached the county by swift rider about noon on April 20. At sunrise the next morning, Col. Paterson's regiment was on the march, fully armed and generally in uniform of blue homespun jackets trimmed with white and buckskin breeches. Col. Fellows' regiment soon followed. The same day Samuel Sloan's company of fifty-nine Minutemen left Willamstown, and the county was represented from one end to the other.

Last week at a meeting of the 1976 Celebration Committee with the culturally oriented groups and institutions in the county, a spokesman for the Boston Symphony Orchestra asked for suggestions as to how Tanglewood might best participate in the bicentennial celebration. What better than to perform the premiere of a specially commissioned "Minuteman Overture," even if not played on April 19? Freedom is more song than story.

In Them Thar Hills

The original April Fool's joke is man's inherent belief that he can get something for nothing. The New England landscape is pockmarked with the holes of those who dug for gold. The first gold strike in America was in North Carolina in 1801; the second was in Georgia twenty-five years later, and that proved so productive that a federal mint was operated there until the time of the Civil War.

But Yankees were digging long before that. In 1760 a gold-digging epidemic swept the whole state of Massachusetts. Speculators in Berkshire took more than twenty leases on land for gold-mining purposes. The land of Levi Pixley in Housatonic was purported to be so rich in ore that bullets would not fly straight there; little matter that the owner was cross-eyed. Those who could feel the pull of a mineral rod, usually a prong from the golden-flowering witch hazel, were in a fine position to capitalize on the hope. Many old deeds indicate how widespread and deep-rooted was this hope by their conveyance or reservation of mineral and mining rights. Thus was the hope foisted by one generation upon the next.

In his *Geology of Massachusetts*, Hitchcock rather hopelessly devoted five pages to debunking gold fever: "Of all the superstitions that prevail among men, those relating to the discovery of precious metals are the most difficult to eradicate." Usually, locations were traced back to the words of some long-departed Indian. Often strange night-lights indicated the mother lode (as they now do flying saucers). Digging was to be undertaken at night with proper silence to outmaneuver the neighbors or incantations to defeat the devil, who had unlimited powers over the treasures of the earth.

"A man ignorant of mineralogy finds upon his farm a specimen of iron pyrites or yellow mica or galena, which he mistakes for gold or silver; he begins excavation under the supposition that metallic veins generally become richer and larger and even change their contents as they descend into the earth."

At Easton, Hitchcock investigated a hole begun in 1815 that penetrated solid granite to a depth of 100 feet. The hopeful mining company expended most of its $80,000 capital and only desisted when two men were killed in blasting. The professor found no traces of ore of any kind on the dumps.

One early attempt to extract gold from the Berkshires (like the latest) was an assault upon Mount Greylock. In that case, a group of Shakers, showing surprising worldliness for the sect, delved long and deep only to discover that their better talents lay in agriculture. For twenty years after 1825 a Captain Billy Badger of North Adams prospected in the nearby hills for gold. Whether the gold he claimed to have found "on a spur of the Hoosacs just four miles from Zoar" came from his clock shop, or not, none ever knew because he died of a stroke before he could be tracked to his strike.

It can never be known how many departed from these fool's-gold hills for the golden mountains of the West, but there were many. In 1849 a group of about twenty North Adams residents formed the Berkshire & California Mining Company. They chartered a vessel, loaded it with lumber, and sailed to Matamoras, from whence they were to proceed to the gold fields by mule train.

Those who remained behind continued to hunt for gold, as excavations in at least twelve Berkshire towns prove. The holes were high as Job's Folly on the Tyringham Cobble or low as Schenob Brook Swamp under Mount Everett, but in all cases they were empty, or worse.

In all fairness and so as not to disillusion any small boys, we do want to state that there is some gold in these hills, if you can find it. Traces have been found in quartz veins in Litchfield. The early scholarly mineralogist Daniel Clark of Tyringham reported it from Berkshire "in the mountains near the line of New York" and in small quantities at the Cleaveland mine on his side of the county. The fact to bear in mind is that the most consistently profitable gold mine in the United States processes three tons of rock to produce a single ounce of gold. Tomorrow, if we are invited to look out the window at a charm of goldfinches in a gilt willow against a golden sunset, we won't look. Gold is not that concentrated in the Berkshires—on April Fool's Day or any other.

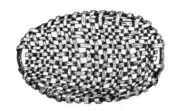

County Carbonari

It seems strange that an industry that once completely altered the appearance of our county can be forgotten in sixty years. Yet, like the glaciers, charcoaling denuded the hills and valleys from Vermont to the Connecticut border, and there are few who remember it.

The ravenous maws of iron furnaces in North Adams, Cheshire, Pittsfield, Lee, Lenox, Richmond, Great Barrington, East Canaan, Lime Rock, Copake Falls, and elsewhere seemed never to be satiated. Millions of bushels of charcoal were consumed yearly, since it took 120 bushels to make one ton of the high-grade Berkshire pig iron; and the Richmond furnace alone could turn out fourteen tons in a day.

Large numbers of woodcutters and colliers were needed to supply the demands of this trade, which flourished most actively from 1815 to 1915. When Yankee labor proved insufficient, skilled French *carbonari* (Italian for charcoal burners) were imported, and later, Irish, Italian, and Swiss.

Almost nothing is recorded concerning this subsidiary industry, so one can only reconstruct the picture by talking with octogenarians in the hills. We talked with one who cut a cord of wood a day for sixty cents when only thirteen; now he "cuts wood for a hobby." Another said his mother cut a cord a day.

This charcoaling was done three ways: as at Richmond, where the cordwood was hauled in to seven dome-shaped brick kilns to be charred and stored—storage capacity 200,000 bushels. Or it was reduced in the woods where cut, and drawn to the furnaces in high-sided carts holding about 200 bushels. Or it was produced in small quantities on the farm as a slack-season occupation.

The second of these was commonest, as evidenced by the numberless circular pit bottoms found all through the county by hiker and deer hunter. These pits were ash-sweetened so much that laurel still skirts them warily, and where the black circles occur in fields, potatoes even now grow scabby.

Whole mountains would be "coaled off" in a season. The gangs of men, some small, some large, would build cabins, withe huts, and even earth dugouts to live in all winter. Entire families lived in the remote woods, and the children would trudge out to the nearest schoolhouse, perhaps to learn English.

If the terrain was not too precipitous or swampy, each woodchopper would cut a swath sixteen paces wide, throwing the branches out and the wood to the center. All kinds of trees, both hard and softwood, fell to axe and saw. Huge trees were split and corded; much good timber was pillaged; and, as in Sandisfield, fine sugarbush was destroyed. On the other hand, much good farmland was cleared in this manner.

When snow was light or had dwindled in the spring, the wood was hauled by yoke or team, or sometimes shot by trough, or cut loose from some ledge in great, chained bunches, "banjoes," to hurtle to a pit area. Here twenty to thirty cords of wood were tightly stacked in four-foot lengths, vertically, in three tiers. The wood was covered with leaves as crack-filler and then dirt, or, if available, sod, laid on grassside in. The finished pile resembled a huge Eskimo igloo.

These piles, many on a mountain, would be tindered by an arch left for the purpose, then shut up entirely except for the necessary bottom draft holes. They were tended carefully and vented at intervals at the top to prevent blowing up. It took about three weeks to transform the pile. The business was beset by fire hazard from start to finish. A small boy climbed one live pile and fell into the inferno, never to be seen again.

After the piles cooled out, they were opened and loaded in high sided carts with the aid of scoop baskets, which are still found in Berkshire barns. Many sticks held their perfect shapes, blackened and shrunken; but they would shatter on their rough trip, if not sooner. It was standard procedure to have a horseshoe bolted to the widest bottom board of the cart, so that if the load caught fire, one horse was quickly unhitched, the traces hooked in the shoe, and the whole load dumped, leaving the other horse to save the cart.

The ironmaster paid about six cents a bushel for delivered charcoal and would reject "coalbran," which had too much wood content. The fine charcoal, being free of sulphur, produced superb iron; but competition from the Mesabi Range ended all this. And just in time, for wood was giving out in Berkshire County, and charcoal had to be imported from Vermont and Pennsylvania.

The Immortal Stagecoach

Anyone who bemoans the inconveniences of the late blizzard has lost his sense of adventure, if not his sense of humor. Civilization tends to go soft and surly as it takes conveniences and conveyances for granted. That was not the case in tavern and stagecoach days when cheery or dreary long winter trips might be remembered a lifetime, but always with the good humor of bravado.

In 1804 Daniel Webster hired a seat in a country sleigh to return home, and wrote: "Stagecoaches no more ran into the center of New Hampshire at this time than they ran to Baffin's Bay." The same could have been said of Berkshire, which stood like a vast, ice-filled punch bowl blocking travel from Boston to Albany. One rim was the pine and snow-clad, granitic, eastern highland known as the Berkshire Barrier; the other was the oak- and scrub-covered, glazed schist of the steep Taconics.

Before 1797, only three roads crossed this snowbound, howling hinterland. The earliest was through Otis, Monterey, Great Barrington, and North Egremont. A 1736 petition of John Sergeant and others stated proudly: "The people living in these parts are now able, and in the winter past actually did pass and repass to and from Westfield, with more than 20 sleighs, well laden, through a wilderness which before that was almost impassable on horseback." In 1742 a branch off this road entered Tyringham and crossed the rugged mountains via Beartown to Stockbridge.

The next road to penetrate Berkshire ventured along the Deerfield valley, over Hoosac Mountain, past Fort Massachusetts, built in 1744. From there Ephraim Williams was required "to keep an open way two rods wide leading towards Albany."

The third road was marked out by Elisha Hawley and two Indians in 1753. It toiled from Kinderhook Creek through the mountains of Hancock, forded the Housatonic between Pittsfield and Dalton, traversed the mountains "very thick set wit timber," and plunged through the Westfield River "in five branches" before reaching Northampton. This horse-path was not widened enough for coach travel until 1793, but six years later, as a turnpike, the Northampton to Pittsfield stretch paid a 12 percent dividend.

From 1797, when the circuitous and precipitous second Massachusetts turnpike was incorporated between Charlemont and Adams, commencing a whole series of turnpikes, to 1845 when the last Berkshire toll was collected, stagecoach and sleigh had a rigorous fifty years over primitive routes. The next fifty saw slight improvement, mostly by the addition of bridges like the long, covered "kissing bridge" at Zoar.

But let the passengers speak for themselves. One question commonly addressed to the driver: "Is this a coach or a hollowed-out iceberg?" A more eloquent traveler wrote: "We traveled all night. The rain and snow descending through the roof, our hats were frozen to our capes, and our cloaks to one another. In the morning we looked like some mountain of ice moving down the Gulf Stream. And this is what the horse-flesh fraternity advertise as their safe, cheap, comfortable, and expeditious winter establishment for Albany."

Berkshire roads were so notorious for frost heaves, ruts, mudholes, and jolts that one tavern master often warned skinflint passengers: "If you should lose your pocketbook between here and

Greenfield, remember you didn't take it out here." Later, when the stage did founder in the bottomless road, the passengers refused to alight and help extricate it. The driver calmly slogged to the road-side to puff on his pipe, finally answering all questions: "Since them horses can't pull that kerrige out o' that mudhole, an' ye won't help, I'm a-goin' to wait till the mudhole dries up."

On the Berkshire run, fares sometimes differed between those who rode all the way, those who walked up the worst hills, and those who pushed. In 1829, when seventy-seven stagecoach lines ran out of Boston, the fare to Albany was $6, or $8.75 on the "Mail Line." The 200 miles required endless tavern stops, occasional passenger exchanges, as to the Dalton sled, and sometimes involved more than 100 horses. In winter the journey took the better part of a week.

Coaches invariably departed at 2 or 3 a.m. One could not see his fellow passengers or tell whether he was drawn by tandem, four, or six until daybreak. Ladies, if they dared travel, often had to clamber over the gentlemen to get the rear seat, the only one with a back. To trim the lurching coach, the driver frequently shouted "Gentlemen, lean left, now right!" The carriages were termed everything from barges to flying machines, but they elicited a singular loyalty. Typical was the remark: "You got upset in a coach and there you were! You get upset in a rail-car or sunk in a steamboat—and, damme, where are you?" One driver spoke truly for an age when he said: "While I am driving this mail-coach, I am the whole United States of America."

A Copake Plow

The old plow rested and rusted in our gravel pit where the last hand had left it years ago. The spot was probably chosen with a mind to next spring's scouring, but that perhaps became unnecessary with the purchase of a new Moline, two-bottom sulky plow.

At any rate, there it was sunken in the grit, hidden by brush and brambles, wooden handles completely gone, yet sporting proudly in heavy letters on the cast-iron beam: "Columbia Chilled Plow, No. 3, 1881, Copake Iron Works, N.Y., U.S.A." At the points of bull-tongue plows like this, the whole country had grown and prospered. Many times had we passed the overgrown furnace and foundry site beside Bash Bish Brook and swum in the flooded ore pit whence came this plow. Suddenly those places gleamed with industry in the mind's eye like a plowshare in April.

The first ironworks in Berkshire County was erected in Sheffield a little before 1739 on the Konkapot River, then called Iron Works River. In that year at Great Barrington, David Ingersoll had begun reducing ore on an open hearth with the aid of a bellows driven by Housatonic waterpower. His 400 pounds per week was shaped into usable bars by trip-hammer and sold at about 80 shillings per hundredweight.

Close by in New York, the first ironworks, and for many years the only one in that colony, was that erected in Ancram in 1748 by Robert Livingston, grandson of the first lord of the manor. This furnace used ore brought by oxcart from Salisbury until about 1830, when the Copake mine was opened.

In Pittsfield some time prior to 1767, the first iron was produced by Captain Charles Goodrich, who secured his ore from hematite boulders strewn by the glaciers. This source, until exhausted, furnished blacksmiths with material for sheathing and plow points to strengthen the old wooden plows.

As may be imagined, ironmasters and blacksmiths were the shoulders of their communities. On their skills and products, such as nails, horseshoes, axes, axles, plows, and muskets, all else depended.

Such a one was Lemuel Pomeroy, aged twenty-one when he came to Pittsfield in 1799 with the family anvil used by eight successive generations. He, more than any other, fostered the growth of Pittsfield. He began by making plows, wooden and iron axletree wagons, and pleasure sleighs. By 1808 he was producing 2,000 stand of muskets, and from 1816 on for thirty years, this amount went annually to the U.S. government. His interests mushroomed to a large clothing mill, real estate, banking, and civic pursuits.

But to get back to the story of the plow, he operated the old Livingston mine at Ancram for ten years until 1845 at which time, under the title "Lemuel Pomeroy & Sons," he established the Copake Iron Works to take advantage of the fine waterpower of Bash Bish Brook and the adjacent ore bed. When he commenced, there was not a house in the place, but by 1878 Copake was an important railroad siding with forty dwellings, a post office, two stores, one hotel, two churches, and more than 200 inhabitants.

The first blast in 1846 produced sixty tons of high-grade iron in a month. The next year, a forge was added to convert the cast iron into wrought iron for gun barrels and axles. A heavy triphammer produced all kinds of rod and bar iron. In 1852 the Harlem railroad reached this little boomtown, replacing the slow oxcart and barge transportation via Hudson. Twenty years later the original old stack was superseded by a larger one, and a new foundry was added for the manufacture of plows and other agricultural implements. A fine steam engine took over in times of waterpower failure. The furnace annually consumed 8,000 tons of iron ore, 1,200 tons of limestone, and 450,000 bushels of charcoal while rendering 3,750 tons of fine quality iron in seven grades from soft to hard.

An old company letterhead speaks modestly and proudly: "Columbia Plow Works Manufacturers of Chilled Plows, Chilled Castings, Chilled Sleigh Shoes, Copake Iron Works, Columbia County, New York, U.S.A." Some Copake car wheels circled the globe, and Copake plows cut furrows around the earth, whilst the plow in our gravel pit came to rest only three miles from its origin. It was not the roving kind.

Biography of a Mountain

Mount Everett should be approached with some reverence when geologists tell us its first upheaval was about four hundred million years ago. The Taconic Disturbance and, about two hundred million years later, the Appalachian Revolution thrust up our present Berkshires. Erosion and glaciers have subsequently ground them down to mere rounded stumps of what were once the highest mountains in the world. In short, Mount Everest has become Mount Everett.

Which suggests the subject of nomenclature. Mount Everett was called Taghconick (with varied spelling) by the Indians of the Housatonic Valley. This name via various interpreters has been said to mean: plenty water, the smaller of two sources of a river, wilderness, and forest. This was the Indian point of view.

The earliest whites, probably describing its outline from a respectful distance, called it the Dome. In the first published reference on the subject, the Rev. Timothy Dwight, first president of Yale College, says: "In the year 1791 I ascended the loftiest summit of this mountain (the Dome) and found a most extensive and splendid prospect spread around me." He goes on to describe the view of five states. By this time the name, Dome, was as widespread as the view.

But others had other ideas. A colony of Swiss living about the base of the mountain nostalgically called it the Peak. Presumably these were people brought in for the charcoal trade, wishing to elevate the mountain to an alp. Some early maps label the mountain Bald Peak.

About 1840 another college president set his foot upon the Dome. This was the Rev. Edward Hitchcock of Amherst, who had been appointed Massachusetts state geologist and who executed the first state geological survey in the country. He was evidently more impressed by the oratory of the Rev. Edward Everett, thrice

Massachusetts's governor, than by the beauty of the Dome. At any rate he changed the name to Mount Everett, using his power of mapmaker. There was much violent criticism of this alteration for many years after. Some said it was profanation "to tack men's names on God's skyscrapers." Catherine Sedgwick wrote:

> Oh call it not Mount Everett,
> Forever 'tis the Dome
> Of the great temple God has reared
> In this our Berkshire home.

The controversy is carried on even to the present in a sort of Shays's Rebellion fashion. The late Walter Prichard Eaton, long familiar to readers of this column, much preferred the Dome; and few have known or hiked the mountain more than he. But the varying opinions of men fail to stir the pitch-pine curls of the sleeping giant, inured to real gales as it is.

There was one occasion when the Dome might have been mistaken for a volcano. During a presidential campaign of the late 1800s (one of the bitterly contested Cleveland elections seems likely), a group of partisans cut the pitch pine and brush from a huge area of the mountaintop and piled it high for burning. The victory conflagration was seen far and wide.

After the turn of the century and after much wrangling over price, William MacNaughton of Boston and Mount Washington, builder of the early Shawmut car, received $8,000 plus accumulated interest for what is the major part of the present 1,000-acre reservation. A county commission was appointed in 1908 to supervise the mountain. About 1910 the present fire tower was drawn by team up the old wood road through the Blueberry Hill property by W. H. Weaver. This ribbon of a road through the lovely laurel skirts of the mountain had been used by charcoalers and later by carriages of sightseers and summer boarders from all over the county. The road ended just above Guilder Pond, so the framework of the tower was boated the last mile to the top over a brushed-out trail. This tower replaced an old wooden tripod of four-by-four timbers.

Five years later the serene Dome again experienced the antlike antics of men. Now that there was a fire tower on top, it seemed prudent to make a way to it. Accordingly, the state sent up a rugged Italian road gang of about twenty men. They must have been rugged; for they worked all through the winter, living in the flimsiest sort of shelter, and fed largely by fish caught and dynamited from Guilder Pond. One unfortunate, his head crushed in by a sledgehammer, started walking the fourteen miles to Great Barrington through the winter's worst blizzard. This Bunyan, with his head swathed in snow and bloody bandages, had made four miles when help reached him.

But even this hardy crew was stopped a quarter mile short of the top by the steepness of the rock. The mountain's passive resistance had triumphed. Mount Washington in New Hampshire, Equinox in Vermont, Whiteface in the Adirondacks, and our own Greylock are all tamed by roads and buildings. The Dome is readily accessible; yet, except for the fire tower looking like an eagle's aerie in a tree, the top has the same monadnock wildness that Timothy Dwight saw almost 200 years ago.

The First Geological Survey

Dr. Edward Hitchcock liked to think of himself as a philosophical geologist. He served four youthful years as a Congregational minister, then, finding himself more interested in things of this earth, switched abruptly to professor of chemistry and natural history at Amherst College. After 20 years in that post, in 1845 he was elevated to professor of natural theology and geology and the presidency of the college.

There probably never was, or will be, a native son who knew the whole of Massachusetts so well. He suggested a geological and natural history survey of the Commonwealth to catalogue all her resources, the first government-sponsored project of the kind in the world. Before he finished the nine-year job, 18 states had undertaken similar work, as well as the federal government, Great Britain and some European countries.

He combed the state from the off-cape islands to the western crests of the Berkshires leaving scarcely a stone unturned as he formed a state collection of 2,873 specimens of rocks, soils and minerals. As he put it: "For ten years—I might in truth say twenty—I have spent a principal portion of my time in wandering over the state. I have climbed all her mountains, I have penetrated her most sequestered valleys and glens. In short I have traveled within her boundaries not less than 10,000 miles; not with railroad speed, but rather with a geological, which is nearly synonymous with a pedestrian pace." His reports published by the state in 1833, '35, '38 and '41 furnish valuable early source material to historian and naturalist alike. The final one contains 825 pages, plus maps, sketches, woodcuts and lithographs. In addition to geology he wrote on the botany, zoology, paleontology and scenery of the Commonwealth.

Among interesting Berkshire observations: He found the iron and limestone to be the most valuable natural deposits in the state making the county the chief mineral district. "Most of the marble is of snowy whiteness, very elegant, and in great demand. ... North of Sheffield blocks 50 feet long are blasted out, and masses of immense size are carried on carts constructed for the purpose, with large wheels, over the Taconic range, to the Hudson." Burning limestone for mortar was also a major industry.

The finest quartz crystals in the state he found on the Phelps farm south of Williamstown, the most beautiful quartz rock for sills, hearthstones and flagstones in Washington, where also there was a porous quartz that yielded millstones worth $80 each. At some of Richmond's 12 iron beds he identified the newly named gibbsite. At Cheshire unsurpassed glassmaker's sand sold at the roadside for six and a quarter cents per bushel. The best rutile used by dentists to color false teeth was in Windsor. In the light of our present knowledge of glaciers it is heartbreaking to see this pioneer geologist wrestle with the facts that he everywhere observed in Massachusetts. How explain the innumerable and vast dumps of sand and gravel?

Why were boulders always strung northwest to southeast from their original sources? What could have caused the deep grooves and scratches starting 200 feet below the top of Mount Everett and on many Berkshire summits? Noah's flood would not have floated boulders over the mountaintops.

The prevailing theory of "aqueous agency" did not satisfy Hitchcock, yet he could not quite abandon it without offering some substitute. Often he flirted near the answer as when he was writing of Mount Everett: "If the rock has a very steep face on its east or west side, that face is sometimes scratched and smoothed as the rocky banks of a river are sometimes smoothed and scratched by masses of floating ice during floods." Of the grooves on the north side, he questioned: "Are they not to be imputed to the boulders that were fastened to large icebergs, which, by the powerful current, were forced over the summit?" The unimaginable forces of glaciation came that near to being first discovered in Berkshire.

Hitchcock was always intoxicated with "the mountain air and alpine scenery of Berkshire." To sketch its vistas, he often took with him his wife or H. J. Van Lennep, one of his Amherst students, or a Miss M who wished to remain forever modest about her artistic talents.

One picture of the seldom visited upper Bash Bish gorge shows Hitchcock plumbing the 194 feet of the chasm with string and stone: "I have scarcely ever felt such a creeping and shrinking of the nerves and such a disposition to draw back as here. Even though I took hold of bushes with both hands, I could not comfortably keep my eye turned long into the frightful and yawning gulf.... When he looks up from the base, a man in such a spot cannot but feel in some measure his impotence for should only one of these overhanging masses fall, he knows that it would grind him to powder."

Other woodcuts notable for showing the earliest views in the county are of Saddle Mountain across Pontoosuc Lake; Tyringham (now Monterey) across Twelve Mile Pond (now Lake Garfield) the view north from Pulpit Rock on Monument Mountain of "the sunny village of Stockbridge and that of Curtisville in the same town;" an Iron covered bridge in Zoar.

Yankee vs. Old Smoke

The imminent championship fight in Miami reminds us that on October 12, 1853, our Berkshires were the scene of perhaps the most colorful bout in American ring history. The southwest corner of the Commonwealth, the county, and the town of Mount Washington, long separated by a mountain barrier, had been ceded by the legislature May 14 to the State of New York. This "District of Boston Corner" comprised 1,050 acres, half steep mountainside and half farmland supporting sixty-one persons anxious for protection.

Isolated as it was from Massachusetts' control, it had become a lawless area, a crossroads for horse thieves, a hangout for counterfeiters, a spot for duels, and a refuge for all kinds of "temporary visitors." No taxes had been collected for thirteen years. Lawlessness was compounded when Congress failed to ratify the territorial transfer until January 3, 1855. For a year and a half "Hell's Acres" became absolute No Man's Land. It was the perfect location for a bare-knuckle bout which otherwise might take place on a barge, island, or the snowy shore of Chesapeake Bay, as had the match between Tom Hyer and Yankee Sullivan in 1849.

James (Yankee) Sullivan, forty-one, so called because of the American flag he wore about his waist when he entered the ring, was a thug from London's East End who had escaped from a penal colony at Botany Bay, Australia. He was lately pardoned from jail by New York's Governor Seward, having been involved in a ring death. He was a saloon owner and leader of one of the three New York gangs. His powerful physique, experience, and audacity more than compensated for his 155 pounds.

John Morrisey, twenty-two, was a solid six-footer at 175 pounds, proprietor of the Gem Saloon on Broadway, and also a gang leader. He was born in Ireland, grew up in Troy, New York, worked as a bartender and bouncer, and as a deckhand on the Hudson River, fought his way to the top of the New York waterfront, thence to San Francisco with the forty-niners, whose gold he took by gambling. The nickname "Old Smoke" was won in a fight of chivalry in the St. Charles Hotel on lower Broadway when his opponent pinned him in the hot coals of an upset stove. He rolled over and beat the man senseless. His flag was black, signifying victory or death.

When Tom Hyer, whose father Jacob had been America's first champion, withdrew from fisticuffs, immediately Morrisey declared he would lick Sullivan in one hour in a twenty-four-foot ring. The articles of agreement were signed September 1 in the Gem: the stakes, $2,000 in gold; the site, within 100 miles of New York; the new London rules to be observed. This meant each round began at the referee's command to toe the scratch. Each round ended by knockdown or the touch of one man's knee to the grass. The fight ended when one fighter failed to toe the scratch.

An unruly crowd of nearly 3,000 New Yorkers jammed the special trains of the newly completed Harlem Line as they steamed for Boston Corners Oct. 11. The illegal fight had plenty of whispered advertising. Eighty to 100 people crowded into cars for forty. *The New York Times* reported: "Men abandoned their business, families, and homes to watch this brutal exhibition between two human beings." All three gangs were present. Many were armed to the teeth with knives and pistols. There was much drinking, fighting, gambling, brawling, and window breaking. Three cars were mischievously cut loose.

Meanwhile, a slightly more sedate crowd of those prominent in society, politics, and sports, including some "ladies," came up the Hudson by steamboat. Others came down the river from Albany and Troy. Farmers, ironworkers, and townsfolk converged from three states by horse, wagon, or carriage. The few homes in Boston Corners were overrun. All the cattle, pigs, and chickens were slaughtered for food. A sandwich cost $5. Most of the crowd spent the night rioting, and the rest slept on the grass.

The sun rose bright over the autumn foliage on Alandar Mountain. The ring had been erected in a natural amphitheater in Vosburgh's meadow, the former site of a brickyard. By 2 p.m. every vantage point was taken by a motley crowd variously estimated up to 10,000. Charles Allire was chosen referee, after his bets had been assumed by Morriney's backers. "Old Smoke" threw his cap into the ring and was shortly followed by "Yankee." Their flags were hung on the east mid-post. Morrissey displayed a frame of herculean proportions when compared with his adversary; his fine condition showed great care on the part of his trainer, "Awfull" Gardner. Sullivan looked remarkably fine and solid as a stone pillar from six weeks of training in weighted shoes.

Some objections were raised by Morrissey's seconds on the size of the spikes in Sullivan's boots, but Morrissey dismissed the matter as a mere trifle, offering to side-bet $1,000 to $800 that he would whip Sullivan, spikes and all. These were the latest odds. Sullivan shook his head, and the hostilities began.

The first five rounds were terrific, according to the *Police Gazette*. Young Morrissey was devoid of all science, while veteran Sullivan was well-posted on all the tricks and dodges of the game. Sullivan appeared able to put in stinging blows at will; on the other hand, Morrissey seemed able to take all the punishment and still land wild lethal swings that might have felled an ox.

Morrissey was a fearsome sight when he toed up for the fifth round. The left side of his face was badly swollen, the eye was closed. His cheek had been lanced to reduce swelling, and blood poured from his eyes, nose, and ears. Even the hardened ladies at ringside recoiled in disgust. But he could still land the thunder-bolts that knocked the "Yankee" back to the ropes. Sullivan had no stomach for more than one of these per round and frequently slipped his knee to the ground. By the tenth round his left eye was closed. He could still outmaneuver his man but took a drive to the ribs "that lifted him clear across the ring to measure his length." Morrissey, though terribly cut about the face and body, seemed to like it better every round; for six hatchet blows, he would return one sledgehammer. In the twenty-third round he "cut Sullivan down like a reed."

But Sullivan gained strength after this, and his backers called for bets of $110 to $50. By round thirty-five, both men were so beaten and cut that only the front rows could distinguish between them. In the thirty-seventh, even Sullivan's friends could see that the tide had turned against him. His backers swarmed to the ropes yelling at Morrissey, who now lifted his man by the neck with one arm, grasp-ing the rope with the other. A riot ensued that probably prevented a strangulation. Opposing gangs swarmed into the ring, and a hun-dred bareknuckle fights ensued. In the confusion, Morrissey was declared winner, though Sullivan, fighting with spectators outside the ring, wished to continue. The affair had taken fifty-five minutes. The purse was still in dispute.

Sullivan was caught by the police later and spent some time in the Lenox jail. Morrissey pleaded guilty and was fined $1,200. Sub-sequently, "Yankee" Sullivan went west to the gold fields, was caught in underworld activities, and three years after the fight was dead in a jail cell, probably from a vigilante bullet.

Morrissey, in the same activities in Saratoga and New York, somehow achieved respectability. He operated sixteen gambling houses at one time. In 1866 he was elected to Congress for two terms and later to the state Senate.

Goliath Boulder Contest

Ever since David slew Goliath, men have been interested in stones; but in this day when atomic bombs have taken the place of slingshots, boulders are more appropriate than pebbles. Accordingly, we wish to urge Berkshire to inventory its ammunition by proposing a kind of internecine warfare among the thirty-two towns. Which has the biggest boulder? Where is the largest boulder in each town located?

After a lifetime of observing the natural assets of New England, in the last year of his life Thoreau penned a passage in his journal that was 100 years ahead of conservation commissions. It states in part: "What are the natural features which make a township handsome? A river, with its waterfalls and meadows, a lake, a hill, a cliff or individual rocks, a forest, and ancient trees standing singly. Such things are beautiful; they have a high use which dollars and cents never represent. If the inhabitants of a town were wise, they would seek to preserve these things, though at a considerable expense. ...

"It would be worth the while if in each town there were a committee appointed to see that the beauty of the town received no detriment. If we have the largest boulder in the county, then it should not belong to an individual, nor be made into doorsteps. Precious natural objects of rare beauty should belong to the public."

Among these natural objects, he went on to include mountaintops and riverbanks. A century later, we are scarcely within a country mile of realizing his thought.

When it comes to boulders, New England was given especial distinction by successive glaciations which removed much topsoil and like pack rats left pebbles in exchange. The larger ones, called "erratics" by geologists, vary in size from the Madison erratic near Conway, New Hampshire, which is approximately ninety feet long, forty feet wide, and forty feet high and weighs more than 4,600 tons, down to the all-too-prevalent wall stones and cobblestones.

Erratics also vary in composition to match New England's heterogeneous base rocks, whether igneous, metamorphic, or sedimentary. So far, none are quality diamonds of pebble size like some found in glacial drift south of the Great Lakes. The big boulders we seek to locate in this Berkshire treasure hunt are ice-transported erratics, not water-scalloped monoliths attached to bedrock like the stone that splits Bash Bish Falls, and not sharp-edged fragments pried by frost action or weathered from cliffs like Pulpit Rock on Monument Mountain. Erratics occur singly or in droves wherever the glacier dumped them. They may be on the surface or deeply embedded in till; they may be at great elevations, like the limestone Elephant Rock south of Perry's Peak in Richmond, or they may be low on the banks of the Housatonic River, like the giant marbles and quartzites rolled out at Bartholomew's Cobble. They will usually show wearing, rounding, or gouging from their rough trip; and they will be greatly or slightly different from nearby outcrops of base or ledge rock. Many erratics, by composition, have been traced back to where the glacier plucked them, in North America, sometimes more than 500 miles northerly; more often, they are fairly local.

Berkshire's most famous erratic is Balance Rock in Lanesboro, immortalized by Melville in his *Pierre* and by Holmes in his *Autocrat*. This triangular perched boulder measures twenty-five by fifteen by ten feet, and by precise cubic-foot calculation weighs 365 tons, in spite of the plaque that long proclaimed 165.

The town of Richmond was especially singled out as a dump by the glaciers. Seven prominent "boulder trains" ("fans" would be more descriptively accurate) were identified as early as 1840 and studied by geologists from President Hitchcock of Amherst to Sir Charles Lyell of London. At the risk of stopping this contest before it starts, the largest Richmond boulder, which may be seen a few hundred yards up a disappearing roadway slanting northwesterly through woods opposite the Center Cemetery, measures fifty by thirty-nine by fourteen feet above ground; it is 143 feet in girth, but it would be as risky to estimate its tonnage as that of your wife.

Greylock

Like massive head and shoulders, Greylock looms central and supreme looking south the length of Berkshire County. To the east falls away the stocky arm of the Hoosacs and to the west the sinewy limb of the Taconic. This loftiest giant of the commonwealth must sometimes laugh at the littleness of men, having known the titanic forces of the Taconic upheaval that thrust it thousands of feet above antediluvian seas, then 200 million years of chiseling erosion, then the violent uprising of the Appalachian Revolution, and another 200 million years of humbling abrasion followed by the polishing of successive ice sheets thousands of feet thick. Little wonder that lightning flickers over its face like a grimace and thunder reverberates there like laughter. As if men could alter the mountain!

Field's 1829 *History of the County of Berkshire* gives the elevation of Saddle Mountain as 3,580 feet; thereafter for many years it was listed at 3,505 feet. The latest geodetic survey in 1951 lowers it to 3,491 feet. Plainly, more practical men are bent on whittling it down to their size.

As if men could change the mountain! The remarkable fact is that they can, the minute their commercial interests infiltrate. The first settler left his mark, still known as Wilbur's Clearing.

From there in 1799, Yale president Timothy Dwight and Williams' first president, Ebenezer Fitch, climbed Saddleback on saddleback, guided by Jeremiah Wilbur, who owned and farmed a large part of the mountain where he lumbered extensively, cut 100 tons of hay a year, and made up to 1,800 pounds of maple sugar. His cattle grazed to the very top whither he had cut a cart-way to take them salt. He proudly showed the sightseers breast-high foxtail grass sown 100 feet below the summit.

But it was not alteration that the college presidents sought. Like the many to come after, they admired the fierce wilderness beauty, the strange coolth in the spruce shadow, the blue shining schist, the small summit pond with two feet of perfectly pure water. They dallied for two hours like schoolboys, climbing for view the wind-tortured trees, "dwarfs stunted in stature and laterally overgrown. ... You will easily suppose that we felt a total superiority to all the humble beings, who were creeping on the footstool beneath us. The village of William-stown shrunk to the size of a farm; and its houses, church, and col-leges appeared like the habitations of martins and wrens."

In the following century, many great and articulate Americans came to the mountain: schoolboys from Bryant to Garfield, novelists from Sedgwick to Wharton, poets from Emerson to Longfellow, sci-entists like Dewey, Hitchcock and Dana.

Hawthorne set his famous short story "Ethan Brand" on the mountain's slope since it was conceived "in a wild road among the hills, with Greylock looking somber and angry by reason of the gray heavy mist upon his head."

Holmes fancied that this mountain of "blue mounds that print the bluer skies" peeked in at his study window as he wrote; while down the road his neighbor Melville constructed a north piazza the better to view the "Purple prospect—nothing less than Greylock, with all his hills about him, like Charlemagne among his peers." Mariner Melville dedicated his spiritual autobiography, Pierre, not to the sea but to "the majestic mountain Greylock—my own more immediate sovereign lord and king—hath now for innumerable ages, been that one grand dedicatee of the earliest rays of all the Berkshire mornings."

Within the scowl of Greylock, Henry James found "a climax, in the Berkshire country of Massachusetts, which forced it upon the fancy that here at last, in far deep mountain valleys, where the win-ter is fierce and the summer irresponsible, was that heart of New England which makes so pretty a phrase for print and so stern a fact for feeling."

Thoreau devoted eleven memorable pages of his Week to a climb and awakening on Saddleback. "It seemed a road for the pilgrim to enter upon who would climb to the gates of heaven." At the students' observatory above the clouds he reflected: "It would be no small advantage if every college were thus located at the base of a mountain. ... Every visit to its summit would, as it were, generalize the particular information gained below. ... It was such a country as we might see in dreams, with all the delights of paradise. ... There was not the substance of impurity, no spot nor stain. It was a favor for which to be forever silent to be shown this vision."

The virgin values of Greylock finally seemed assured in 1898, when 8,660 acres were constituted reservation under three commissioners "vested with full power and authority to care for, protect and maintain the same on behalf of the commonwealth." Since virgin mountains are difficult to protect and since commissioners may be dwarfs beside their charge, it is unfortunate that words proscribing *all commercial interests* were not written into the original act. For there is the entering wedge.

Many wise and perceptive Americans, with wilderness still common about them, cherished the unique, untamed, untrammeled virtues of Greylock. Can we, with wilderness shrinking on every side, do less?

Ice Glen

Three dryads came trippingly down the woodland path from Ice Glen. Possibly they were New York or Stockbridge actresses; at any rate, their query as to where the trail went showed that they did not know where they had been. "Just a big jumble of rocks," one of them said. Her cosmetic veneer looked strangely out of place in the cosmic setting of knee-deep ferns, gigantic boulders, and columnar trees.

We wanted to sit down on a mossy log and tell them where they were; but dryads, being creatures of the moment, don't care. They skipped on down the trail, their voices becoming faint as

the murmurs of a blackburnian warbler in the arrowy pine steeples overhead.

It might have interested them to know that another actress,
Fanny Kemble, had trod that path before them, and also a host of
other notables. Indeed, Ice Glen ever since the inception of Stockbridge had been a local wonder and attraction known to villagers
and visitors alike.

One summer night in 1841, Dr. Samuel P. Parker, the Episcopal
minister, led his schoolboys armed with flares through the wild,
rocky cleft between Bear and Little Mountains. The expedition was
so successful, in spite of (or because of) the difficulties, that it
became an annual affair. The gorge, one-eighth of a mile in length,
was a confusion of cabin-sized boulders and giant, tumbled tree
trunks, many easier to crawl under than over. Ice often stayed in the
darker holes well into summer, and always coolness was there.

On August 5, 1850, a distinguished party of authors that had
ascended Monument Mountain in the morning dined at host
David Dudley Field's and in the afternoon "scrambled through the
ice-glen, under guidance of J. T. Headley," as Nathaniel Hawthorne
put it in his notebook. That word "scrambled" proved fruitful for
American literature, because the adventures that day brought
together for the first time Hawthorne and Melville and joined them
in a catalytic, lifetime friendship at their creative peak. Later that fall
Sophia Hawthorne with her husband and children "went to a
bridge where we could see the torchlight party come out of Ice Glen
and it looked as if a host of stars had fallen out of the sky and broken into pieces."

The autumnal, nocturnal expedition at mid-century grew into a
gala community festivity usually beginning at the Stockbridge House
(now the Red Lion Inn). A costume parade moved by torchlight to
Laurel Hill, where there was dancing and singing around a huge
bonfire. Then the more venturesome, meaning all who were not too
old or too young, crossed the rickety footbridge over the Housatonic, and by beacons of colored Bengal lanterns made their way up
to the glen.

One participant remembered for posterity "the merry shouts and ringing laughter, how the mad glen re-echoed with a thousand Babe-lish discordances, until our senses were almost dazed when we came out into the moonlight that rested upon the dewy meadow and misty river.

The Ice Glen madrigal persisted until the turn of the century, after which it was revived a few last times by those who cared. Rachel Field, still too small to participate in some of the last, recalled the great occasion forty years later: "Nothing quite equaled that for commotion and color. . . . It came with turning leaves and the first frosts of fall. The street was alive with gypsies, peasants, Indians, and pirates, and they formed a long procession that disappeared into the woods and on into the mysterious depths of Ice Glen. The torches made glorious flares, and the familiar features of neighbors took on strangeness in that pulsat-ing light. I watched fascinated, feeling vaguely awed and excited as if I were witnessing some pagan rite, so old that no one could remember its reason for being."

The faint laughter of the three dryads brought back the twenti-eth century momentarily, but soon we were back out of it again and entering Ice Glen with its fern-capped rocks, mossy grottoes, cool caves, and log bridges that spoke of all centuries. For all the clamor that had gone before, only the chipmunk, the red squirrel, the wood thrush, and the solitary vireo spoke now. A partridge and her bum-bling, half-grown brood exploded from a sunny glade floored with shinleaf in full waxen blossom. We looked and listened. A half hour later, after passing under acacia trees planted by Matthew Arnold, we were back in the twentieth century on the Stockbridge main street, not necessarily in pursuit of the dryads.

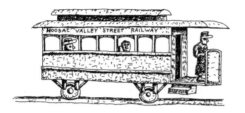

Trolleys Arrive

Walkers off the beaten track in Berkshire woods and fields often come upon grassy embankments and long, straight woodland aisles that may puzzle them. Obviously carefully graded, these alleyways are interrupted by slides, washouts, brush growth, fallen trees, fences, and missing bridges. Sometimes they disappear altogether in hard-surfaced roads.

Of the three living generations, only the oldest will be stirred by memories of pleasant trolley excursions over a Berkshire network that ranked with the longest in the nation and ramified into three neighboring states.

The electric trolley era began in Richmond, Virginia, in 1888; but electricity-conscious Berkshire was not far behind. On October 15, 1889, the first electric car in the county ran between Adams and North Adams on the old Hoosac Valley horsecar line.

Two years later the Pittsfield Electric Street Railway Co. began running trolleys from Union Station to Park Square to Pontoosuc Lake. That first July Sunday of operation 3,700 skeptical passengers traveled. The overloaded cars had difficulty making Benedict Hill, and the future of electric propulsion seemed so uncertain that the company maintained five horsecars and a sleigh for more than a year.

As power and equipment improved, tracks extended like tentacles so that by 1904 there was clackety Toonerville service to South Mountain, West Pittsfield, Lake Avenue, north to Cheshire, and east to Dalton and Hinsdale.

The boom era really began in 1902, when Ralph D. Gillett came from Westfield to join Thomas D. Peck in what became the Berkshire Woolen Mills. The Pittsfield company refused to build a spur line to accommodate mill employees so Gillett established his own Berkshire Street Railway Co. with a capitalization of $2 million; and a "trolley war" commenced. Competition for customers spurred expansion in all directions, the first prize being Cheshire. The Berkshire line beginning at Park Square and running out East Street won, although the Pittsfield line, extending via Lanesboro to Cheshire, captured the first connection with the Hoosac Valley line, thus furnishing through service to North Adams.

Gillett turned his attention to South County, running tracks out Appleton Avenue, along Holmes Road, and down the Housatonic River. There were countless public hearings, town meetings, petitions, and injunctions over franchise and property rights. Lovers' quarrels embroiled farmers and industrialists, selectmen and aldermen, state commissioners and legislators. Some towns like Lee and Great Barrington wooed the tracks right down Main Street; others like Lenox and Egremont were coyly approached by spurs off the main line. Stockbridge proved demurest of all, splitting equally between "trolleyites," comprising farmers and younger citizenry, and "anti-trolleyites," made up of "cottagers" and the oldest village-improvement society in America. The town could never agree—as the "cat-fight" fountain affirmed.

Representative of both sides was Cyrus's nephew Stephen D. Field, holder of 200 patents, who was experimenting with a ten-foot, two-seater, third-rail trolley in his own backyard; nevertheless, he cautioned his fellow townsmen not to allow "the invasion of our beautiful street by a so-called trolley; such a proceeding would at once change our town from the only Stockbridge to a dull commonplace station on a second-class trolley railway." Gillett intensified pressure by building tracks to the town line, north and south, then invoking connecting-link legislation.

Scrappy Stockbridge healed its schism by raising $18,000 for property rights and an extra bridge, and the trolley was shunted along the riverbank. The first Pittsfield passengers jounced into Great Barrington November 23, 1902, amid general rejoicing.

The trolley war ended in 1910 when the older Pittsfield Electric Street Railway, with nearly twenty-five miles of tracks within city limits, was consolidated with the far-flung Berkshire Street Railway. The same year the New York, New Haven & Hartford Railroad acquired control of the merged companies and the Hoosac Valley Line, and continued operation as the Berkshire Street Railway Co.

Track extension continued to a peak of 150 miles, broken lines being last added and first discontinued. Seventeen Berkshire townships and six outside of the county were linked. Bennington was reached in 1907, Egremont and Canaan in 1910, and Huntington in 1917, by the fabulous $2 million "Huckleberry Line" that endured for two seasons only.

Trolley Excursions

The Berkshire trolley system, which extended from Canaan Connecticut, to Bennington, Vermont, with offshoots to Hoosick Falls, Briggsville, Hinsdale, Huntington, and Egremont, flourished over a mere twenty years, but it gave the county a sense of unity and an awareness of assets that horse and buggy, trains, and local newspapers had never been able to do. The trolley cars were cumbersome, Victorian carry-overs filling the transportation gap between the old horsecars and modern autos and buses, but their effects were significant.

In their brief time, county population more than doubled. And no one who ever rode on a trolley forgot it, from the three little hill-waifs whose pails originated the name "Huckleberry Line" to the Astors, Carnegies, Vanderbilts, and Whitneys whose fifteen-cent fare was regularly collected on the "millionaire trolley" that shuttled the two and a quarter miles from Lenox Station to Lenox village, or from the conductor who was sued by a Dalton woman who backed off a moving streetcar and broke her leg, to the Pittsfield motorman who was jailed for running down Governor Crane and President Theodore Roosevelt, killing the latter's aide.

The Berkshire Street Railway at twenty m.p.h. was billed as being the fastest and safest in New England in 1902, although its President Gillett probably blinked the fact that the coasting trolleys hit forty-five m.p.h. on downhill straight-aways, and sometimes, to the delight of cheering passengers, passed trains where tracks lay parallel. The seventy-pound rails were laid carefully to avoid sharp curves and grades exceeding 5 percent. In spite of this, the Huckleberry Line attained an elevation of 1,742 feet in Otis to become New England's highest. The oaken cars, open in summer and closed in winter, were forty-eight feet long and weighed thirty tons. Central power for 13,300-volt transmission was generated at the main station in Pittsfield and supplemented at four substations along the line, a fifth being portable.

To please the rising influx of "cottagers" and summer boarders, excursion trips were added to the local passenger and freight service. In 1903 a plush mahogany-and-plate-glass masterpiece known as The Berkshire Hills was added to the rolling stock at a cost of $20,000. Its exterior, white as a yacht, was trimmed with buff and lined and lettered in gilt. It proved so popular that another luxury Pullman, The Bennington, followed. Each day in season, from 1910 to 1916, these palatial trolleys, one starting from Canaan, the other from Bennington, made a seven-hour round trip through Berkshire. They were retired from service in 1922.

The ladies with their fans and the gentlemen with their cigars enjoyed drinks from a built-in icebox. Fares were $1 over regular rates, plus a twenty-five cent charge for a wicker chair upholstered in tapestry. Capacity was thirty passengers. As women's suffrage was about to come in, chivalry was about to go out, for it was becoming trolley rule that "ladies must get on as best they can."

A tour guide was offered, keyed by number to wooden signs along the route. These pamphlets, printed in lots of 50,000, described sixty-two points of interest up and down the county—places of scenic, literary, historic, and industrial significance.

In addition, recreational parks were provided for the public, the largest being Berkshire Park near Coltsville, to which twenty extra trolleys sometimes ran on weekends. Vaudeville acts, balloon ascensions, burro rides, baseball, picnics, theatre, dancing, and fireworks were some of the features. Other such parks were on the south shore of Pontoosuc, north of Great Barrington, and south of North Adams.

Trolley days were not all good times, however. It took herculean efforts to keep winter tracks open for the "running refrigerators." Air brakes could fail, and at first were abetted by a pole pried against the wheel through a hole in the floor. Accidents were numerous, as when a trolley smashed the bridge at Lee and hurled the motorman onto the frozen Housatonic. The wrecked car had to be burned.

Complaints became as noisy as the trolleys. Lee and Great Barrington restricted the cars to 5 m.p.h. in their streets. The company countercharged: "The streets are crowded like Boston; it is absolutely outrageous." Pittsfield found the trolley bells, whistles, and wheels "a screeching nuisance." There were wrangles over pavement rips and rights. Then wartime brought higher fares and a strike by 400 employees for increased wages. Schedules were curtailed and interrupted, and lines were gradually discontinued and abandoned.

Old ghosts now speak along sunny embankments and in dim forest aisles where the trolleys once ran. Pines whisper comments of yore: "The cars seem almost alive as they glide through this fairyland of mountains and dales. One enters Stockbridge, and the breath of aristocracy seems to be rising among the hills."

Or: "Each turn of the road is like the turn of a kaleidoscope presenting some new phase of scenery. Praise comes from outsiders until the native-born, moored in his own dooryard, begins to realize what an Eden his lot is cast in."

How can we preserve this legacy? By awakening these Rip van Winkle roadbeds from their fifty-year sleep. By linking their remnants in a hike-and-bike trail the length of the county. How better?

Berkshire Epitaphs

Epitaphs, like wildflowers and birdsongs, are lively reminders that all is not death in the graveyard. It is unfortunate that their grace notes have now passed out of style, for they uniquely recorded traits and trends in the history, the poetry, and the philosophy of other times.

The most prevalent epitaphs are oft-repeated Biblical quotations or overworked and worked-over lines from widely circulated epitaph books, with brevity to satisfy the stonecutter, truth to console the bereaved, and bouquets to flatter the deceased. Old diaries show how our ancestors faced up to life; epitaphs show how they regarded death, though they seldom wrote their own. If they had, we would have more lines as startlingly pensive as poet Frost's: "I had a lover's quarrel with the world."

Odell Shepard, in his *Connecticut, Past and Present*, detects a definite evolution in the art of New England gravestones from the early Puritan skull and bones, to the winged skull, to the cherub's head, to the urn and weeping willow. A collector of epitaphs might easily develop a corollary in thought trends, but let us look instead for diverse traits. This sampler offers out-of-the-ordinary lines gleaned from rambles among many sunny memorials. The reader is challenged to find some common denominator as he goes along.

Stern words of warning are cut in Berkshire marble as Calvinist sermons were impressed on character. In the Lenox hilltop cemetery, for William Andrus who died in 1786, we read:

When you my friend are passing by
And this informs you where I ly
Remember you ere long must have
Like me a mansion in the grave.

For Adolphus Hyde who died four years later, age twenty-one:

Nor sex nor age can death defy.
Think mortal, what it is to die.

In Lee for Elizabeth Jenkins who died in 1788, we find:

Behold my friends while passing by
This stone informs you where I lie.
Tho I have lived to ninety one,
Yet you may die while you are young.

On a roadside stone between these same towns, as if to caution speeding motorists, is the inscription: "On this spot was found the lifeless corpse of Mr. D. Blossom of Lenox, May 8, 1814, in the 22nd year of his age. Walking here he was suddenly called into eternity without any earthly friend to console him in his last moment or to close his dying eyes. Reader, pause and consider the vast importance of being prepared to meet thy God. For thou knowest not the time, the place, nor the manner of thy death."

Resignation may be expected where belief in predestination was commonplace, but sometimes it is found in peculiar measure, as at Lenox for Nina E. Dodge, age fifteen months: "This bud was broken off just as it began to unfold in great beauty. Jesus wanted it."

One wonders at the terse resignation of two Sheffield inscriptions: "Katie Lee, died 1886, age 11. Young but ready to go." "Ira O'Brien, drowned June 1851, age 18 years. It is well."

In Sheffield's Barnard Cemetery, for the illustrious Maj. Gen. John Ashley, who died in 1799, we find:

Make the extended skies your tomb,
Let stars record your worth;
Yet know vain mortals all must die,
As nature's sickliest birth.

Promises of the great reward are as numerous as past pastors of
the Berkshires. Here are four, all from the Lenox cemetery. For Dr.
Anson Jones, the last president of the Republic of Texas, born in
Great Barrington in 1798: "Tis not the whole of life to live, nor all
of death to die."

John Uriah Judd, age 17 mos.
Death may the bonds of life unloose,
But can't dissolve my love
Millions of infant souls compose
The family above.

Our Georgie, age 5 years
Sweet little flower
So soon to die
So soon to bloom
Above the skies.

Elizabeth H. Eells, died 1843, age 21 years
Partner of my bosom go!
Jesus calls you home away,
While I mourn thy loss below
Thou dost dwell in endless day.

In the Old Burying Ground at New Marlborough is this quaint
figure of speech for Mrs. Elizabeth Sheldon, died 1809, aged 24:

Oh may you scorn these cloths of flesh
These fetters and this load
And long for evening to undress
That you may rest with God.

Part 2

Berkshire Nature

Over the Snows

Like white rabbits on broad, furry pads or partridges on feathered feet, we shuffled silently up Mount Everett over two to four feet of snow, leaving a trail of snowshoe prints like spider webs pressed into the surface. A half-inch fall of frost flakes during the night had given that special pristine brilliance seen best in morning sunlight, a cut-glass scintillation in pinpoint flashes that my comrade, being an artist, despaired of bringing to canvas unless it could be done by sprinkling bits of mica flake on the flat oils.

The woods were filled with reflected light. Splashes of sun filtered through hemlocks, dappling the snow and illuminating dark trunks with surprises of light; the columned alcoves became halls of mirrors. At no time of year are the woods so filled with snow and light as when February turns to March.

This is true underfoot, in the immediate woods and at a distance. Hawthorne noticed it 100 years ago, looking from Stockbridge Bowl at the very mountain we climbed: "The transparency of the air at this season has the effect of a telescope. ... In the early sunshine of the morning, the atmosphere being very clear, I saw the dome of Taconic with more distinctness than ever before, the snow patches on its round head being fully visible. Generally it is but a dark blue unvaried mountaintop. There seems to be a sort of illuminating quality in new snow, which it loses after being exposed for a day or two to the sun and atmosphere."

When we reached a point where we could see surrounding ridges and hogbacks, it was noticeable that even in the middle distance the hills harbored a special quality of light. Ledges, laurel, and underbush being for the most part snowed under, their sides and flanks gleamed through bristling trees suggesting great somnolent porcupines, the snow quilt being the white underquill.

The artist, ever watchful to get things right, noted that the horizon sky seemed to pick up the snowy luminosity in a circling white that, somehow with no gradations, mounted to intense blue at the zenith.

Then we noted in the open oak woods beside the mountain road a shadow phenomenon that, if painted as it was, would not look right, indeed, would scarcely be believed. The last heavy snow was borne in on a wind that had scooped the usual holes about every tree. The sun was up enough to obliterate all shading of these wind-scoops so that from the road they were invisible. Each prominent tree shadow, therefore, ribboned up toward the base of its tree and abruptly stopped one foot short. There was no optical illusion; there was just no shadow for that last significant, connecting foot. Obviously oak trees do not jump away from their shadows like hopscotch boys. Should the artist fill in the missing link to satisfy expectations, or should he "paint the thing as he sees it for the God of things as they are," risking all credibility?

We shuffled on, lest several trees should fall, soon arriving at Guilder Pond muffled in deep snow. The windswept surface was tormented in places, as it would be in summer, by cat's-paw breezes. There were wavelets of snow with knife-edges that lapped about our snowshoes as their counterparts would at the prow of a canoe in summer. Snowshoe and canoe, two Indian inventions that have not been bettered for their purposes. Like two Indians we were out for winter tracks. There were none at all about the pond, not even the punctilios of deer. The reason for this was plain when a broken branch indicated four feet of snow in the marginal woods. There had been some browsing on last-choice, low hemlock branches, but those deer were now pastured or yarded elsewhere in lesser snows.

The meek had inherited the earth. The tracks of white footed mice were all that we saw that morning, not exactly their tracks but the strung intaglios of their bodies connected by faint tail impressions as they sprang along in the deep powder, always straight for some upright stem or trunk and then on to another. They tunneled up through all that snow like little derelicts through Pompeian ash or denizens of Egyptian

ruins through drifts of Sahara sands, only to turn about shortly and
descend again to the familiar leaf mold and wreckage of woods. Why
did they struggle thus to surmount the snows where they found no
food? Why were we snowshoeing up Mt. Everett?

Measuring Spring

How measure spring, that essence so various, so
changeable and intangible? When no one springtime is
ever like another, can we define it in degrees, colors, distances, weights, shapes, and decibels?

We can only hope to define the spring at hand, every man being
his own doctor as he watches the thermometer as if it were under his
own tongue. It is a mercurial disease, this spring fever, gone one
minute and back the next.

Like love, it is subtly realized and simply perceived in little hints
and blushes. The drab olivaceous winter plumage of the male gold-
finch suffuses with the spring yellow of willow twigs. The immature
purple finch muddies to the rosaceous of osier withes in a sunlit
swamp. We might fancy that these birds had perched among those
twigs and that wet colors had tinted their feathers. But the mutual
colors mounted more subtly than that: they were mingled on spring's
palette by a brush of sunlight stirring sap and blood alike.

It might be possible to put the surveyor's chain to a spring at the
inlet of an ice-bound pond, to measure the progression link by link
where water warmed by the pulse of sunlight lapped forward with a
dark tongue, slowly sapping white ice in a lengthening channel that
would eventually rive the pond.

Such an incursion we observed as early as March 4. Birds and animals were watching the place also. The first redwings, feeling the disease,
gargled their notes along the cattail perimeter and from encroaching
alders. A brace of geese cruised sedately as two steamboats along the

open channel. Four black ducks attended the opening, significantly in pairs, two squatting on the edge of the ice and two dabbling in the water. Two muskrats poked hopefully along the margin, dark pelts warmed by spring sunshine that nudged the mercury into the fifties.

It looked like termination of the flood of winter days. The water had begun to lap on Ararat, and two muskrats were the first ashore. The measure of spring was two by two.

Next morning the pond was frozen solid again, and a stray herring gull sat stolidly on the ice cooling webbed feet, his pied bill pointing into a northerly breeze as if he were a stuck weathervane, not a dove with an olive branch.

A week later, snow fell during the night; the temperature was twelve above zero. March had taken one step forward and two backward. It was the seesaw weather to bring on sap flow, the tides of March. Spring was being measured in every sap house in gallons of syrup and in pounds of sugar. That was a measure many could understand. It showed in figures in the bank account.

The account of snow banks was just as graphic, if less noticed. The balance between white and brown-blotched landscape shifted each day. Slowly the strange-shaped continents of snow dwindled at the edges into seas of flattened, brown grass as everywhere winter trickled away. On the warmest days chipmunks scampered over the pasted leaves, measuring distances between shrunken islands of snow. They were the Magellans of spring.

Sounds of spring were as various as its other manifestations. We recognized them by their suddenness and newness. They were hardly to be put to musical measure: the maundering of crows with new leisure to philander, the honking of geese in opening oxbows, the cacophony of a hundred redwings in a squashy bottomland.

Again, they were as brief and softly musical as the first essay of a brown creeper whose fine, sweet notes of partial song emanated invisibly from the trunk of a tree where the little bird, investigating a lichen rosette, detected a new green and almost exploded with the news.

Surprise may be the essence of spring. Who would ever expect to measure it by counting the swimming strokes of two green frogs on the fourth of March? That was how early it came and how we measured it this year. Henceforth, that may be as memorable as the Fourth of July. Frogs may date their freedom from it.

There they were sitting in our own heavily ice-covered meadow pool. A little opening had been forced at the edge where the spring water ran in. There they sat, noses protruding from the surface, basking in sunlight, awash with the slightly warmer waters of the spring, one a female with throat white as meadow daisies, the other a male with bib yellow as buttercups.

Disturbed by a footstep, they disappeared with three gliding strokes beneath foot-thick ice. Inadvertently we had set spring back by the measure of two frogs.

Blizzards of Blackbirds

At mid-March when the renowned blizzard of '88 becomes the perennial talk of the town, ever optimistic, we watch for a storm of another kind, an inundation of the earliest spring birds. Into the piebald landscape of half snow and half stubble they come, harbingers of halcyon days that will not be held back.

Before the vernal equinox signals spring, there comes a day, sometimes just one, this year several, when the air warms with the vibrant expectancy of a tuning fork. Inevitable notes will be heard, melodious as the ritual of the song sparrow, plaintive as the warble of the bluebird, discordant as the split whistles of the rusty blackbird.

There had been omens earlier like the clangorous, wavering V of geese that followed the north-pointing ridges of the Taconics and the gaggle of fifty geese that tarried on the south-flowing Housatonic for rest and palaver. There had been a few rather silent robins and bluebirds.

But that day everything broke loose in a torrent released by the sun. Sunrise temperatures in the forties rose to afternoon sixties. Water ran everywhere from under the gray, icy heels of old snowbanks. Gullies burbled. Culverts spouted. Ditches, puddles, and pools filled. Brooks gushed for the first time in several years. Pond ice flooded and lifted slowly.

Meanwhile, in a counterflow almost as obvious came the birds, not so much to the still snow-filled hills as to the squashy bottoms of the river valley, one stream thrown back upon the other; as the snow went out, the song came in.

Song sparrows trilled stylized solos from sunny thickets along the riverbanks. Bands of redwinged blackbirds, all males sporting red and gilt epaulets, blared in the tops of any tallish trees like Salvation Army bands at corners of ash, elm, or sycamore. Flurries of juncos scratched and chattered in winter-pasted leaves, some venturing their first spring jingles. Over a partly open pond there coursed a sally of swallows, if three tree swallows can make a sally.

Where a giant dead elm thrust broken arms akimbo, an early flicker investigated the polished, silvery remnants of branches, cackled once and flew off in a flash of golden wings. The loud, liquid song of a cardinal sounded somewhere in the offing. On a dry pasture hilltop that at first seemed barren of birds, by their scurrying in the brown grass, we located an exaltation of larks, both horned larks and meadowlarks. The land was coming alive with restless birds and running water.

Around the greening edges of a sizeable meadow pool there played a coquette of killdeer, six of them, cavorting in the expanding circle between the snow and the water. Their attentions were to each other more than to probing in the mud. They bowed and scraped, uttered long, melodious warbles, rather than the familiar plaint, fanned rufous tail feathers, and fluttered hither and yon like courtiers and jesters about a regal pair of mallards that dabbled disdainfully in the water.

Then, emerging from the darkness of the old covered bridge in Sheffield, like a woodchuck from the burrow, we came face to face with spring itself, unmistakable and irreversible: a continuous flow northward of redwings and grackles streaming low across the road from the trees and brush bordering the frozen oxbows on the one side to the muddy field and patchy snow spiked with corn stubble on the other. We counted a few hundred, but it was useless; there were several thousands.

The noise was incessant, the sputtering of the grackles blending with the gurgling of the redwings to produce a *sacre du printemps*. Neither voice alone would have been particularly impressive, but the vast medley chorus was startlingly so, like a symphony of bagpipes and hurdy-gurdies.

On the ground, the two intermingled species were easily distinguished by size; in the air, the larger grackles dragging long, keeled tails suggested sluggish rowboats flailing upstream. We studied them on the ground with binoculars at close range to determine if there were any purple or Ridgway's grackles among the bronzed, since all three do occur in Sheffield. The iridescent backs shimmered and glinted bronze in the sunlight; neither of the more southern varieties appeared to be among these early arrivals.

Mudtime

New England is divided into two camps: those too young to remember mudtime and those who wish they didn't have to remember it. Mudtime was that inevitable stretch, beset with sinkholes, extending from ice-cutting time to trout fishing. It hit the sugaring season right at the root and altered the date of many a town meeting.

Hard-surfaced roads have played hobs with mudtime just as they have with the railroad and trolley car. It is hard to believe such natural phenomena can pass from the scene so quickly. Robert Frost once foresaw that sometime even his lucid lyric "Stopping by Woods on a Snowy Evening" would need a footnote; there would be those in the space age who would not understand "harness bells." Already there are inexperienced Yankees who wonder at "Two Tramps in Mudtime." For them this hipboot note.

Mudtime was a time to stay home. It was all the difference between getting stuck in the clean snow and getting stuck in a hog wallow. We have heard of those bottomless swamps where a roadbed has gradually been built upon the carcasses of sunken trains, such as the swamp south of Stockbridge where surefooted deer have disappeared. Similarly the spring roads of any small New England town might properly be known as the tar pits of the Model T.

We cannot speak firsthand of days when the snow was packed and rolled in the roads by sled and team rather than plowed. That compounded the mud with slush, often preventing travel for six weeks, necessitating a summer term in the one-room schoolhouse. But the thrifty Yankee family took advantage of the spring spell; the children got done with chicken pox, mumps, or measles; mother caned the chairs or the children; and pa and the hired man got out the winter-cut logs or the maple sap, taking full advantage of the greasy ground so favorable to pung and logboat.

Our experiences with "mud luscious spring," as E. E Cummings called it, were of the late Model A era up to the time when Chapter 90 finally made the town roads passable. When home-butchered pork and potatoes palled and stock or flock feed began to run low, a man might be forced to the road. The six miles to a hard-surfaced highway could easily be an all-day adventure. Necessary equipment included shovels, at least two jacks, tire and log chains, an ax to cut poles, and the more plank and blocking the better.

The strategy was to choose the best set of ruts and give the engine her head. Often, two wheels could be run along the frozen remnant of snow in the ditch or on the bank and the other two down the center of the quagmire; the spattered vehicle proceeded like a heeling sloop. When she settled in to the hubs and hung, then the pilot really learned about spring in New England. Nothing sounded as pleasant as a bluebird's warble or as derisive as a honking wedge of geese as when one was down in the mud trying to work a tipsy jack to a point where it would push a stone down and a car up. The legendary turtle out in the middle of space holds the whole earth up more easily than this. And the turtle stays clean.

After all four corners were jacked and stoned up and the nearest stonewall had been distributed in the ruts, the vehicle might advance enough to jump the road entirely and travel in a hayfield for a ways. Some farmers walled barways to prevent this and to ensure spring work for the tractor, drawing the unfortunates through.

Now good gravel gets us through most back roads, unless we happen to slip into a ditch. It is possible to speed through mudtime without hearing the melody of a single fox sparrow. Speed was always a poor bargain, but so was mudtime.

Philohela Minor

If we had been permitted the creation of birds, there never would have been a woodcock. Imaginations, except for an occasional Lewis Carroll's, are not that fanciful. Indeed, our birds like the dodo would probably never have gotten off the ground.

Now here is April playing its fool's jokes, its annual spring pranks, making its feats look easy, almost natural, like the skunk cabbage and the woodcock. Before the snow is gone the mysterious woodcock is back in favorite alder swamps and pussy willow hollows where some earth remains unfrozen. Here he probes the mud with his disproportionately long bill that Thoreau called "a sort of badge they wear as a punishment for greediness." With this bill plunged up to the forehead in mud, the eyes of necessity have evolved almost to the back and top of the head, so that even in his awkward position the bogsucker cannot be surprised.

His food is chiefly earthworms, and one captive bird is reported to have eaten almost double his weight in worms each day. Like the robin, the woodcook hunts partly by ear. The upper bill-tip being flexible and sensitive enables him to locate and seize a worm, and not make mistakes with roots. Doubtless he could have furnished Darwin much information for his classic treatise on earthworms.

Most woodsmen know this bird from hunting experience and regard it as king of the game birds because it lies so close, suddenly flashes to the alder tops, then zigzags off. We seem always to shoot at a zig when it is on a zag. For us it is more interesting in the spring.

Across the road from our house any clear evening down in the alder swale may be heard the nasal *peent* of these crepuscular gnomes. The name, Philohela, means loving the sun's heat, which certainly is a misnomer; the woodcock rises as the sun sinks. It is at dusk the male begins his remarkable courtship song and aerial dance, which seems unknown to most hunters. Many times we have stolen down the shadowy meadow to witness the performance, making advance as the bird sang high overhead and crouching still as he descended to land, sometimes within a few feet.

He makes impetuous little rushes through the leaves and grass, occasionally strutting like a ridiculous, diminutive turkey cock, short tail feathers erect and spread, wings drooped, and bill sheathed in his breast-feathers, or sometimes pointed skyward. His ground note is that uncouth, guttural *peent* so like the nighthawk's "barbaric yawp" that Whitman heard over the city rooftops.

But let us get our bird off the ground, for his spring flight song has been compared to that of the skylark. He suddenly whirs up with that characteristic whistle of wings, probably caused by the scythe-like primary feathers, ascending an ever-widening spiral staircase of dusk. If there be sunset glow, his whistling circles are easily discerned; and as he reaches his zenith almost out of sight, he bursts ecstatically into a melodious chippering, twittering song, one note cascading upon another long after his breath should have given out.

During the last part of the song he begins an erratic bat-like descent, sideslipping and volplaning steeply downward to his landing within a few feet of us. The performance lasts a little over a minute, but, after a few *peents*, is repeated. Through our window on favorable moonlit nights we have heard this serenade till daybreak.

But if the timber doodle seems one part foolishness, one part angleworm, and one part song, it is also one part courage. One spring we found a nest in the alders near a brook, simply a gathering of what leaves were at hand with the four speckled, pyriform eggs to hold them down. The mother would actually remain on the eggs, allowing us to stroke her. Rex Brasher told us of a bird that sat thus repeatedly in the center of a logging road, while two horses and a loaded log boat passed over her. How is that for a game bird?

So if we would exercise ourselves and our imagination of an April eve, let us dare to get two feet wet and visit some alder run or bosky dell. There nature hangs her tassels and demonstrates what she can do. Her little vespertine voodoo, all "mimsy in the borogroves, will gyre and gimble in the wabe." Between bird and man which is then prosaic, foolish one?

Along the Edge

Early spring is the season of edges. The season itself is the edge between winter and summer. The garment of winter like pond ice frays at the edges to the nudge of spring, and at night it freezes again. At perimeters the two forces meet. Look north, and the sinister wind tingles the teeth; look south, and the dexter sun caresses the cheek.

At the edges things begin to ameliorate. Look not for spring deep in the woods, within the fastness of the swamp, in the middles of wind-blown fields and pastures, nor in the centers of icy lakes. Those reinforced seats and elbows will come out in due time. Look now along the selvage; that is where to feel the fabric of spring.

Shore lines, riverbanks, bog margins, fence rows, stone walls, roadsides, escarpments, woods' edges, all borders come alive with tasseled catkins, beaded twigs, greening shoots, animal rustlings and bird notes. One swallow may not make a spring, but three do, and we saw three tree swallows on April 1 at Twin Lakes, fluttering low along the edge of the offshore ice, inspecting the wrack and ruin of winter at the seams. They were no joke to be snatched away like a purse on a string from a sidewalk. The following week the ground was like a sidewalk; the temperature stuck between 12 and 32 degrees, and $20 million worth of peach blooms blasted in the Carolinas and Georgia. But the swallows were free agents, harbingers with no strings attached, feeling influences in their hollow, mercuric bones.

Along the same ice crumble, crows and grackles picked at flotsam and jetsam, knowing full well that the best morsels appeared along this rip between seasons. At the sunny, sheltered edge of the lake, red-wings and rusty blackbirds explored along the splashed stones getting wet feet like small boys and uttering excited split whistles that cracked upward like adolescent voices.

Though the wind was chill, nearby where a yard bordered the woods a tufted titmouse was moved to sing over and over his loud clear trebles calculated to tip the balance from brown grass to green. In the edge of another wood, the thin sweet lilt of a brown creeper defied the cold wind off the lake and seemed impetus enough to relax tight bud scales. A cardinal flirted with us along the roadside, not stirred to sing, but as bright red and full of sanguine palpitations as the red osier twigs that offered him perch.

At the south verge of swamps, skunk cabbages poked forth from the mud like so many noses of spring, purple with cold, their green handkerchief leaves still missing. On south-facing cobble ledges scouted by phoebes for nesting possibilities, aquilegia, saxifrage, and other plants splayed basal rosettes like brooches about multi-carat, central buds. In frozen backwaters of the Housatonic, drab pairs of black ducks dawdled on the ice as if waiting for it to melt, while white shoals of sheldrakes bobbed like ice cakes and disported happily midstream or sunned on sandy spits. Everything was a manifestation of the edging of spring.

Sparrows are to the edges of April as warblers are to the middles of May. Along any margin some kind of sparrow will be scratching or singing. We may list a dozen common varieties and up to half as many rare ones in a spring. Their very names evoke the season: tree, song, fox, white-throat, field, swamp, savannah, chipping, white-crowned, grasshopper, vesper. The house sparrow is not included in this spring paean, being an outlander that prefers city middens to edges. The first one ever to reach our property lingered about our sheds the last two weeks of March, cheeping piteously for a mate that never came. Finally the minstrelsy of song sparrow, fox sparrow, and white-throat shamed him from the premises.

Beside a stonewall where New England asters had dropped their seed, we watched a song sparrow scratching for more than half an hour. He hopped and clawed with both feet simultaneously, working the integument of the earth, circling one small spot like a farmer hoeing his garden, except that he harvested meanwhile and trilled an occasional lisp to the April breeze. His seed might not bloom to asters, but it would be translated into songs. After he flew, his tiny designs remained etched on the glebe, hieroglyphics of spring, words of affinity born of old necessities.

Consider the Dandelion

The next time you are down on your knees grubbing the first spring dandelions from the lawn, pause a moment to reflect that many others, from scientists, doctors, and epicures to children, poets, and philosophers, have genuflected to this lowly plant, and for reasons quite other than eradication. By its own virtuosity the humble dandelion has preceded or accompanied civilization around the earth, and interest in it has been similarly widespread. Indeed, a letter from California has requested this panegyric from a New Englander who has, in fact, some dandelions in his lawn and garden for love of them.

The Greeks had a word for dandelion, *Taraxacum*, meaning disquiet or disorder, not because it caused but because it cured those conditions. A bitter medicine was made from the root and a diuretic from the milky juice. Our word comes from the French *dent de lion*, lion's tooth, used by practically all nations and referring to the jagged leaf edges. The dandelion has collected other colorful common names in its vagabonding such as "peasant's clock" and "tramp with a golden crown."

Its epicurean uses have been many. The dried roots have been a coffee substitute and adulterant, as has its cousin chicory. The young, succulent, spring greens impart flavorsome bitter-sweetness to a tossed salad. The early leaf rosettes boiled with some diced lean and fat salt-pork are far superior to spinach, and six weeks and a country mile ahead of any garden produce. New Englanders used to put them down in crocks or put them up in jars by the bushel. Nowadays their special spring qualities preserve well in the home freezer.

The blossoms, besides furnishing early pollen and nectar to the winter-starved bee, can be made into a delicious wine. We especially recommend dandelion fritters made from the young flowers rolled in a batter, then pan or deep fried; we have had these mistaken for fried oysters. But a mess of greens, ah, complementing crisp, six-inch, native brook trout, with a piece of maple sugar fresh out of the pan for dessert: There's a distillation of spring days that will get one through a winter just thinking about it!

George Washington Carver, deeply distressed by the starving plight of some of his fellow men, showed them how they could sustain life by eating the weeds about their hovels. The dandelion was one of these, so to some it has been a veritable necessity. Yet the child, who has split the stem and run it over the tongue to make curls or used the hollowness to link a golden bracelet, necklace, or crown, knows it as a toy.

Another April, Thoreau wrote: "Dandelions, How surprising this bright-yellow disk! Why study other hieroglyphics?" And also from his journal: "I was ready to say that I had seen no more beautiful flower than the dandelion. This flower makes a great show, a sun itself in the grass. How emphatic it is! You cannot but observe it set in the liquid green grass even at a distance."

A poet who wrote in our Berkshire Hills had a special affinity for this adaptable flower that may cower on the lawn to bloom beneath the mower or tower over a tall stem to blossom among the skyscrapers in the meadow jungle. That was Edna St. Vincent Millay. The following unpublished lines from a poem she wrote at age fifteen are here first printed by permission of her sister, Norma Millay Ellis of Austerlitz:

> The world is covered with a carpet fair,
> And blooming all around
> Are dandelion buttons, buttoned there
> To keep it on the ground.

At Austerlitz in her last April this poet wrote, in a letter to the postmistress, of her husband: "How excited he always was when he saw the first dandelion! And long before the plants got big enough for even a rabbit to find them, he had dug a fine mess for greens."

Seven Spring Sisters

Put to it to list the first seven wildflowers that signal spring in New England, seven botanists would surely give seven different answers. Put the same question to the earliest flying bees and flies and their answer would be one and the same since their lives depend on it.

Growth in a plant is good but insufficient evidence of spring. The traditional emblem, the pussy willow, may show a silver tip in the *ber* and *brr* months. Thoreau, who made such universal affairs his daily business, did not regard the pussy willow as a spring sign until the ament projected more than the length of its covering scale. This was a sophist's rule of thumb.

The more knowing insects do not heed and flock to the pussy willow until later, when it begins bearing nectar and shedding pollen.

That is a spring sign with intrinsic meaning, not simply old growth, but new essences and new beginnings in response to new impulses.

Take then this manna and honey on March and April bleakness, pollen and nectar for criteria. We arrive at these seven sisters, listed alphabetically to avoid priorities. It is a seven-way tie if one judge can be simultaneously in seven places. All have shed pollen in late March or early April.

Arbutus shyly thrusts forth pink buds and pinkish-white, waxen blooms from trailers of leathery, evergreen leaves, half-hidden in withered oak leaves, moss or pine needles, often at the very edge of the dwindling snow. Its modest presence along wood roads and field margins is announced by the sweetest fragrance on the breeze.

The prostrate plant, first to greet the Pilgrims after their first hard winter, was hopefully named mayflower after their ship, which in turn had been named from the English hawthorn.

The skunk cabbage, humble relative of the regal calla lily, proclaims its streaky, mahogany presence in the mud by stench, not by fragrance. Its cupped hand, formed underground the season before, sometimes pokes up through swamp snow and ice looking purple with the cold; yet within the sheltering spathe will be found the thumb-like spadix with its minute, foetid flowers already shedding pollen. The entrance may be webbed by a spider awaiting the first fly.

The coltsfoot, looking like a spindly dandelion in ditches, wet places, and even in the middle of trout brooks, shows its yellow head long before the leaves, which gave it the name. In fact, early botanists supposed flower and leaves to be two different plants. Coltsfoot is now a widespread, naturalized, European plant that since the days of Pliny in the first century symbolized all herbal medicines, its leaf shape having been painted on many an apothecary door. Coltsfoot tea, syrup, lozenges, rock candy, and tobacco are still used to relieve coughs, asthma, and spring fever.

The dandelion, cosmopolitan composite of spring sunshine, has been found blooming every month of the year in the Northeast, so it cannot be omitted from first flowers. More than 100 species of insects that seek its nectar and pollen would object.

The hepatica, grace note of winter-beaten, forest leaf mold, surpasses all early blossoms in loveliness as arbutus excels them in fragrance. The earliest butterflies such as spring azures of matching hue may dally with them in March wind, then depart like petals in April breeze.

Last year's tri-lobed leaves hidden about the gathering of fuzzy stems proclaim the Doctrine of Signatures whereby this plant was indicated the best cure for liver ailments.

The beaked hazelnut shows its tiny vermilion stars only to the initiate who will explore with the fox sparrow along hedgerows and stonewalls where the chipmunk has seeded it. There the bushy withes swing short, tan tassels that cast pollen upon these least but brightest of all spring flowers peeking like rubies from drab, bud settings.

The pussy willow, with spring peepers trilling about the hummock-base and with redwings gurgling in the twigs as they dislodge pollen like gold dust from their epaulettes, brings us back to the point of beginning.

For all their diversity in habitat, color, structure, and size, these seven sisters share one trait in common: without the chlorophyll preliminaries of new-leaf building, they immediately set about seed production. They put first things first.

Through the ages how many have grouped the infinitely distant Pleiades as seven sisters! Yet this may well be the first time these flowers of mundane affinity have ever been clustered, other than by spring. Find all seven firing pollen powder before Patriots' Day and you will have seen spring come to New England, with ancient meanings in new beginnings.

The Spring Deluge

Generally, April brings us at least a few warm showers and, along with them, a gradual blooming of wildflowers and a steady infiltration of migrating birds. This year, like last, April sulked in the thickets and refused to play her cards. We had snow and more than enough cold but no showers at all, and very few flowers and birds.

Then, all at once, in the first week of May, the dam broke and the spring flood poured in with showers and all of April's birds and flowers. For those who notice such things, it was overwhelming, too much to keep up with. We like our springs to be slow and easy—like a courtship, not like a whirlwind.

On May 2, about forty glossy ibises were discovered in the marsh north of the Pittsfield sewer beds. This typical denizen of Florida swamps has been mysteriously extending its range northward in coastal marshes during the last decade. Heretofore, the only Berkshire records, both in Sheffield, were a single individual in the spring of 1966 and four in 1971.

The northernmost record, a dozen ibises seen last fall on the Ontario shore of Lake Erie, indicates the erratic wandering of this grotesque dark bird whose sacred white cousin appears in the Bible and in the bulrushes of the Nile.

The Berkshire flock could be approached quite closely where they were dabbling and feeding in the mud among green sedge clumps at the edge of last year's cattails. Their unbirdlike, low-pitched grunts sounded as if more from frogs they were swallowing. If it was difficult to count the moving, jostling birds on the ground where they could not all be seen at one time, in the air it was equally impossible. With legs and necks outstretched, the big birds continually shifted within the wheeling flock, which itself now thrust out a neck of birds or again offshot a wing or trailed a leg of them. As lief count a fluid school of fish.

In the following three days, the flock broke into lesser fragments of from eighteen down to one which were seen at various points in Lenox and Pittsfield along the flooded Housatonic River.

On May 3, even more astonishing was the unprecedented flock of some 100 cattle egrets that appeared on dairy farms in the northwest outskirts of West Stockbridge. These African aberrants made a mysterious Atlantic crossing about fifty years ago, began nesting in South America, and were first found breeding in Florida in 1952. They have spread along the Atlantic and Gulf coasts, finding domestic cattle quite as accomplished at kicking up meals of grasshoppers as were the wild elephants and water buffalo of South Africa.

These white egrets with yellow bills, legs, and feet and buffy crest and nape first appeared in Berkshire near Bartholomew's Cobble in 1962. A dozen together is unusual; and our favorite bird-watching companion, on an African photography safari, saw no regale of egrets on their home veldt that approached the West Stockbridge concentration.

This flock was seen to mill over and suddenly settle around a flooded pasture pool. Like fishermen who knew their business and almost as if manning a net, they all waded in toward the center simultaneously, evidently seining out every spring peeper that had been heard in that dell during April. They lingered in the vicinity in variously fragmenting flocks for three days.

There had been no unusual storm to waft these surprising numbers of egrets and ibises into our hinterlands. Perhaps we can only conclude that in an excess exuberance of spring they overshot their mark. The migration flood, too long impounded by a reluctant spring, at last broke through, and Noah's Ark came riding into our hills.

The sudden influx of all the usual April arrivals along with the warblers of May makes it possible to tally eighty species where, before May Day, it was nearer forty. The anomaly is that May birds have now come into a retarded foliage-and-weather pattern more typical of April. One hardly expects a bobolink singing in an unleafed tree, nor a scarlet tanager in an unbloomed magnolia, nor that warmest-weather bird of all, an indigo bunting, singing in the dooryard; yet all were witnessed the first week in May.

The many insectivorous birds finding little or no food in tight-budded branches were forced to the ground to forage. This caused such incongruities as treetop warblers appearing on cattail flotsam in the swamps and deep forest birds hopping like sparrows at the roadside.

But who ever complained because one spring was not just like another?

The May Wildflowers

For perfect company to the passing parade of in-between spring birds, nature has provided a host of flowers that can also be grouped conveniently, though unscientifically, as "in-between" wildflowers. Too late for May baskets in Berkshire, they follow the earliest spring company that includes the shorter and daintier arbutus, hepatica, anemone, bloodroot, Dutchman's breeches, trout lily, and spring beauty. They are generally taller and more generous in leafage than the earliest flowers, but not so towering or tough-stemmed as the ranker June flowers. They are apt to grow hither and yon in the loose scatterings of a lawn party or regal court rather than in crowded masses. Their hallmark is a certain elegance, ranging from the kingly bearing of the Jack-in-the-pulpit to the queenly moiety of the May apple.

Most of these are woodland flowers upsprung from the rich leaf mold of the forest floor before the fully extended, leafy canopy of June has cut off the sunlight. April's flowers wanted full sunshine filtered through budded twigs; May's flowers want dappling sun cast through half-sized leaves.

Under the forest clerestory, a few provide their own shade. Some good examples, all now to be found at such places as Bartholomew's Cobble, Pleasant Valley Sanctuary, Fernside, October Mountain, or Greylock, if not in your nearer woods, are the May apple which raises two broad parasol leaves above its large, solitary, white flower; the true Solomon's seal that swings its pairs of golden bells along an arching stem beneath a double row of leaves; the modest nodding trillium whose petite, recurved, white petals peek from under a leafy triad, said to be the commonest trillium though certainly the least known among such show-off country cousins as the red, the white, and the painted. But most retiring blossom of all is that of the common wild ginger that can be found only by probing in the leaf mold under its signaling pair of heart-shaped leaves; closeted as Emily Dickinson, this winey chalice would remain unsung, were it not for green leaves.

The majority of May flowers are, like the marsh marigolds, as conspicuous as orioles; like the columbine, as declaratory as the throats of rose-breasted grosbeaks; and, like the clumps of bluets over lawn and field, as forthright as chipping and field sparrows.

They do not form impenetrable tangles like goldenrods and asters. They do not lacerate like wild rose and tear-thumb, nor prick like thistles, nor assail like burrs. They are the comely and the beautiful, buxom as marsh marigolds, lissome as columbine.

They represent many flower families. As the May morel is first and tastiest of the mushrooms, so one of these is first and choicest of the orchids. Indeed, the showy, gay or spring orchis deserves the title of queen of the in-between flowers.

Its flower spike tops a fleshy, five-sided stem that rises five to ten inches between a glistening pair of silvery green leaves. The three to six florets are striking with their upright purple or rose sepals and lateral petals contrasting with white lip and spurs. They are snapdragon traps baited with nectar to reward the bumblebee for its vital service of cross-pollination.

Look for this rarity now in rich, moist woods, especially under scattered hemlocks. Memorable will be the place and the day that you find it. Such a day stands out almost fifty years ago when a mother took her small son gathering wildflowers for a school contest. They chanced upon a company of showy orchis beside a woodland spring. It was obvious even to an eleven-year-old that these were something special and too precious to be picked. He drank deep at that spring, picked one which won the contest, and has never been the same since.

Warbler Days

Now leaves unfold everywhere in old patterns in mid-May. Any gatherer of autumn leaves knows how difficult it is to find a perfect leaf to press. All have insect perforations, wind tears, blights, or even barnacles like the witch hazel gall. Now all leaves are pristine, glistening red, yellow, and green flawlessness. But this is only for a fleeting babyhood, for even before many buds are fully opened, an equivalent insect hoard is hatching, hungry for salad. The entire leaf crop seems in as much peril as a chokecherry stripped by a nest of tent caterpillars.

Then comes the warbler invasion, wave on wave, returning to nesting grounds, migrating northward. They appear in every tree and thicket, looking like animated blossoms as they flit about in quest of insects. They have been infiltrating since arrival of the yellow palm and myrtle warblers in early April. Now they appear everywhere in mixed companies. The thin buzzing songs drift down from the oak tops like that of the blackpoll, or they bubble up from the swamp like that of the yellowthroat.

The *Parulidae* or wood warblers comprise about 114 species essentially confined to the New World. Of these, almost forty have been recorded in the Berkshires, and about two dozen have been found nesting. The family is a puzzle, a challenge, and a delight to bird watchers. The beginner will have his eyes full simply identifying males in spring regalia, learning common songs, or focusing field glasses quickly on a feathered flash in an oak top.

The veteran will renew old acquaintances—and refresh his memory of songs with the ever-present hope of adding some rarity to his life list, such as a cerulean warbler. He will scan every golden-wing and blue-wing he hears in hope of seeing one of the two hybrids that a mixed mating can produce.

He may establish a record early date for some species for himself and his region, if not for science. He may discover a new range for a species, as we did back in 1937 by finding worm-eating warblers in four widely separated locales about Mount Washington, which still remains the most dependable site in the state to find this uncommon species.

By June first the various warblers settle down into favorable breeding environments. The noisy, ventriloquil yellow-breasted chat sometimes returns year after year to the same swamp. The lovely black-throated blue warbler will be nesting in the laurel behind our house. The top of Greylock is a southern outpost favored by a few warblers that usually go farther north, such as the Canada (also on Mount Everett), the magnolia, the mourning, and the blackpoll, which seems to make this its extreme southern limit. A dozen warblers will leave us altogether.

But these last two weeks in May they are all here, which is not to say they will all be seen and identified. Thoreau in his lifetime never could identify a mysterious night warbler that often tantalized him at dusk with its ecstatic flight song over the treetops. Doubtless it was the common ovenbird whose quite different daytime "teacher, teacher, teacher" sounds outside my window at this moment. Thoreau finally acquired a primitive spyglass, and his friend Emerson cautioned him not to book this bird, lest life henceforth should have so much the less to show him. He never solved the mystery; perhaps he never really wanted to.

The warblers are interesting for their variety. They are slender-billed, small birds mostly in yellow and olive patterns, often with gay bonnets, sashes and trimmings. But the minute one generalizes, exceptions pop up like the yellowbreasted chat, which is as big as a catbird, being giant of the family. Several species have no yellow at all. Almost all have helpfully diagnostic markings of black, like the mask of the yellowthroat, the cap of Wilson's, the hood of the hooded, the mantle of the mourning, or they have significant streaking like the chestnut-sided and prairie.

Some are common, some rare; some early, some late; some bright, some dull. Some are ground and thicket birds; others inhabit the highest treetops. The Louisiana water-thrush will only be found along rushing mountain streams; the redstart is everywhere.

Songs can be a great aid in identification and can be remembered by putting words to the music. Once a blackburnian warbler, bright as a Christmas ball, lit on a dark hemlock tip by a cord of wood we had cut. With head thrown back in full sunlight, he sang "ouija, ouija, ouija," while his brilliant orange throat pulsed like flame. We got the message in this sunshine seance, and remember the song.

Peregrine

The duck hawk is a bird of wind, sky, cliff, and skyscraper, the epitome of daring, fierceness, and wildness. As its scientific name, Falco peregrinus, indicates, it is the wandering sickle, rocketing through the skies of the world armed with eight rapier talons and a scimitar peak.

It was inevitable that such a bird should be chosen in days of chivalry by kings and emperors for their sport of falconry. Only nobles of the rank of earls and higher were allowed to fly these rare birds, which brought fabulous prices. This recreation was practiced in early Christian times by the Romans and for ages by the wild tribesmen of Persia, Tartary, and China.

The fierceness of the bird could never be tamed. The falcon was only controlled for the sport by keeping it hooded and jessed. Then it had to be starved before release so it would set about devouring the struck-down game and could be recovered. But even these holds were tenuous. One classic instance of escape was a prize falcon belonging to Henry II that flew after a little bustard at Fontainebleau and was caught next morning at Malta over 1,000 miles away.

But it is the duck hawk nearer home that we are interested in. Why is this bird so rare when it is probably the fastest bird that flies and the best equipped to take its prey? From 1860 to 1915 the depredations of egg collectors undoubtedly reduced the species. The hawks invariably chose ledges on the face of a sheer cliff for their nesting sites, but the rarity of a set of eggs lured collectors to these perilous places, which were reached by rope from above.

Sets of eggs brought up to $50. One man living near Mount Tom estimated that in forty-eight years he had taken thirty sets of eggs from the precipice.

Finally the noble birds received legal protection. The Massachusetts state ornithologist for a time tattooed the eggs to destroy their value for egg collection, and the hobby gave way to more intelligent bird watching. Now the falcon's one enemy is the gunner who ignorantly shoots every hawk he sees.

There are half a dozen nesting cliffs in Berkshire County, two within a few miles of our house, but none have been used lately. Many times we watched these remarkable fliers in the sky and at the eyrie. In flight they resemble a huge barn swallow with three- to four-foot wingspread, but with long pointed tail; they have the swallow's blue-black upper coloring, but beneath, speckled brown on a cream-colored breast. The jet-black cap and mustache ever-white bib and tucker give aristocratic appearance.

These graceful flyers make sport of a March gale, riding in long strides with slicing, powerful wing beats in its very teeth, then circling or sailing before it, spanning whole mountains in a moment's glide. Their telescopic eye spots any bird above treetop level. With wings partly bent the hawk plummets like a meteor at speeds estimated beyond 120 miles per hour; and few birds can elude this "stoop," which has been known to tear the side right out of a tough merganser. Even the chimney swift, all wing and speed, has been taken.

Once, high over their nesting chasm, we saw a pair obviously at play in the sky. One dropped a flicker he had killed. The other, with instinctive timing, dove and recovered it a hundred feet above the waiting forest.

Another time we ventured to climb down to the eyrie on a ledge 250 feet above a chute of white water and a green-blue pool. There were four large eggs, heavily blotched reddish brown. The tercel circled screaming high above, but the intrepid female dove slantwise at the cliff as if bent on self-destruction, or that of the interloper. The last instant, without seeming effort or wing motion, the bird shot skyward straight up the cliff and hundreds of feet into the air. She repeated this astonishing flight maneuver several times, cackling menacingly, and we were glad to come out alive.

From Boston to Bangkok when a rabble of starlings defiles the buildings, when a squabble of English sparrows gossips in the cornice, and when pigeons take over the park, it is gratifying to know that nature, as always, has provided a check. From the wildest cliffs and chasms arrives the duck hawk, to make the skyscraper his watchtower over the city canyons. He is the sword of Damocles suspended over the unwary and the unfit.

Native Brook Trout

Middle May to the twentieth almost always brings that idyllic day to the mountain that recoups in one sprint the ten-day headstart that spring gains in the lower elevations. The new leaves, more red than green, change to green. Apple trees burst into private snow storms. Shadbush, serviceberry, and hobblebush hold over melting white blossoms, and now play host to warblers instead of white-throats.

Such a day invariably calls us on an annual trip to some wild trout stream so inaccessible that no poster and rarely a footprint mark the bank. We may as well confess now, for those who wish to leave early, that this is strictly worm fishing, there being no space for sophisticated casting about in such a wilderness glen. Indeed, one had better be boy to get there at all.

Equipment needed is simply a sharp knife, two or three small hooks, a short line, a small-meshed orange bag for creel, a can of worms, and a liberal application of bug dope. We missed some of the brook in taking pains to select a green, willowy wisp of pole, with the finicky air of one viewing glass rods in a sports shop. Yellow birch was too heavy, red maple too curvaceous, witch hazel too zigzag, ash too jointy. Finally the perfect tapered pole, a lithe moosewood, appeared at the stream edge, camouflaged by natural green-and-white streaking and certainly familiar to the shadowy trout darting below. Two turkey buzzards circled overhead like hovering clerks as we selected and trimmed the pole.

Now we were invited downstream from one pebbly, clear pool to the next. Only the loudest birds were audible above the brook noise: the ovenbird, the northern water-thrush, and sometimes a partridge drumming. Brook trout were plentiful, although never stocked in this stream; several had to be thrown back for each "keeper." It was difficult to understand how such a clear stream could feed so many fish unless they ate gravel, and that proved more fact than fancy, for a few opened stomachs revealed that the main supply of food was caddis-fly larvae, those soft little bodies that encase themselves in sarcophagi of gravel or bits of vegetation for protection. But the sharp-eyed trout were not fooled by the stratagem, and the larvae were ground up by their own selected grit in gizzard-like stomachs. The trout were obliged to swallow more grit than grist on this menu.

Farther down where the brook took longer plunges toward the valley, there were deep, dark pools formed among the tumbled boulders. Yew, evergreen woodfern, polylody, and moss grew luxuriantly among and upon the rocks. The mountain arose steeply on either side, so steeply that giant hemlocks had pitched headforemost downward. Down these shaded slopes cascaded the fluted melody of the hermit thrush, only to be heard when one swung away from the cataract momentarily to circumvent a cliff.

In these darker pools the trout were black and almost invisible as they swirled up from the depths. Their yellow flecks, red speckles, and orange fins edged with black and white appeared the brighter, as if they could still afford bravura on such scanty fare as the crystal water and scoured rock provided. A similar analogy in the plant world presented itself here and there where the brook at flood had casually tossed up a few tons of stone, sand, and gravel. On these bare bars bloomed a scattering of small violets, both white and purple. Thus by apparent alchemy does nature produce the brightest colors in the most unexpected places. The garnet is brighter in the trout's speckle, and the quartz whiter in the violet's bloom.

Having run out of fishworms and having fed far more small trout than "keepers," we took to fishing with bits of the gills. One deep pool looked most promising. A white flume plunged in at the head, creating the usual streams of bubbles that followed the vagaries of the current across the black water. A cast at the edge of the froth brought an immediate, fierce strike that bent the moosewood to the pool. It was the monster of the day—nine inches. He had a three-inch trout in his stomach, indicating that only cannibals could grow beyond the six-inch norm. Doubtless such a natural wild stream could support very few tiny trout, and very few cannibals also.

Rattlesnake Hunt

W e three met again, not in thunder, lightning, and in rain, but on a partly cloudy day, for a rattlesnake hunt with camera. The sleek, handsome timber rattlesnake has become something of a rarity, having suffered a steady persecution since the temptation of Eve. It is estimated, for example, that in the entire State of New York there are only sixteen locations remaining, rattlers having been reduced to one-third of their normal numbers.

The way led steeply upward onto a rocky shoulder affording a fine view of Mount Everett above and the Sheffield valley below. It was here that famed herpetologist Raymond Ditmars discovered an albino rattler; and here also that he learned rattlers could not withstand sunlight for very long, when his catch expired inside a burlap bag. He and his fellow hunters were in the habit of keeping their snakes temporarily in the bureau drawers of Mount Washington boardinghouses.

The afternoon was warm despite a hard frost two nights earlier. It seemed likely that the coolness of late May would hold the snakes close to their rocks well into June. Azalea and pink ladyslippers had come into bloom. Various migrating warblers were in song on the dry hillside: the redstart, the Nashville, the Canada, and the black-and-white.

To the searching eye, the top of the rocky shoulder presented a conglomeration of soft colors. The slabs of gray schist were strewn helter-skelter through the wood like shingles blown off a roof, their forms blotched with gray lichen or with the dark brown of rock tripe. The soft Turkish rug of leaf mold was brightly foiled with low patches of new growth blueberries. A light tessellation played over the forest floor as the branches and new foliage stirred in the breeze. Laurel and scrub oak cast patchy shadow, their stems sprawling prostrate like snakes. Beneath each pine was a russet carpet of needles perforated with lilies of the valley and starflower rosettes. Fallen sticks and bark, old trunks and stumps added to the confusion of the parti-colored background. Meanwhile, argosies of small clouds passing overhead continually altered the patterns of sunlight and shade.

In short, searching for a mottled rattlesnake in this setting seemed like hunting for a straw in a haystack, and there was no certainty that the snake would be straw-colored, since half are of a dark phase.

On this shoulder a week before, our veteran had grabbed an escaping snake by the tail and found his hand full of rattles as the thick, four-foot creature disappeared under a rock. After some poking about with sticks, we heard a shout from him and converged with the photographic equipment to find a very dark rattler quietly coiled upon light leaves beside its flat rock shelter. Disturbed by the placing of the tripod, the snake sounded a dry buzz and slithered under the stone, which was too large to move. Our intrepid Marilyn cleared away the leaves, peered under and looked the snake in the eye while he rattled, but, not being Medusa, failed to lure him out. She left him rattled.

The next omens were propitious: some bleached woodchuck bones, chokeberry in blossom, and a buzzard shadow passing amongst us. Marilyn thereupon spotted another rattlesnake, a yellow one; but he had gone before we could commence the brew or click the camera. The lugubrious notes of a cuckoo chortled through the wood. The snakes were skittish. It was just not the day for pictures or poison potions.

Then suddenly in front of Alvah a whippoorwill flushed from the dry leaves. There, in the middle of nowhere, found by the chance of a footfall, was the seldom-seen nest, or rather no nest at all; for not a twig or leaf had been drawn up to contain the two lavender-blotched eggs. They lay upon the fallen leaves, protected by the camouflage of the bird and the laws of chance, a lifetime longshot to come upon in woodland vastness. They were in the sunlight beside the shade of a pine sapling, and they were wreathed by a thin circlet of lilies of the valley, as if nature were furnishing the nest.

One other find awaited us as we descended the toppled stairway of boulders on the lower slope. That was the rare wild clematis, purple virgin's bower, spreading graceful leafy vines over the gray stone. It was a luxuriant patch, sizable enough to make the scarce plant seem ordinary, but the pendant, translucent, lavender bells dispelled that notion. It was a lavender day.

Rattle Tales

There is no house in Mount Washington without its snake stories, its set of rattles or its stretched skin on the wall. The retiring timber rattlesnake approaches the northern limit of its range here and precariously maintains its last stronghold in the Berkshires. Three remaining hibernating dens form an equilateral triangle with apexes about two and a half miles from the Town Hall.

After exhausting the food supply of mice and chipmunks in the den areas and impelled by summer droughts, the rattlers radiate outward from their dry ridges in search of better hunting grounds. If they were not forced to cross roads, we would hardly know they were around. That is where they generally meet their doom. Ever since the serpent caused the downfall of Eve, Adam has been out to get him.

We have heard of ladies who would not get out of their cars in this town for fear of snakes. Actually, they would be safer if they did, because cars are far more lethal. Herpetologist Raymond Ditmars, who studied snakes over a period of twenty years in the Berkshires, heard of but three cases of snake bite, each due to unusual carelessness in places where rattlers were known to lurk, and only one of these ended fatally.

Rattlers, besides being rare, are extremely shy, much preferring to trust to concealment or quietly steal away. Their fangs have primarily and mercifully evolved to subdue their rodent prey instantly. None of the constricting or slow swallowing of live game for this species. Only secondarily, and when there is no retreat, are their weapons used for defense, and then only after a warning rattle.

We saw a good example of this two weeks ago when we took a rattler for a museum specimen near our yard. The snake was seen crossing a wood road by our sister-in-law. We reached the place about ten minutes later. An oak top left from lumbering lay in a laurel tangle, and it seemed likely the snake had retired under it. Five minutes of trampling and poking in the dry leaves failed to elicit a buzz. Then we spotted it coiled, quietly watching us, under the outer branches of the tree, a darkly blotched individual of the yellow-color phase.

A yard away lay a freshly killed chipmunk with a drop of blood on the back where it had been struck. The snake, trusting to mottled camouflage and to stillness, was hoping we would pass by. It did not rattle until the fork pinned its neck to the ground.

A week later another rattler was taken in the town road with the same length of forty-four inches, this one of the handsome dark-black phase, making a perfect pair.

Six other rattlers that we know about were killed in the town in the first half of July. Such a number in so short a time is probably more a result of the drought than indication of any increase. Whenever numbers do increase inordinately, there are always too many hunters willing to raid the dens in spring and fall.

During late summer the females return to the dens where their six to twelve young are born. Henceforth some mysterious sense of direction, as with birds in migration, guides rattlers back to their original cradles. Perhaps by painting the rattles we could determine how much, if any, interchange there is between the three dens.

With each set of rattles there is usually a rattling good tale. One from this July occurred when a breathless teacher hurried in to a summering doctor's to get help for a nearly drowned camper. The doctor was in New York, but his daughter went to help. On the way, the two ran over a rattlesnake and instinctively jumped out to kill it. While beating the snake, the daughter shouted to her companion "What are we doing killing this snake while someone is drowning?"

Wife Barbara topped that one a few years ago when she stepped on a rattlesnake in our raspberry patch, and, though bare-legged, did not get bitten.

Our own best tail was of a snake sixty-one inches long, eighteen rattles, and a button. But that was twenty years ago. They seldom live that long now.

The Showy Moths

As butterflies are the accents and punctuation of summer sunlight, so are the moths the illuminated manuscript of the night. They flit through the filmy realm of starlight and moonlight as through the pages of some dusty, medieval tome on a monastery shelf, unseen by most of us. Theirs is the classic beauty of Aida, not the prettiness of Madame Butterfly.

We get only chance glimpses into their mysterious, nocturnal world, as when we see a giant *Cecropia* softly battering a street lamp, or a bright underwing, attracted by the house lights, at rest upon the screen. A stroller in a garden at dusk will occasionally encounter hawk moths and sphinx moths darting like hummingbirds among the phlox. These may easily be caught for a better look by holding a floret of the blossom where one hovers, and gently pinching and taking him by the tongue as he dips for nectar.

The large velvet-winged moths marked like Indian blankets with bright hieroglyphics on softly shaded backgrounds are far less common than formerly, largely because of pesticide programs, though their numbers were diminishing in the '30s before such things started.

We recall one wild cherry tree that was regularly hung with the silvery cocoons of the *Promethea*, each half-wrapped in a leaf and fastened by the stem, reinforced by silken strands, to a twig to swing all winter. The moths would emerge early in the warmth of the house. Collector John Bonn once took four *Io* moths from his window in Sheffield in a single night but never saw one again. The *Io* is the stocky sulphur-yellow moth with dark owl-eyes on the underwings like those of the much larger *Polyphemus*.

Another spectacular moth listed as common and well-known by Holland in his moth book of seventy years ago is the *Luna*, that lovely pea-green swallowtail that most of us encounter about once in a lifetime by our porch lights. When they were more numerous, countless moths were attracted by headlights and killed by cars. It is our hunch that the automobile is more destructive to these phototropic species than their natural enemy, the ichneumon fly. It was B.C. (before cars) that they were prevalent.

The *Cecropia*, our commonest native silk moth, is familiar to every museum visitor, but it is admired more often on the pin than on the rose. Its cousin *Cynthia* was introduced to America in 1861 as a possible silk producer. The silk could be carded but not reeled successfully.

Wherever ailanthus trees abounded, our generation caught this beautiful fawn-colored moth; not so our children.

The real silk moth was smuggled from China in the sixth century
for the Emperor Justinian by two monks who secreted the eggs in the
hollows of their bamboo walking canes. From this chicanery evolved
all the silkworms of Asia Minor, Africa, Europe, and America, including those introduced to the Berkshires in the 1820s by the Berkshire
Agricultural Society. Mulberry became nursery stock in our hills, with
twigs bringing as much as $5 apiece. Berkshire speculators, handi-
capped by rugged winters, lost their shirts in sericulture, while the
Cheney brothers in the more salubrious Connecticut Valley soon
made their shirts of silk, by importing the raw material. The *Bombyx
mori* is not to be found in our woods now.

The best way to discover which showy moths remain is the collector's method of long ago. A witches' brew is concocted of three or
four pounds of sugar, a bottle of stale beer, some molasses, and a
dash of rum. This syrupy mix is splotched on a few dozen tree trunks
at dusk, perhaps along a field's edge where the trees are large and
various. On a calm, humid night the emanations will drift far into
the wood and across the fields, luring the winged beauties to a Satur-
nalian feast.

Later, making the rounds with a flashlight, you may be surprised
to find that not all the moths are gone. Some shapes will be seen on
the tree trunks like bits of damask in the dusk, like swatches of dim-
ity in the moonlight. You might even see the ghost of a *Bombyx*!

Summer Auction

It is easy to know the summer season. The summer folk flock around like murmurations of starlings by day and like flotillas of fireflies by night. As pole beans begin to climb, the auction tents go up, and their red flags beckon gaily as baskets of strawberries along country roads. The droning of the auctioneer is heard once again in the land, matching the repetitive intonations of the bullfrog in the nearest swamp. Now the city man covets his country cousin's possessions, and what was once a handmade necessity or a beloved heirloom becomes debased to a cocktail conversation piece.

The auction at Fred's Red Shed was out of the usual run in that it was no sale of home or farm furnishings, which inevitably waste much time on mixed junk. It was the entire contents of an antique shop, which meant that everything to be sold had been selected once by an appraising eye.

It meant also that dealers would be plentiful in the tent. We foresaw that bidding would be very competitive, but also that prices would be fair because dealers would only go high enough to allow for a profitable markup.

The stock was strong in our own special interest of early American tools, household and farm gadgets, in wood, iron, tin, etc. But our chances looked dim in view of a self-imposed ceiling of $15; and so they proved to be, because everything started at $5 and very little went for less than $10.

A miscellaneous sampling may show what your attic and cellar troves are worth: burl bowl, $45; hanging wrought-iron bear trap, $5; Connecticut trade ax like an Eric Sloane illustration, $50; very small milk-glass hen, $12.50; flat butter mold, $7.50.

Interrupting the bric-a-brac, a handsome four-poster, tiger-maple bed with canopy sticks (estimated about 1830) was contested hotly by two bidders. The young bride in front of us dropped out at $700. At this point, the auctioneer announced the license number of a car that the police were about to tow away for obstructing traffic; it proved to be that of one of his six assistants, much to the hilarity of the bulging crowd.

A shiny, eighteen-inch brass bucket fetched $30, and a graceful china-headed doll of about 1880, $62.50. An Indian-made burl bowl with hex sign shown in Mary Earl Gould's book brought $100; a little upright wooden churn, $37.50; a small trough table that the glib auctioneer dubbed "a gout bench," $12.50. Bidding got hot over the lion-pattern glassware, and the smallest pickle dish went for $40 as men fought over lions for a change.

The wily auctioneer, amid laughs, bade his assistants: "Take some of the junk off this tray so we'll sell it better." Or, by turns, he would throw in some incompatible object to compensate for a missing porcelain chip or a wobbly leg. Perhaps in one of the oddest combinations, we secured an early cranberry scoop without handle, but had to take a horse muzzle to get it.

Some large furniture went at low prices, such as a nice Sheraton sideboard for $150, whereas small items often went dear, like a primitive wooden cup with carved handle, $35. A bracket lamp "without the kerosene" brought $17.50; a New York wagon bench in maple, $160; a tiny pewter pot, $40; an ancient lock with large key, $47.50.

The smooth-tongued auctioneer was obviously enjoying the dealer rivalries; he declared himself willing and able to break up the oldest friendships. "Here's the first chest that we ever sold that the drawers won't fall out of." It went for $85 after standing in the rain all day. "Here's the homeliest child you ever saw," he said, holding aloft a toddler's nude portrait. Amid much laughter, a sympathetic mother behind us took pity for $75. A primitive portrait of a grandmother in a lace cap and shawl reached $85. Gramp brought $65.

Weather vanes are plainly Americana desiderata for the false garage cupola, although few modern settings can effectively support their prodigious size, their graceful artistry, their consummate craftsmanship, or supplant their original barn perches and steepled heights.

A jaunty gilded rooster on a large gilt ball stepped down from the farm world for $110. For the same amount, a carved wooden horse with flying mane and tail left his familiar barn and sky. A carefully carved beaver vane, perhaps from the Maine woods or the Adirondacks, entered the world of the auto for $120. A second golden cock, missing the letter E where sunrise had burned it off, brought $140. A whale weathervane (and who knows whether it may have caught the eye of Melville) reached $275.

We would like to have presented that to Arrowhead Farm, just down the road, where *Moby Dick* was written. That would have been a fit setting. Instead, we came home hugging a three-legged milking stool that some pioneer farmer low on boards had painstakingly fashioned from a forked tree. We wished the $10 could have gone to him back in the 1700s.

A Miracle and a Marvel

Have you held a spark of life in your palm? One ten-year old boy will never forget it. He was plying a butterfly net about the honey-suckled lattice of the summer cottage when all at once he had "the tiny, pulsing, burnished, green-gold gem" that is a ruby-throated hummingbird. He rushed to show it to the one who had given him his own spark. Little fingers opened gingerly, and the mystery, held for a moment, vanished into summer air, gone but not forgotten.

It so happened that as the first astronauts were about to settle upon the great white moon, once again we were watching a hummingbird, this time a white-bibbed female, settling down upon her own diminutive, white, bean-sized egg.

The nest was just out of reach at the pendulous tip of the lowest branch of a lofty pine, over spacious lawn, amid many flowered gardens. The little mother turned gently on her soft, plant-down lining to

watch the interloper fearlessly, her long bill matched to the pine needles. The wristwatch nest was upon a finger twig to which it was carefully bound by fibers and cobwebs. It was appliquéd and camouflaged
with the usual bits of lichen which gave it a lively green appearance, as
if it were part of the tree. It was a fitting cradle for a spark of life destined to outshine all the fertility the moon could boast.

While millions watched the first *pas de deux* upon the moon, hummingbirds in New World gardens from Hudson Bay to Tierra del
Fuego were performing their elaborate pendulum dances or simple
dalliance with flowers. How easy it was to be carried away by the distant mechanical marvel; how easy to fail to see the backyard miracle!

As late as 1703 "a person of learning and piety" in England maintained that birds migrated to the moon, requiring sixty days for the
trip. Now man has bettered that flight of imagination. But the real
miracle remains the infinitesimal, ruby-throated hummingbird that,
without $24 billion and with only 940 feathers, regularly migrates up
to 2,000 miles, including a 500-mile passage over the Gulf of Mexico,
on swivel wings that beat a fantastic seventy times a second. This mite
is literally a winged heart, one-quarter of its weight being wing muscles
and a fifth being heart.

The "glittering fragment of the rainbow," as Audubon called it, has
recently been discovered to have the highest metabolic rate and greatest
metabolic range of any vertebrate creature. Its daytime temperature of
112 degrees may drop at night almost half, to within a few degrees of the
environment, as it approaches torpor with only pilot light burning. Little wonder it fuels largely on nectar, the food of the gods.

William Wood, coming in 1629 to the New World, to which all
388 species of hummingbirds are confined, in Massachusetts saw the
ruby-throat, which is the only one east of the Mississippi; it was sufficient miracle for him to pronounce it "one of the wonders of the
Countrey." His ship may have been a marvel, but his "humbird" was
the miracle.

Are we not too much inclined to subordinate natural wonders to
mechanical marvels, which is a form of idolatry? The real miracle is
life itself, fluttering in the lattice of our ribs, not in the empty module

on the barren moon. A hummingbird in the hand is worth all the
Eagles on the moon.

Still, the difference between a miracle and a marvel does not
debase the space program. We may need that for an anchor to wind-
ward as a way to haul the precious spark elsewhere, if we increasingly
fail to respect it here in all its forms.

Mushroom Days

When August heat coincides with a wet season to bring on dog days, when the earth is a
steamy stifle of humidity, then into their own
come mushroom, puffball, toadstool, rot, blight,
mildew, and the host of fungi. Biding their time for reproduction all
the long year, sometimes through many a year of drought, beneath
leaf mold, under piles of old boards, in cellars, in devious passage-
ways of dead roots, in fallen tree trunks, or where a mere sparrow
fell—anywhere there is organic matter to be reduced to basic, reus-
able components—there they have been stitching their unseen fila-
ments of hypha into white cobwebs of mycelium, the enduring part
of the plants, which one damp day will thrust up the pallid or gay,
spore-casting, mature forms that we recognize, from delicious morel
to destroying angel.

This summer has been a banner one for the mycologist. Above-
average rainfall and long spells of sultriness proclaimed that times
were right for the mushroom. Accordingly, when we received a call
about a rarity, we made haste to go. The place was Steepletop, former
home of poet Edna St. Vincent Millay. The caller, her sister, could
be trusted in outdoor matters, for the three Millay sisters had shared
a rural Maine upbringing whose ABCs included amanitas, blueberries, and codfish.

The species was the seldom seen *Amanita Caesarea*, more common in Europe where the Romans had named it for Emperor Claudius Caesar. The variety was a delicious, edible exception to the poisonous Amanita family; yet it proved fatal to the emperor when his wife, Agrippina, "seasoned" his mushroom dish with mineral poisons. Otherwise known as food of the gods, imperial or royal agaric, Kaiserling, orange mushroom, or amanita, this delight of epicures was destined to bear forever the name of the one man it killed. Still, this may be good warning to the careless amateur who could possibly mistake for it the sometimes-scaleless, like-colored, lethal fly amanita.

Into the shady wood we started with gathering baskets and cameras. The rich-smelling leaf mold was springy underfoot. Mushrooms in all sizes, shapes, and colors, spaced at discreet intervals, clustered, or in irregular lines, polka-dotted the ferny forest floor.

Above a mossy tree bole stood the scarlet elfin caps of *Hygrophorus conicus*, small but edible. Nearby were some blood-red buttons and rosy tops of *Russula emetica*, generous in flesh but quite poisonous. Peppery *lactarius* stood white as milk, bearing a little rubbish it had raised from the ground. *Clavaria* resembling branching coral appeared in cream and gold and purest amethyst. *Boleti*, brown as biscuits but larger, grew along the brook. One delicate, vivid-green mushroom, a pixie cap on a slim stem, we could not identify by any book. Bright-orange chantarelles looked like gay umbrellas blown inside out. The warty pinecone mushroom somehow suggested a hedgehog. These and many more we saw, including the ghastly-white, deadly amanita and the fly amanita rising from symbolic death cups. Some passé varieties had deliquesced into black Rorschach blobs on the dead leaves; read into them what you would.

Among the throng, up to now, forty of the rare orange amanitas have appeared. They were in all stages, from the initial creamy-white egg, to the ruptured cup revealing a cherry-red cap, to the finally expanded, waxy, orange parasol. The largest was ten inches tall, slightly less than seven inches in diameter and almost one-half pound in weight. The gills and stem were faint lemon-yellow. It was easy to see why it has been called the handsomest of its race.

A few mushrooms, typically the oreades, grow in "a fairy ring" started by a single mushroom, which drops its spores in a circle about its base. Since nutrients are used up within the circle, the next generation and every succeeding one expands outward like ripples from a cast stone. Gansevoort, a relative of Herman Melville, reported a circle forty feet in diameter near Albany. Fairy rings in Colorado are estimated to be 600 years old.

Caesar's mushroom occasionally grows in this manner, though, in this case, the woodland had disfigured and interrupted the circle. Nevertheless, within its compass was a small woodchuck very much the worse for wear. His only motion was his heaving and breathing. He was either high from mushroom hallucinogen or low from mushroom toxin. The blue-bottle flies suspected the latter.

Many insects, birds, and small animals feed avidly on mushrooms. We like to think that infallible instinct guides them. But may not their greed also misguide them, as the cow in apple time? That small woodchuck in the fairy ring—was it Hansel or Gretel? Like them, next day it had vanished.

Drama at Daybreak

It was one of those pristine August mornings, so sparkling with dew that it looked to the beholder like the first morning that ever was. The rising sun peeped over the ridge, picking out, spire by spire, newly minted, glistening gladioli, foxgloves, and cardinal flowers. A rubythroated hummingbird, choosing between dewdrops and nectar, sipped at bright goblets about the garden, while a late sphinx moth on invisible wings of night still dallied over florets of phlox, pink, blue and white.

Suddenly a black-and-white cat walked onto the scene with the stately grace of generations of leonine ancestors. Every move was perfect, although there seemed no purpose in the prowl until he was seen and denounced angrily and vociferously by a chipmunk in the garden wall. His muscles tensed; the yellow eyes, slitted with black, fixed the spot; he stood still a moment on four soft pads full of scalpels.

The wall like a medieval castle surmounted a bank just its own height. It was completely hidden by a cover of woodbine that sent creepers of five-fingered leaves down the bank, which itself was redoubled with lush, dew-drenched ferns as tall as the cat. The chipmunk in his parapet knew where the cat was, but the cat did not know where the chipmunk was.

By playing the game in age-old style, the cat set about reversing that situation. Gingerly in the wet grass he edged over to the bank, using the very defenses for his offense. Then, on his belly, he crept along under the overhang of ferns, like an Indian at the foot of a palisade, to a point directly below the scolding chipmunk, who could not now see him. He crouched, facing up the bank, every muscle tense as a drawn bow, his ears no longer turning hither and yon for every sound as when he first walked in, but pointed directly at the quarry, his whole being focused like a black-and-white eye.

The two were no more than one leap apart, but the chipmunk was in a wall aperture masked by woodbine, and the cat had his interfering eyelashes of wet fern.

The watcher in his window ten feet away held his breath. For the chipmunk this morning and all mornings hung in the balance. It had been fifteen minutes since he first and last saw the cat. His scolding chips were less frequent now and soon ceased altogether. He had two ways to go: down out of the wall or back into it. There could be a cat or hawk without and a rattlesnake or weasel within. He turned indifferently and disappeared in the wall. Now neither knew where the other was, anymore than they knew they were being watched from the window.

The cat relaxed into a patient vigil and began turning his head with each diverting bird or insect sound. His tail twitched, jarring dewdrops from the grass. The first stirring of morning air, like the fanning of some great, unseen moth or hummingbird, moved the garden clumps into restlessness. The cat, too, became uneasy, arose, put forepaws up the bank into the wet ferns, stared into the woodbine, turned, and stalked off as he had come. The drama was over.

Or rather there was no drama at all, unless one realized the meaning of the watcher being watched and that, on a dewy morn made perfect, whitefanged injustice and cat's-paw inequality were as much a part of the scheme as Gandhian luck and Schweitzerian innocence.

The Autumnal Equinox

This year on September 23 at 12:38 p.m., the center of the sun in its cycle southward crosses the celestial equator for an instant, marking the autumnal equinox by shining vertically upon the earth's equator. Exactly one half of the earth's surface is illuminated by the sun's rays, while the other half remains in darkness except near the poles.

The time of this celestial event varies from the 20th to the 23rd of September because of the difference between the conventional year of 365 days and the actual or solar year of 365.242195 days. It is the one time all year that solar time exactly agrees with sidereal or star time. At least, we in our self-centered precision so state.

In the larger perspective of interstellar space, apparently the sun is drifting eastward across the limitless star-fields dragging its inconsequential planets with it. No one out there would know that the sun was moving southward in relation to anything, any more than they could fathom our arbitrary time arrangements. In our way we are as egocentric as primitives who believed the earth was the center of the universe.

To escape our cosmic lostness, if we think of it at all, we seek fixity and order in natural, social, artistic, and mystic realms. These are the rocks we cling to, and no voyager can prove that one is less than another since each is a manifestation of the others.

The autumnal equinox, as well as being a dependable buoy in space, is an earthy phenomenon as natural as a pumpkin. It concerns us little that those in the Southern Hemisphere or elsewhere in the galaxy know it not as we know it in New England.

As well as marking time it marks ripeness of leaf, fruit, and landscape, suffusing this favored cheek of the old globe with the tints of a maiden-blush apple, scenting the land with musk of honey, vine-ripened melon, and wild grape, vibrating the clear air to a thousand cricket tambourines. After the muggy heats of summer, it signals the cool, goldenrod and silverrod days of September to be followed by the white, blue- and purple-aster and gentian days of October.

At night, with feet firmly planted in some frost-sparkling meadow, we can look aloft to a firmament as starry, scarcely knowing where one begins and the other ends. Now, at eve low on the eastern horizon, Orion, the brightest constellation in all the heavens, appears for the first time, rising higher and higher each successive night in the oldest autumn encounter of all.

Giant Orion, with a club in his right hand and a slain lion's skin in his left, confronts Taurus, the bull. Marking his right shoulder is the red star, Betelgeuse, with a volume twenty-seven million times greater than our sun. Marking his left leg is the bright blue Rigel, with a luminosity 10,000 times that of our sun. From his belt, glistening with three second-magnitude stars, hangs Orion's sword, another triad, the central star being the Great Orion Nebula, a magnificent luminous mass of gas and dust with a diameter 700,000 times the distance from earth to sun. At his heels are Orion's two dogs, major and minor, the larger marked by bluish-white Sirius, the brightest star in the entire sky whose companion star is so dense that a teaspoonful of its matter would weigh an earth ton.

In slight flirtation with the universe, man looks up and pins down the autumnal equinox like a monarch butterfly, names the stars as if they were his dogs, and reduces astronomical volume, luminosity, distance, and density to kitchen terms so he can comprehend them.

All well and good, if he were as adept at understanding himself and his fellow man. All the astronomical numbers are not in the heavens. A recent mundane statistic states that normal men have killed 100,000,000 of their fellow normal men in the last fifty years. Truly an implausible accomplishment for a creature with stars at his head and asters at his feet. Or is it? Not only at the autumnal equinox is half the world illuminated and the other half in darkness.

Gossamer Days

Certain rare autumn and spring days sparkle with a special brilliance unknown and unnoticed by most people. Even artists with their awareness of highlights do not seem to know of this seasonal scintillation. If they did, they would despair of reproducing it. On these warm, quiet, dividend days the air sometimes glints and glistens as if chosen light rays were executed in silver. Only when we look in the direction of the sun do we perceive this dazzlement of day ribboning from low grasses, goldenrod plumes, bushes, trees, or even free-floating in the air. Look in another direction, and you will not see it at all. Walk through it, and you feel nothing.

Still, it is real enough and more than a light phenomenon. The day being somehow salubrious, myriad small spiders are moved by wanderlust. With deliberate intent, they climb to some weed top or elm-tree eminence, there to spin out their long, invisible strands that will bear them off on the slightest air current. Light as milkweed floss or thistledown, they float away to destinations unknown. Like animate seeds they disperse their kind to fresh fields and pastures new.

It is usually very young spiders of many different species that exhibit this aeronautic proclivity. Their weightier elders are shackled by the webs they spin. Chains for the one prove wings for the other, as if it were the privilege of the young to soar.

On their self-spun silken chutes, favored by upward air drifts, there is no telling how far or in what direction they may be carried. Should they fall upon water, they do not drown like parachutists in the Great Lakes. Their infinitesimal weight will not break the surface tension, so they may be wafted ashore or aloft again. These little Argonauts have been caught in ships' rigging hundreds of miles at sea.

There are many unanswered questions about the gossamer phenomenon. Spider books do not offer much on the subject. Exactly which species resort to this means of locomotion? Are they all juveniles, or are some the adults of very small species? Is this a manifestation of overpopulation? How long are the silken strands that flash here and there in the sun? What do the little spiders do at the end of their Indian rope trick? Do they reel in and eat this part of themselves as female spiders eat their mates?

It was once our good fortune to have an entomology course with a world authority on arachnids, Professor Petrunkevitch, who passed many a happy hour searching Berkshire fields, barns, and cellars for rare specimens. The trouble was that, like most college students, we did not know enough to ask the right questions. But that did not matter to a teacher who wanted his pupils to see for themselves.

The good professor must have been presiding over an Elysian field one day when we happened to be plowing it. It was one of those frosty, russet, October days that warms up at noon like a roasting chestnut. The turf overturned smoothly, showing the gleam that the plowshare imparts to moist sod. The ridges lay neatly, one against another, like so much hempen warp awaiting the woof.

When we returned from lunch, the woof had been supplied. Driving into the sun, we saw that the field was a-glimmer with cobwebs, trailing crosswise, one furrow to the next. Like the share's polish, the shimmer was never seen widespread, but reflected to the eye in narrow area like the wake of the moon upon water.

It was a strange weaving, this tapestry of agriculture and sericulture. Evidently a vast number of spiders had attempted to set sail from the disturbed sod, but their lift lines, perhaps blown by the merest zephyr, had grounded. Or was it thus? Search as we did, we never found a single spinner in all that glimmering gossamer.

Autumn Mowing

The report of 1752 to the Massachusetts General Court describing the first farms settled by the Dutch in Berkshire County in the mountains west of Sheffield shows how agonizingly slow was the battle against the wilderness. Six of the forty-four men in the list testified that their lands had been cultivated for sixty years; yet none had more than eighty acres fenced and improved. The aches per acre must have been about 43,560, or one per square foot. Long stonewalls bear mute testimony.

These lands which were cleared and won so painfully may be lost by default in seven years, since gray birch and alder will be an inch in girth in that time, and too tough to graze or mow. Woods have thus taken back much of New England's cleared land as any wall trailing off into the woods and hills indicates. Lost, woodland cellar-holes are the sunken graves of many a farm.

Since we live on a part of a pioneer farm in this report, dating back to 1692, we have made it a project of the past week to hold the acreage a while longer by a seven year's mowing. A horse-mowing machine of the early '20s that has rusted away in the goldenrod for the last twenty years served admirably when fitted out with a tractor drawbar, a new pitman, and a few new knives.

The extensive fields at their edges were invaded chiefly by gray birch, aspen, white pine, willow, and alder seedlings. Being wind-dispersed, these also dotted the middles. Tough thickets of meadowsweet, some still in bloom, steeplebush, shrubby five-finger, and sweet fern were clumped everywhere. The mower quite naturally becomes botanist, learning the names of the wooden soldiers as they fall.

Jungles of Canada and flat-topped goldenrod indicated the areas of richest soil. Honeybees worked this last variety industriously to beat the frost, that universal mower. A scattering of asters in shades of washed-out purples to pure white decorated the old fields also, but, surprisingly, no gentians appeared.

The shuttle leveled all with its clickety-clack, sometimes taking the top off a mounded anthill, out of which poured the little communists. Now and again the bar passed over deer beds pressed into the grass, where it was easy to picture the dewy creatures asleep beneath the stars.

The margins of the fields presented their special hazards. There were tumbled walls to batter the bar, blackberry tangles to clog the knives, split rails, fallen branches, or rusted wire to break the teeth. But the worst hazard, and one which could not be anticipated, was yellow jackets. We were hatless and stripped to the waist when the first nest boiled over, peppering us well with that fiery poison that drop for drop is as potent as rattlesnake venom. This was the week two New Jersey women had been killed by single stings. Our tolerance differed, fortunately.

We rammed the tractor recklessly out of the hotspot, losing eyeglasses as we fought off the swarm, then jumped from the tractor seat, and rolled in a cool bed of ferns at wood's edge, accompanied in misery by the ever-present Labrador, Ebony. One of us suffered eight stings; the other licked but couldn't count; and we both slunk home till things quieted down.

After lunch we set forth once more in another field, having added a protective cap and shirt and substitute glasses. While mowing heavy goldenrod along one of the few zigzag split-rail fences left in these hills, we misjudged the bar length, shook up the fence, and brought forth another whirlwind of yellow jackets that stung us six times along the cap line. It became obvious that these fields, won painfully, were going to be preserved painfully also. At least we did not have to deal with panicky horses in our retreats.

The next day in a hilltop field, a friend, rough-riding the rusty mower seat, was routed by the sting of a white-faced hornet that struck him like a bullet in the lower lip. As each successive swath entered this sector, we noticed uneasily that the dog was skirting it warily. The reason became apparent. While we watched goldenrod topple, of a sudden a gray paper-bomb cut down in the previous

swath lay in front of the machine, having been straddled by the tractor. Hornets crawled all over it.

This seemed no time for holding the field. We sped over it and away
in high gear, drawn in as much like a turtle as possible. Those first Berkshire settlers had only to fight stones and stumps and Indians.

Hawk Hegira

The broad-winged hawk has been a favorite
among bird watchers since 1840, when one sat
quietly unafraid while Audubon painted a life portrait of
it. The bird was brought to him, nest, eggs, and all, by his brother-in-
law, who fetched it from the nest tree merely by covering it with his
handkerchief.

Broad-wings when you see them today are more apt to be lone,
graceful, soaring specks in the summer sky, that announce their presence by split whistles like the signal of a peanut vendor. These beneficial mousers have learned respect for a civilization that too often
greeted them with a fusillade, as in Minnesota in 1925:

"Toward evening a vast flight of hawks arrived and settled in the
numerous trees from Wheaton to Herman on a front of at least 25
miles. The appearance brought out every man who owned a gun in
both towns and most of the farmers in the surrounding country. It
was estimated that at least 3,000 hawks were killed at Wheaton and
1,000 at Herman. No one can venture a guess as to how many hawks
were in this vast flight. It would seem all the broad-wing population of
the north country must have been traveling in company."

More than any other hawk, the broad-wing, last of the hawks to
arrive in spring and first to depart in autumn, is notorious for
"bunched up" migrations. These are only occasionally observed
because we are not in the right place at the right time, and because
we are too much like cows. (Thoreau once noted that he had seen

but one cow contemplating the sky.) Yet in New England, in mid-September, with favorable wind and weather, and along certain routes, there are spectacular overhead parades that make a stiff neck worthwhile.

Authorities have wondered what causes these concentrated flights and why they follow now one route and now another. This fall the first coordinated hawk watches held in Massachusetts and Connecticut may shed some feathers on the subject. Many members of many bird clubs participated by manning stations at long-recognized vantage points.

September 19 proved to be the big day for broad-wings. After a spell of adverse rainy weather that was pushed north by a hurricane, the overcast cleared, and brisk winds swept in from the east.

Watchers at eight stations in the Connecticut River Valley recorded the amazing total of 8,082 migrating hawks; the highest count of broad-wings was the 2,378 seen from Mount Tom.

At Ridgeway Avenue in Pittsfield, watchers who kept records for the entire month scored a high of 1,723 broad-wings on that particular day. The hawks came streaming and "kettling" from Windsor Mountain, making for the southwest. Total for the month was 3,599-plus hawks, including 51 falcons and 15 accipiters.

Watchers on Mount Everett, like all the rest on the big day, kept count by each half hour. Broad-wings began coming overhead, at eye level and below, by 9:30 a.m. The numbers skyrocketed from 11:30 until noon, when 1,103 broad-wings were counted. For about ten minutes large "kettles" were everywhere, those westward over New York State being like swarms of mosquitoes, completely uncountable. The majority appeared to drift from West Stockbridge and Monument Mountain due south.

A group of Connecticut watchers stationed at Cooper Hill near the state line four and a half miles southeast of Mount Everett estimated 4,300 broad-wings during the day. Their high count also came between 11:30 and noon, when two definitely separated flights of over 1,000 broad-wings passed overhead and streamed off to the southwest.

Much more work needs to be done correlating all the gathered information. However, these scattered figures are enough to indicate that the September passage of broad-wings in the Northeast may be more intensive and on a far wider front than heretofore realized. It also suggests that stations should be established at more numerous intervals on an east-west line from the Massachusetts coast well into New York State. The problem comes in picking the right day and even the right hour. How many were aware of this sky spectacular that was there for all to see?

Lest the numbers lead any to believe that hawks are common, be it remembered that these ten-minute concentrations may well represent virtually all the broad-wings from almost two million square miles of eastern Canada. Raptors by natural laws occur in low numbers, but only by man are they extinguished.

Indian Summer

What a felicitous Americanism—Indian summer—a phrase that arose within the original states, spontaneously and indigenously expressing the unexpected halcyon days of golden autumns. Yet, for all its roots in the past, how appropriate for this or any autumn when lavender haze gauzes the hills, when geese go honking south in sky-splitting wedges, when unseasonal warmth loosens the acorns from the oaks hailing them down on a merry-go-round of squirrels, when cranberries in unfrosted pockets of sphagnum ripen their last white cheeks in slanting rays of sunshine, when the harvest is home—at least for the chipmunks and for those who still grow something.

Indian summer was not brought from the Old World. It was not coinage of the realm in any respect, for there is no usage of Indian summer written into the voluminous records and diaries of Colonial times. The first written appearance of the happy combination occurred eighteen years after the Declaration of Independence, though obviously it had to be in the vernacular before that. It probably comes closer to being the first pure American idiom than does Yankee Doodle, antonym for Englishman.

A military journal kept by Maj. Ebenezer Denny of Pennsylvania records under date of October 13, 1794: "Pleasant weather. The Indian summer here. Frosty nights." It is almost as if he were defining the term; and no dictionary has improved upon his entry.

Unfortunately, the second written record broadens the term to a point that has caused confusion. In June 1798, Dr. Mason F. Cogswell of Hartford, describing the preceding winter, wrote: "About the beginning of January the weather softened considerably, and continued mild for several days. Most people supposed the Indian summer was approaching (a week or fortnight of warm weather, which generally takes place about the middle of January), but, instead of this, there succeeded to these pleasant days a fall of snow about a foot in depth." Was this a slip of the quill, perhaps the doctor intending "January thaw"?

The French traveler Volney, who visited America between 1795 and 1798, describing the American climate, mentioned Indian summer as coming toward November; he equated it with St. Martin's Day, being November 14. These seem to be the only written references to Indian summer from the eighteenth century.

The term must have spread gradually among the people after 1800, although one weather researcher could discover only six more written examples of its use before 1820. It made its first appearance in the *Farmer's Almanac* in the issue of 1818. That Massachusetts publication probably popularized the expression more than anything else could. After 1820, it became as commonplace in writing and literature as before it had been in parlance.

The picturesqueness and poesy of Indian summer appealed to writers on both sides of the Atlantic, and as early as 1830 in England DeQuincey wrote of his friend Bentley: "An Indian summer crept stealthily over his closing days; a summer less gaudy than the mighty summer solstice, but sweet, golden, silent; happy, though sad; and to

Bentley it was never known that this sweet mimicry of summer—spiritual or fairy echo of a mighty music that has departed—is as frail and transitory as it is solemn, quiet, and lovely." Has anyone better evoked the opium of Indian summer?

By the end of the century, the poet laureate of England, seeking to bless Queen Victoria on her eightieth birthday, could find no greater benison than the phrase "the Indian Summer of your days." Using these two quotations, that great English teacher George Lyman Kittredge concluded his case that "few Americanisms have had so triumphant a progress."

It is one thing to locate Indian summer in the vernacular and quite another to pinpoint it on the calendar, or even to define it. It baffled that self-appointed observer of all natural phenomena, Henry Thoreau, who wrote: "Methinks that any particularly pleasant and warmer weather after the middle of October is thus called—the year renewing its youth.... May my life be not destitute of its Indian summer, a season of fine and clear, mild weather."

From the same Concord, we find him writing in the first week of a September: "It is nothing but Indian summer here at present." Yet in late November, seventeen years later, he wrote another friend: "Don't wait for the Indian summer; but bring it with you."

In New England, where a hurricane is more predictable than an Indian summer, one can only hope. There are no guarantees. There may be some dividend days, even weeks, or none or few. But you cannot miss them as you look over autumn's landscape veiled in a smoky haze as of burning leaves. Remember that Indian summer is all your own, harking back to the cradle days of an infant Republic. Those inexplicable lavender mists upon the hills may be part smog. Once they were part smoke of widespread conflagrations set by the Indians to clear the forests of underbrush. Once they were part smoke from the numberless pits of the charcoal burners. Once they were wood smoke from hearthstones and chimneys long since vanished in the hills. Call them the mists of history.

A Hornets' Nest

About Halloween every year when the trees stand starkly leaf-bare, like gaunt skeletons against the Hunter's Moon, we may spy among the empty branches of farm sugar maples the gray Japanese lantern of a hornets' nest that was all summer in the making. More ominous than a pumpkin jack-o'-lantern, it holds irresistible attraction for the small boy who must, at all risks, stone it down or shoot off the supporting twigs with a boxful of hard-earned 22s. If the day be warm, the intriguing nest may return his fire with an unerring volley of black-and-white bullets.

The white-faced hornet, potentate of sting, is really the farmer's friend. It clears his barns and sheds of flies to feed its thumping grubs, even taking a few harmlessly from his bald head while he snoozes on the porch. Robert Frost once saw one strike repeatedly at a nailhead; he toyed with it by rolling out blueberries on which it pounced like a kitten, seeming to mistake them also for flies.

In his *Letters from an American Farmer*, de Crevecoeur reported that settlers often hung a hornets' nest in their cabin to rid it of flies. This account is corroborated by another in 1869 which said: "They soon made a clearance of the obnoxious flies, and so long as you do not meddle with them, they will not meddle with you."

These humbling members of the wasp family prefer sugar maples but lodge in many other trees. We have seen a nest attached to the shiny bark of an aspen. They may nest high in a lofty elm or just off the ground in laurel, blueberries, or goldenrod. They have a predilection for sheltering eaves, as many a farmer knows who has nearly set some building afire burning them off. We have seen nests beneath rock overhangs and once on a church blind. Our truck remained idle one summer with a large nest under the hood. But the prize location of all was that of an unselfconscious queen who started her nest on the pane of a neighbor's bathroom window. The glass pane between hive and house created an observation hive for hornet and human alike.

History tells us that the first paper from wood pulp was made at Curtisville in the Berkshires. This may be true as far as man goes, but the white-faced hornet has been doing the same thing for hundreds of millions of years.

Every spring large, fertilized queens stirred by rising temperatures emerge from hibernation retreats. Last June we watched one begin her nest under our sunporch eaves. In countless trips she returned to the chosen spot with her masticated cud of weathered wood fibers, plant stems, and the like. Each mouthful of the salivary-mixed papier-mâché was strung out darkly along a paper edge where it was pressed to suit by white mandibles and forefeet. In a few days there was a gray paper nest the size of a golf ball containing some hexagonal cells that would cradle the first few workers. At this early stage the queen, who would later specialize in egg laying, was obliged to perform all duties of the incipient colony. She was designer, papermaker, builder, mother, nurse, guard, and gamehunter until her offspring could assume those duties.

Skipping quickly to November and having just opened the large nest in a kind of Russian roulette (there were about forty bullets left), we can assess the accomplishment and geometrical progression of one queen as well as the durability of the race.

The tapered-globe nest was sixteen inches tall and eleven inches in diameter. The outside paper cover had a shingled appearance, as of oystershells appliqued in vertical rows, all curves arching downwards. One could not imagine a better design to shed water.

The annular rings of the shells varied in shades of gray to some of white, depending on materials. The narrow bands of color clearly showed how much paper one hornet had made in a single mix. The wall of the nest had up to seven sheathings of paper with a three-eighths-inch air space between each. This is said to be as efficient an insulator as a sixteen-inch brick wall.

Inside, suspended by firm attachments, were five tiers of paper comb opening downward and built from top to bottom. This last fact led the philosopher in *Gulliver's Travels* to suppose that men should be as wise as hornets and commence their houses with roof and garret.

The first-generation, upper stories of comb were of small cells for the rearing of sterile workers only. Later, as the colony prospered and summer shortened, enlarged cells at the edges and the entire lower level were devoted to the raising of males and queens. A close estimate revealed 2,280 cells in all, and since average use of each is about three times, one nest of this large size could produce about 6,000 hornets in a season—so many papermakers and never a paper tiger.

Like hornets, all men are not born equal, but they are never so equal as when facing a hornets' nest.

Comfort Me with Cider

If the Bible had been written in New England, Eve never would have been the original sinner for passing Adam the apple. It would have been vice versa as John Alden, first to set foot in the Massachusetts garden, passed Priscilla Mullens a glass of cider. Yankees did not invent cider, but they certainly made the most of it.

Apples originated somewhere along the slopes of southeastern Europe or southwestern Asia near the Mediterranean. But the virtues and vices of their juices never got much further among mead, wine, and beer drinkers than to become the word *shekar* in Hebrew, *sikera* in Greek, *sidre* in French and *syder* in Old English. It took Yankees to make cider, and make it hard.

Dutch and English colonists, who had never been great water drinkers in the old world, found it difficult to grow hops and grain in the new; on the other hand, their apple seeds and scions grew apace and often began bearing within six years. The cherished orchards of Winthrop and Endicott in Massachusetts, Blackstone in Rhode Island, Wolcott in Connecticut, and of patroons in the Hudson Valley were so speedily multiplied that by 1670 cider was plentiful and cheap everywhere. That year Josselyn recorded: "I have had at the tap-houses of Boston an ale-quart of cider spiced and sweetened with sugar for a groat."

Everyone drank cider, men and women, old and young, in all places and on all occasions, from baptisms to funerals, and from church-raisings to ordainings. Babes in arms drank mulled hard cider at night, a beverage that might put a modern infant to sleep forever. Every schoolday, students at Harvard and Yale passed cider from hand to hand in two-quart tankards down the commons tables. Delicate women drank hard cider. Farm hands laced it with rum. While John Adams was president, he said: "If the ancients drank wine as our people drink rum and cider, it is no wonder we hear of so many possessed with devils." Still, to the end of his long life, he always began the day with a tankard of hard cider before breakfast.

The first Berkshire township, Sheffield, was purchased in 1724 from the Indians by Capt. John Ashley and his committee for "460 Pounds, Three Barrels of Sider, and 30 Quarts of Rhumb." But even before that, in 1692, a few Dutch families, namely Brazees, Halenbacks, and Spoors, were planting apples in the hilltown of Mount Washington. According to a sworn statement in the year 1752, their descendants on the same farms produced "49 bbls. of syder."

Not that this was any record. Judge Dudley wrote of the Bay Colony in 1726: "Our apples are without doubt as good as those of England, and much fairer to look to. Our people of late years have run so much to orchards that in a village near Boston, consisting of about 40 families, they made near 10,000 barrels of cider."

With the advent of cold weather, the New England countryside became aromatic with Roxbury russets, pungent with Newtown pippins, and redolent with Westfeld seek-no-furthers. At first, cider was made by pounding the apples by hand in wooden mortars. Then various types of leverage and screw presses appeared according to the ingenuity of the farmer. Next, homemade mills were constructed using hollowed logs (often apple wood), with a revolving springboard. Kalm, the Swedish naturalist, traveling through the Hudson Valley in 1749, saw several styles of horse presses in action.

Neighbors turned out gladly for "apple cuts" or "apple bees" to keep the hungry mills fed. As likely as not, the meal afterward consisted of cider and apple pie for all. Another traveler writing to Europe in 1758 reported: "Apple pie is used the whole year, and when fresh apples are no longer to be had, dried ones are used. It is the evening meal of children. House pie, in country places, is made of apples neither peeled nor freed from their cores, and its crust is not broken if a wagon wheel goes over it."

Cider lent itself to infinite strengths and recipes. One tavern favorite was flip, a concoction of hard cider, rum, beaten eggs, sugar, nutmeg or ginger, and lemon peel. Smoothed to a cream by a red-hot poker or loggerhead and served hot, a quart of this nectar was commonly styled "One Yard of Flannel." An even more potent cider mix with rum was called "Stone Wall."

Cider-royal was made by boiling four barrels of cider into one; this was termed "gumption." More preserving of the essence was freezing; many a barrel was frozen as often as seven times, lanced at the bung with the loggerhead, and drawn off each time minus its water. This "Jericho cider" made a raw day in January seem like midsummer.

At the other extreme, ciderkin or water-cider was made by pouring water on the mill pomace and pressing it out again. This was deemed especially suitable for children, as cider and cider brandy were not.

There was even a cider soup. This was boiled and thickened with sweet cream and flour, then served with croutons of bread or toast. Ah-mmm!

The Prognosticator

Wooly-bear caterpillars and almanac compilers have a good deal in common when it comes to long-range weather forecasting. They are each prickly as a hedgehog and dyed-in-the-wool when defending their opinions; but there are differences. The compiler, being intelligent and human, errs at least half the time; the caterpillar, being instinctive and accustomed to bite off what he can chew, never errs at all.

He curls up in a bristly bundle looking for all the world like an abbreviated red-and-black wheel. Howsoever you bet, he knows that winter will be warm at both ends and cold in the middle or that it will be cold at both ends with a January thaw in the middle. In either case, he takes no chances and crawls under the nearest pile of boards, brush, or rubbish, and remains 100 percent right.

The wooly bear is, of course, the common black and rusty banded caterpillar seen scurrying with the blown leaves across lawn and sidewalk in autumn. He is the same length as the word "prognostication" and twice as accurate.

Most caterpillars choose to winter incognito in cocoon or chrysalis or both, but the wooly bear with the courage of his convictions elects to hibernate in person. His evenly clipped, prickly coat and habit of curling up in a defensive ball caused the wistful colonists to name him the hedgehog caterpillar. He was, however, as indigenous as the Indian, being restricted to the United States and Canada. There are only three species in his genus of tiger moths. The others are oddly far-flung on the earth's surface, one being in Argentina, the other in Turkestan.

When or how the wooly bear acquired his reputation as a winter forecaster is a mystery buried in the old calendar leaves of New England. Certain it is that Thoreau, who took particular delight in Yankee sayings and folklore, knew nothing of it; at least he never mentioned that special proclivity in his voluminous writings, although he once entertained one of these humble fellow-travelers in his hat.

It happened this way. Under a journal entry dated January 8, 1857, he wrote: "It was 18 degrees when I went out to walk. I picked up on the bare ice of the river, on a small space blown bare of snow, a fuzzy caterpillar, black at the two ends and red-brown in the middle, rolled into a ball or close ring, like a woodchuck. I pressed it hard between my fingers and found it frozen. I put it into my hat, and when I took it out in the evening, it soon began to stir and at length crawled about, but a portion of it was not quite flexible. It took some time for it to thaw. This is the fifth cold day, and it must have been frozen so long. ... I demand of my companion some evidence that he has traveled further than the sources of the Nile—Did he ever get out of the road which all men and fools travel? You can call yourself a great traveler, perhaps, but can you get beyond the influence of a certain class of ideas?"

Awakening from winter sleep, the wooly bear changes his ideas with his habiliments. After devouring some new spring greens, he spins a thin silken cocoon that entangles his own shedding hair and, after a period of pupation, he emerges as a lovely tiger moth called *Isia Isabella* with wingspread about the same as his former length. Poet John Keats caught this reincarnation in three lines: "All diamonded with panes of quaint device, /Innumerable of stains and splendid dyes /As are the tiger moth's deep damask wings."

You are apt to catch him of a summer night clinging to screen or siding beside your porch lights and rendering the other small moths drab by comparison; his forewings are margined and cut into intricate, black geometry by prominent, creamy lines; the underwings tinged with orange-red are canceled lightly with dark spots, and the tawny body is tiger-streaked down the mid-line. He will be befuddled by the light.

But he is not so befuddled as the almanac maker. A spot check of the recent November days shows that one compiler hedged with the words, "Dandy, Andy." Actually a hard nor'easter blew in on those days with winds gusting up to sixty-six miles per hour. In four successive waves, twice it dumped as much as a foot of snow over parts of New England, causing power failures and some minor flooding; one weather report called it the worst November snowstorm in New England history. Perhaps it was dandy if you happened to be a skier named Andy. The snug wooly bears laughed it off in their sleep.

A Buck Walks in Danger

Massachusetts Wildlife points out how hard it is to shoot a deer. We scarcely need to have that shown to our myopic eye, but the way it was proven was to fence thirty-nine deer in one square mile of typical deer cover. With snow-tracking conditions ideal, it took six hunters four days to see a buck. Fourteen hours per man were expended for every deer shot, while it took fifty-one hours to kill a buck. Enough on the difficulty.

Now on the methods, with deer week upon us in Berkshire County. A single hunter will usually do well to acquaint himself with the locale ahead of time and take a stand before sunrise on a busy deer run where it enters a feeding ground furnishing wild apples, yew, acorns, or some other favorite fare. Here he may sit till his patience runs out, till he freezes, or till sunset.

Two or three hunters usually employ an Indian style of stalking or trailing. This requires the highest degree of skill, keen eye and ear, and a "Thoreau" knowledge of the wind, the woods, and the deer. Even this type of hunter on retracing his path will occasionally find heart-shaped prints upon his clumsy footprints where some curious deer has followed and mocked him.

The usual method, that of the meat hunter, is to organize a drive of some swamp, mountain, or valley; this may require one or even two dozen men, half of whom act as dogs to yap and drive while the rest form an impenetrable line.

There are variations and combinations of these methods, as well as highly individual styles. One very successful hunter customarily nests in a large pile of leaves on the forest floor with his head out like a periscope. A neighbor drove a more reckless type from his woods for taking "sound shots." Only last year in the nearby Catskills, another hunter watching from the branches of a hemlock was mistaken for a bear and shot in the stomach; his groan was taken for a certain bear, and the second shot brought him down dead. One hunter, we presume not from the Berkshires, brought a heifer into a deer checking station; another proudly lashed a goat to his bumper.

There was a time about 1900 when for years there had been no deer in Berkshire County. The first deer seen in our town, by a native born in 1865, was a doe standing in Bash Bish Brook about 1915. Posting of private land, conservation measures, and limited hunting now threaten to bring overpopulation with consequent increased crop damage and starvation from competition in some areas. We have seen enough crop damage to potatoes, apples, and grain so that our sympathy lies somewhere between the hunter and the hunted, as may be shown by this personal hunting experience.

Two of us set out for an Indian-type hunt along a wild ridge on a sunny December morning. There was no helping snow, but everywhere deer had scuffed the oak carpet in search of acorns. As we reached the top, dim with hemlocks, the sudden hue and cry of an unexpected drive raised to the south. We had no choice but to sit in the middle of it, along with the deer. We chose a hemlock staddle for cover, near a cliff edge along which any deer might pass. My partner was on the ridge backbone. Here we crouched in high expectancy.

As the drivers approached, it became apparent from the barking that they held a fairly tight, straight line. Suddenly, without a sound, a great antlered buck appeared moving leisurely along the cliff, looking over his shoulder from time to time in the direction of his pursuers, with an air of contempt that came from holding that crowned head so high. The light through the evergreens dulled and glinted by turns on the flinty antlers as it did on the gun barrel. The buck was treading the brink of eternity, though he knew it not.

It was not buck fever, but the gun failed to fire from a jammed trigger mechanism. This chance meant life to the buck. He saw the pounding at the gun, wheeled a circle with almost the gun barrel for radius, and headed toward my partner. A shot rang out, but the buck escaped and somehow slipped back through the drivers. Nor did we tell them a twelve-point trophy had slithered through their net.

Later that day, the last day of the season, at sunset a veteran hunter saw that monarch at the edge of the wood we had been hunting. He said it was the biggest deer he had ever seen. By luck and by craft it was safe for another year.

Cold Turkey

The thermometer rose and stuck at around zero the day after the blizzard. If the wild turkeys could survive it with naked heads and feet and part-feathered legs and necks, we could endure it with hoods and insulated boots.

The old wood road beckoned with white invitation. Any print in the snow would be new now, and around any curve might appear those telltale, palmate tracks as big as a man's hand. Or, more likely, we might not find them at all. These great, shy birds, now beginning the fifth year on the mountain since first introduced, are always a surprise.

A veteran hiker, Justice William O. Douglas, described one of his more memorable moments, which occurred on the lower western slopes of Mount Everett. Half-lost and alone in October dusk, he was rustling his way out to civilization when suddenly this whole roosting flock burst from low trees overhead, reminding him that he was still as deep in wilderness as one could get east of the Mississippi.

The blizzard snow lay only drumstick deep, and on the south-slanted slope no wind had dislodged the last-fallen flakes from the brittle hemlocks. The air had that intense chill that somehow distills a few frost crystals, allowing them to drift lazily downward glinting like gossamer, the special brilliants of winter's coldest days.

Beneath one hemlock the snow was strewn with the brown flakes of shredded cones where a flock of pine siskins had stormed the tree. Reedy *sherrees* sounded through the clear air where they teetered among the needles of another tree.

Presently we came into a clearing with a thick, squat pine at its center. Under it the snow was trodden out with turkey tracks somewhat snowed upon. Evidently the flock had huddled here during the blizzard. A fox passed through the trampled yard at night, but too late; the birds had gone to roost. We followed the blurred phantom tracks further into the wood where the turkeys had paraded the old wood road, hardly expecting to find them.

They saw us before we saw them, for every head was at alert, necks moving sinuously like so many bronze Indians peering through the dimness of the hemlock staddle separating us. They were in the full light of the low winter sun. Their heads were pewter blue, and their dark-bronze plumage scintillated with metallic lustre. Slowly and soundlessly they stalked off into the woods Indian file. By rough count there were about sixteen, but so magically they moved and blended through the dark brush and tree trunks that it was like counting ghosts. Never did we get the same total.

Leaves, grasses, and snow were stirred up together where they had been scratching the sunny slope through five inches of snow. For what? There seemed no food value there. Perhaps those amazing gizzards capable of grinding whole hickory nuts could work on the biggest shell of all, the frozen earth.

At any rate, the flock had survived and increased, though only one of the original nine banded birds remained after two years. Furthermore, they had produced enough extras to start colonies elsewhere.

We followed the stately birds for a quarter of a mile through the woods without seeming to alarm or hurry them. They flowed like a snake dance along the serpentine bluff high above a brook, always at least fifty yards ahead of us. Their steps often measured off a foot of snow and might or might not be marked by links of toe dragging.

Usually a large, bearded gobbler brought up the rear like a lagging sentinel.

As the stately procession began to circle back whence it had come, we parted ways and tramped half-frozen from the snowy woods. It was below zero now as the shadows lengthened.

When we were far across the brook, one clarion gobble split the chilly air like an ax. One blue head was not yet tucked under a wing.

Beaver Swamp

T o see how frozen were the locks of winter, we made an excursion through a nearby beaver swamp tucked away in the hills. The temperature was close to zero, but the chill wind sounding on the mountain did not strike in the hollow, and the afternoon sun cast that special glow that seems restricted to winter swamps and southern slopes. Probably no animal can alter its environment as dramatically as the beaver. These industrious creatures felled timber, built dams, dug canals, and practiced flood control and water conservation long before man. A pair of beavers was introduced to this particular swamp about twelve years ago. The location was a secluded narrow valley near the divide of a watershed; one small trickle ran northerly, through Bash Bish eventually to the Hudson; the other ran southerly through Sage's Ravine to the Housatonic. The valley was filled with alders and a mixed growth of trees, but there was no open water. Now there are four sizable ponds and additional acres and acres of swamp.

Many sub-zero nights made it easy to explore what at any other season would be a watery sanctuary for beaver, wood duck, and trout. The snow-covered ice floor was everywhere penetrated by alder stubs from the drowned-out clumps. Similarly, gaunt, drowned trees stood armless in the swamp, furnishing nesting sites for woodpecker and tree swallow. Denuded, cinnamon stalks of the royal fern arched above the snow. The deserted swamp had the air of a blasted battle-field; the vegetation could not survive the three to four foot rise of water engineered by the beavers.

Only by the vast decimation could we tell that under all the ice and snow lived a warm-blooded, breathing colony. In that medium of ice water all industry had subsided to a routine of sleeping, swimming, gnawing submerged bark, and waiting for spring thaw.

In the first pond there were two large houses of mud, sod, and sticks, one sixteen feet in diameter. Somehow through all the zero weather, the beaver had kept a hole open in the ice. One set of tracks, blurred by the dragging tail, wended out through the snow and returned after a few hundred yards. No doubt it was cozier in the dry, dark shelter with others to maintain warmth.

At the end of the pond were two parallel dams about seventy-five paces long and ten to twenty paces apart, above them another pond and extensive swamps. There was no winter house in this higher level, which evidently had been created to broaden the feeding grounds. Why the two dams, where one would accomplish as much? It seemed like excess work, or sheer exuberance of animal spirit, as if these little dynamos just couldn't be idle. It made us wonder how they could wait out the winter.

Over the divide were two younger ponds with fifty-five- and sixty-five-yard dams, the work of crowded-out grandchildren. Each pond had one large house with chewed-off sticks pointing in all directions. Breathing holes at the tops indicated that there was indeed life in these frozen igloos that looked as dormant as a bud.

Here the main supply of food was black cherry. Many trees were felled and a good deal peeled; many others were deeply cut and left standing. One huge cherry twenty-two inches in diameter was half cut, as if the beaver expected the wind to finish the job. One small cherry was lodged firmly in a nearby crotch, showing that these toothy engineers were not infallible, but that was the only mistake we discovered. It was like looking on the pyramids of Egypt.

Miracles demand a miraculous explanation. One Swiss naturalist of medieval times quotes authorities thus: "The tree being down and prepared, they take one of the oldest of their company, whose teeth could not be used for the cutting, or, as others say, they constrain some strange beaver whom they meet withal, to fall flat on his back … and upon his belly lade they all their timber, which they so ingeniously work and fasten into the compass of his legs that it may not fall, and so the residue by the tail draw him to the water side, where those buildings are to be framed, and this the rather seemeth to be true, because there have been some such taken that had no hair on their backs, but were pilled, which being espied by the hunters, in pity of their slavery or bondage, they have let them go away free."

Whispering Evergreen

Going, going are all the hearty memories of Christmas trees, when the farmer and his son trudged out through fresh snow to select a shapely pine or an aromatic spruce from the woodlot. Now, too many go up to the attic for a synthetic, collapsible, fireproof substitute. Progress, maybe, but the symbolism grows vaguer. A tree is no longer a tree unless we can stand outdoors with it, measure ourselves by it, see it rooted, wind-tossed, snow-flecked, and pointed upward like a steeple toward sun or stars.

Today we stood under a giant spruce on our small parcel of land that was once a part of the six-mile square of "baronial territory" known as Ponoosuck and bought by Col. Jacob Wendell at a Boston land auction in 1735. Wind soughed; a red squirrel chattered, and a nuthatch fluted in the heavy horizontal branches. The chapel-like grove, of which this tree was one column, had been planted by Oliver

Wendell Holmes more than a century ago on the 280 acres called Canoe Meadows which he had inherited from his great grandfather's original 24,040.

In 1848 the imaginative doctor built "a perfectly plain shelter," still standing but much enlarged, on a knoll overlooking, to the south, his meadows straddling "the fantastic windings of the amber-flowing Housatonic, dark streak, but clear, like lucid orbs that shine between the lids of auburn-haired, sherry-wine-eyed demi-blondes;" and viewing, to the north, Greylock: "the twin summits, suggestive to mad fancies of the breasts of a half-buried Titaness, stretched out by a stray thunderbolt and hastily hidden away beneath the leaves of the forest."

When the good doctor took over the ancestral acres on the Middle Road to Lenox (now Holmes Road), the property was almost destitute of trees. Standing under that spruce, we recalled what he had written to a friend shortly after he left Pittsfield for good, in 1856: "Seven sweet summers, the happiest of my life. One thing I shall always be glad of: that I planted 700 trees for somebody to sit in the shade of." We sat down in a surrounding ring of saffron cones.

Dr. Holmes had a pantheistic veneration for trees, especially for towering elms and evergreens. His five-foot-four frame may have had something to do with that. He thought of himself as "a pretty well-seasoned old stick of timber." He joshed: "I call all trees mine that I have put my wedding ring on, and I have as many tree-wives as Brigham Young has human ones." The "wedding ring" referred to the thirty-foot pocket tape which he carried, and actually wore out on rough bark like that of the spruce murmuring overhead.

"I have a most intense, passionate fondness for trees in general, and have had several romantic attachments to certain trees in particular.... I always tremble for a celebrated tree when I approach it for the first time. Before the measuring tape the proudest tree of them all quails and shrinks into itself in the presence of the awful ribbon which has strangled so many false pretensions."

A hemlock blew down at Canoe Meadows in 1852 which Holmes found to be twelve and one half feet in girth. He counted 342 rings, which showed that it had sprung up in 1510. "The tree was 7 inches in diameter when Shakespeare was born; 10 inches when he died. This thread marks out Johnson's life, during which the tree increased from 22 to 29 inches. Here is the span of Napoleon's career; the tree doesn't seem to have minded it."

The diminutive, sylvan doctor, who had considered carving on his Boston shingle: "The smallest fevers gratefully received," next to the American elm, revered the white pine "marked in its form, its stature, its bark, its delicate foliage, as belonging to the nobility of the forest."

His prize tree at Canoe Meadows was a titan pine which graced the meadow southwest of the house. It stood a few rods back from the Middle Road on the way to neighbor Melville's Arrowhead. This, his favorite tree-wife, topped 100 feet in height, exceeded ninety feet in spread of branches and measured over seventeen feet in girth when it crashed in a windstorm only five years ago in 1962.

The tree remained engraved upon Holmes's memory all his life, because thirty years after departing Pittsfield, he wrote: "As we passed the gate under the maple which may stand there now, we turned and looked at the house and at the Great Pine which stood in its solitary grandeur and beauty,—and Goodbye."

Since then the land has passed through many owners, always with the singular stipulation in the deeds "that the tree known as the Holmes pine standing by itself in the meadow to the south of the homestead shall be allowed to stand as long as Nature permits; that it never shall be cut down or moved while it remains in a live or healthy condition."

We arose from the wreath of cones lying about the massive bole of the spruce planted by Holmes 115 years ago. Its great stem tapered skyward like a spire; it spread arms lusty as the crossbar of a crucifix. Here was a Christmas tree that was a Christmas tree. It needed no protection of a deed. It was its own deed. As lief try to cut down an inspiration.

Black Spruce Swamp

Christmas trees look best decorated with a light fall of new powder snow in some black spruce swamp. Such a swamp lies in the hills at the south boundary of our county. It is a botanist's paradise, a virtual island of Hudsonian tundra in our more temperate clime. Botanical clubs from New York, New Jersey, and Boston, staying at the Mount Washington boarding-house farms, visited there in the 1870s. The bog has probably changed little in the interval, being practically inaccessible in winter and visited only by an occasional botanist, blueberry picker, or hunter at other seasons. It may have quietly added another inch of peat in the last 100 years.

At the heart of the bog is a shallow pond about half a mile long, lily-spread in summer, snow-quilted now. Water depth is insufficient for a dog to retrieve a wood duck, but the black muck is bottomless. Around the edges in the quivering sphagnum grow cranberries, pitcher plant, and sundew. Quaking mats of leatherleaf and tamarack roots support the cautious explorer in summer. Now winter freeze permits easy exploration, and the snowshoe rabbit browses the new supply of leatherleaf shoots at his leisure.

Back from the margin begins a dense tangle of woody shrubs that would confuse, confound, or constrict the best botanist: Labrador tea, high-bush blueberries, swamp white azalea, various viburnums, and other species, as interlaced as Gray's *Manual*. Backing up this maze are the dim aisles of black spruce eternally shading mosses, ferns, goldthread, twinflower, creeping snowberry, and other plants seldom found locally. Native rhododendron grows nearby.

Besides its Christmas trees, this swamp has other Christmas attractions, in name at least: holly and mistletoe. The mountain holly (*Nemopanthus*) is now bare of leaves and berries. In August its unshining but vivid red berries hang on long stems among the greenery like a scattering of little Christmas balls out of season, making a pleasant contrast with the swamp's plentiful blueberries.

The mistletoe is a dwarf variety (*Arceuthobium*), an inconspicuous parasitic plant with tiny scale-like leaves. Old botany records show that it flourished in this particular swamp; it probably still does, but was too miniscule for us to find. It victimizes the black spruce twigs, causing hexenbesen, or witches' brooms. The month to look for it is June, not January, and it would be poor judgment to let your kisses depend on finding it.

Although these plants are not at their Christmas best, the black spruce, patched with snow, more than compensates. Besides bearing its own mistletoe, a black spruce Christmas tree may provide its own confection by exuding aromatic gum. While not as colorful as a striped peppermint cane, this spicy chewing gum is a more traditional New England candy, once sold in rural general stores, a penny's weight for an old large penny.

The black spruce ranges from the least seedling to the modest matriarch of forty to fifty feet. To stand among the columnar trunks is to hear the wind as never before. The dark branching clerestory tames winter winds to a susurrus. Each tree has the stateliness of a steeple pointing to a star; and once again, as in pre-Christian days, here every evergreen is symbolic of enduring life.

PART 3
Birding and Botanizing
Poems

Phoebe on Forsythia

A forlorn phoebe on forsythia
Clutches a yellow spray, a spring idea,
Clings fast to what there is of early flowers
When April gives us snow instead of showers.

He fixes with alert flycatcher eye
Each flake, as if it were a frosty fly,
And contemplates the slow insistant push
Of smothering snow upon a burning bush.

Snow wraps the world in soft white chrysalis,
Leaving nothing of emergent spring but this:
A lowly yellow bush and strident song
To show the doubting heart the snow is wrong.

Woodlot Warbler

In fog walls of our laurel-furnished room,
Misty and topless, the blackened tree trunks loom.
My rhythmic axe strokes ring against a tree,
While you sing a reedy *zwee. zwee. zwee.*

Singing to stake a claim to this dense growth
Of laurel, for some mate still in the South,
With voice not very musical or strong;
But on this day I welcome any song.

Ours is a camaraderie of fog,
Each watching each on the same wet log,
As for an interval we both relax.
Bird with beak and woodsman with an axe.

It seems to be your wish-fulfilled to show
No song is sweeter than the here and now
In this dark dripping woodlot where we strew
Chips and songs, bedraggled black-throated blue.

Black-capped Philosopher

On winter's coldest days
Through lonely woodland ways
I never fail to see
The cheerful chickadee.

With tumbling snow-flake flight
On nearest twig he'll light,
Unconscious of me yet?
Ubiquitous coquette!

Then tapping with concern,
He'll topsy-turvy turn;
No gravity in that,
Small spritely acrobat!

Though bitter be the cold,
His enemies untold,
His food scarce, and drink ice,
His courage will suffice.

His size is quite absurd
Even for a bird,
But spirit plus a feather
Will weather any weather.

Early Saxifrage

Inconspicious little plant
Cradled in a cleft,
Unable with the rest to vie,
You take the place that's left.

There you spread a leaf rosette
And raise a modest stem,
And toss in breeze above the rock
Your small-starred diadem.

Many flowers are rarer, fairer,
But there are none as meek;
And though the multitude pass by,
You're found by those who seek.

Your transient simple beauty,
Like your seed, will outlive stone,
As lovers' legends linger
When epitaphs are gone.

This Morning-glory

For many things learned
But few understood,
I will botanize *convolvulus*
Then seek it in the wood.

Disdaining wealth
And customary worth,
I will kneel down
For a handful of earth.

Because of common things
Like wind, leaf and stone,
I will sometimes pray
When I am alone.

For moments treasured
But transitory,
I will bring you
This morning-glory.

A Late Robin

Shy robin, wherefrom all your fear
Never letting me come near
In this leafless time of year?

Before, you built your very nest
Outside the window where I rest
In a confidence expressed.

Now you make your exit hence,
Leaving me on this snow-topped fence
To wait out the difference.

Southbound stranger, erstwhile friend,
How silently you fly to end
A season's dividend.

In spring each watcher saw your first
Arrival break the birdless past
I, only, saw you last.

Winter Leaves

White oak and beech brave snowy woods
Knee-deep, and wind-ripped all their height,
Still clinging to last summer's leaves
To weather winter night.

When all but evergreens are bare,
The great green cloak of these has shrunk
And faded to a leathern coat
That tatters at the trunk.

Their leaves may guard the swelling buds,
Catch cold sun and keep it near,
Serve to reline a squirrel's nest,
Or camouflage a deer.

Whatever need there be, or none,
These hold their penny-colored trove
Of last year's leaves that will be gone,
Tenaciously as love.

As I cling to this dear hand
To withstand season's grief,
Knowing it as shaped and veined
And holding as a leaf.

PART 4

Berkshire People

Voice in the Wilderness

The hills wore red and gold regalia October 12, 1734, when the youthful John Sergeant first rode into Housatunnuk with Rev. Nehemiah Bull; but to the young minister, after a night spent in the woods without fire or shelter, it appeared "a most doleful wilderness."

Only a youth with a dream would have come at all, for this was a remote frontier offering none of the comfort and security of teaching in New Haven. Only one dedicated in selflessness would have undertaken "the salvation of the heathen" in this mountain-surrounded outpost where the forty-odd Mahicans far outnumbered a few settled whites. For a doubtful prospect and a salary equivalent to one ounce of silver per year, the twenty-four-year-old Sergeant was about to trade the last fifteen years of his life.

Obstacles were many, the unwritten language of the Indians being first. Ebenezer Poopoonuck interpreted Sergeant's first discourse to about twenty Indians on the east side of the Housatonic somewhat north of the Great Barrington fordway, this being halfway between Captain Konkapot's wigwams at Stockbridge and Lieutenant Umpachene's at Sheffield. Ebenezer was then baptized, vowing that "he would rather burn in the fire than forsake the truth."

The Indians were deeply impressed with Sergeant's earnestness and personality. Within two weeks they cheerfully erected a large wigwam at this middle ground to serve for meetinghouse and school, and about it built their huts for the winter. Leaving Timothy Woodbridge as schoolmaster, Sergeant returned to Yale to complete his own commitments, taking the chieftains' two sons with him that they might learn each other's languages. On July 5, 1735, he was back for permanent residence in the wilderness.

The young minister's immediate success with the Indians stemmed largely from his living so closely with them. From this developed a mutual sense of belonging never achieved by Jonathan Edwards later on. When the Indians departed into the woods in the middle of February for the annual six weeks of maple sugaring, Sergeant went with them, since he did not want them so long without prayer and instruction.

The Rev. Samuel Hopkins, his friend and biographer in Springfield, wrote: "The snow now was about a foot and a half deep in those woods, and the weather cold. A deerskin with the hair on, spread upon some spruce boughs, and a blanket spread upon that, was his bed; and three blankets spread over him was his covering; where he slept very well. And though their diet was low, yet it was cleanly and well dressed, by the Captain's and Lieutenant's wives. Their drink was water." At this time Sergeant wrote wryly of his isolation: "Perhaps we shall be so taken with them and their way of living that we shall take a wife amongst, and sadly disappoint all other fair ones that may have expectations from us."

In January 1736, the mission was moved into Indian Town north of Monument Mountain, where Sergeant resided with schoolmaster Woodbridge "who had built a house and brought home a wife, etc." A year later Sergeant had his own home and boarded twelve Indian boys for a year of instruction. By this time the Indians were proudly saying: "Our minister speaks our language better than we do ourselves." Nevertheless, he found it to be a dry, barren, imperfect dialect, unsuited to abstract Christian terms. His Sabbath sermons in gutturals may have induced the throat canker that brought his early death.

The mission in Stockbridge was beset with continual difficulties. Sergeant wrote many letters to the outside world and the General Court pleading for funds to sustain his efforts. Response was small and sporadic. The Dutch traders supplied the Indians with rum, "their beloved destruction," and endeavored to convince them that the English were enslaving them. Chiefly, the problem was one of transforming an entire alien culture. It must be said that in his short allotted time with this small group, Sergeant was as successful as anyone has been in a similar situation.

At his death in 1749, his model village contained fifty-three

Indian houses, twenty built after the English mode. There were 218 Indian inhabitants. He had baptized 182 and converted many more in neighboring lands. There were then only a dozen white families in the town, but the name change ten years before, from Indian Town to Stockbridge, had been for them. Sergeant's dream, passed on to Edwards and to his own son, dissolved westward.

Stockbridge Theologian

Our Berkshire neighbor Reinhold Niebuhr has been somewhat embarrassed by comparisons with Jonathan Edwards, who lived in the town of Stockbridge exactly 200 years earlier. He states frankly that Edwards was the greatest theologian in American history, while he was simply a teacher of social and political philosophy who happened to teach in a theological seminary. It is not our intention to violate the humility of greatness by any comparisons. The men's times were extremely different. Each might have thought as the other, give or take 200 years, though it is as hard to imagine a liberal Edwards as a conservative Niebuhr. The differences in their thought may be more numerous than the parallels in their lives, but few would agree with the provincial cleric visiting the Stockbridge Library who said: "They may have lived in the same town, but they are not going to the same place."

Archbishop Temple of England and John Baillie, Principal of New College in Edinburgh, agree that the two are the greatest native theologians that America has produced.

Both were the sons of small-town Protestant ministers, Edwards born in 1703 at East Windsor, Connecticut, and Niebuhr born in 1892 in Wright City, Missouri. After a rural family upbringing, both matriculated at Yale, Edwards graduating in 1720 and studying two more years for the ministry, Niebuhr graduating from the divinity school in 1914.

Both were called into parish work that ultimately brought them into first-rank prominence on the American scene. Edwards was pastor in Northampton for twenty-three years in the largest and wealthiest church in the colony outside of Boston. His concern in many revival sermons was with the salvation of the individual by return to the old high Calvinist faith, acknowledging God's "absolute sovereignty." His originality was in the great stress which he laid upon subjective experience. He finally endeavored to turn the clock back by restricting communion only to those who had experienced inner awakening, thus bringing about his own dismissal.

In 1751 Edwards at age forty-eight removed to Stockbridge as minister to twelve white families and missionary to 250 Indians. The town was no more than a tiny outpost on the wilderness frontier. The Indians could scarcely fathom the discourses, delivered by interpreter, designed to save their souls from drink and unknown hells. It would seem that Edwards had been effectively silenced.

For seven years he lived in the midst of white feuding and Indian savagery. His little son never spoke English outside the home that was sometimes a fort, since all his playmates were Indians. His visiting daughter, Esther Burr, recorded: "I hant had a night's sleep since I left New York. ... Proposed to My Father to set out for home next week, but he is not willing to hear one word about it, so I must tarry the proposed time and if the Indians get me, they get me, that is all I can say."

In this uneasy environment the dedicated minister closeted himself thirteen hours a day in his new four-by-eight-foot study, reading and writing at the six-sided escritoire now in the Stockbridge Library. By 1752 he had completed the first book to be written in the Berkshires, a polemic entitled *Misrepresentations Corrected and Truth Vindicated*. There followed in 1754 his *Freedom of Will*, which marked a turning point in systematic theology, granting as it did man's free choices but limiting these choices by motives beyond man's control, the will being thus passive and God-directed.

The next book completed was *Original Sin Defended*, after which he began work on *A History of the Work of Redemption*, which was to set forth the whole body of divinity. This was interrupted by call to become president of New Jersey College (Princeton).

In 1758 Jonathan Edwards preached a farewell sermon to the Indians and another to the whites, the last being on the text: "For here we have no continuing city, but we seek one to come," whereupon he departed from Stockbridge over the January snows. Two months later he was dead.

The modern world gives little heed to the brilliant framework of logic harking back to Plato and Aristotle, which Edwards employed to give metaphysical coherence to fragmented Calvinism. Alone in his time, he furnished a solid backlog for the pulpit and fresh kindling for the pew. A sundial on his home site in Stockbridge designates sunny hours to an inscription reading: "My times are in thy hand." And his interpretation of religion in terms of private, personal experience endures.

Joe Pye

On our Housatonic canoe trip we very nearly passed the giant Lenox frog on the riverbank without seeing it, though our portage passed under its very nose. The gaily painted, seven-foot rock crouched concealed in a dense patch of joe-pye weed, the five- to ten-foot skyscraper of summer wild flowers. Feathery, wine-colored clusters of flowers topped the erect stems, which were regularly marked off by whorls of leaves at the different story levels all the way up to fifteen. The whole patch was bright with butterflies.

This plant, which thrives from New Brunswick to the Gulf of Mexico and westward to Manitoba and Texas, bears the name of a Stockbridge Indian. Very few wild flowers have been named for individuals, though it is common practice with cultivated roses. It so happens that the scientific name of joe-pye weed, *Eupatorium purpureum*, also comes from an individual—Mithridates Eupator, the ancient king of Pontus who, according to Pliny, found one species to be an antidote against poison. Various common names for our plant of wet roadside, low field, and river bank are trumpet weed, gravel root, purple boneset, and queen of the meadow, but the favorite in common parlance is joe-pye weed.

Various botanies, pirating from each other, report that Joe Pye was a Massachusetts Indian medicine man who earned fame and fortune by curing typhus fever and other horrors with decoctions made from this plant. The dried flower heads, along with boneset, still hang from some New England rafters, ready to be brewed into a nauseous cure-all.

An old tavern ledger kept by Captain Isaac Marsh in Stockbridge shows a charge for Joe Pye on July 26, 1775, for 1 quart rum, 1 shilling and 6 pence. There are other rum charges and two cash advances that year. In 1782, debts are partly erased by credit of one hat and one bushel of wheat. Joe Pye is listed, along with the other Stockbridge Indians, as debtors from whom Captain Marsh received in 1789 a parcel of land in Vermont in full settlement. This became the town of Marshfield, near Montpelier.

It is clear that the Stockbridge Indians were having their troubles with rum and money, for eighteen Indian Revolutionary volunteers petitioned Congress that their wages be paid in trust to Timothy Edwards and Jahleel Woodbridge of Stockbridge, to be paid out in necessity. Captain Marsh also had his troubles, eventually selling his tavern and two acres of land for 47 cents. What became of Joe Pye is unknown.

There is further evidence, however, that he was a Stockbridge Indian and not just a transient. The Indians had a fierce tribal pride of locality, which heightened the tragedy of their removal from their ancestral lands. The main body of Stockbridge Indians, otherwise known as Mahicans (from *muhhekaneew*, meaning wolf), moved in 1785 to a tract of land in New York given them by the Oneidas.

When this land became too valuable, they were shunted to the Green Bay area of Wisconsin, where an 1848 act of Congress lists seven Pyes as heads of families. Ten years later eight Pyes were listed as having shares in $18,000 due the tribe from the State of New York. Next, they were pushed to a reservation in Minnesota. So the name Pye was eventually spread to very near the range of joe-pye weed as the medicine man's grandchildren were forced west. His unusually brief name among Indian polysyllabics stands as firmly rooted in the Stockbridge tribe as the plant is in the banks of the Housatonic.

It seems unlikely that much else can be discovered about Joe Pye at this late date. We can only guess that his rum purchases went into his remedies and not into his stomach. He must have attained all possible eminence for an Indian doctor among Yankees to have his name attached first locally to a wild flower, then spread country-wide. Wherever the tall purple blossoms blow, there is immortality of a sort for Joe Pye.

Pioneer, Patriot, and Abolitionist

John Ashley of Sheffield may well have been the only individual in American history who participated in the concerns of the Colonial, the Revolutionary, and the Civil War eras. In his ninety-two years from 1709 to 1802, he saw that much history telescoped and in great measure helped to shape it. He was the Winthrop, the Jefferson, and the Garrison of Western Massachusetts.

Col. Ashley's roles in settling the first town in Berkshire and in formulating a Declaration of Independence three years before the national one have been related; but his part in abolition eighty years before the Civil War may not be so well understood. It can be misinterpreted because he appears to have resisted at law the very freedom for his slaves which he had advocated for his white brethren. Actually, he was changing his mind.

In reverse of the usual trend from liberal to conservative, it is significant to note that all John Ashley's experience demanded that he be conservative, while his thinking demanded that he be liberal. A case in point was his loyalty to Britain, lived over sixty years, clung to almost forlornly when he joined the infamous nineteen Rescinders in the General Court, then completely abandoned as he led the patriot cause.

It was the same for him when the matter of civil rights came up at age seventy. Mum Bett and his several other slaves had been well-treated, respected members of the household since their youth. Like many others, Ashley seems to have believed that freedom in society would remove their protection and livelihood.

The new Massachusetts constitution of 1780 echoed his own words seven years before when it stated in a prefatory phrase: "All men are born free and equal." Mum Bett had heard those words discussed in the Ashley house for years without thought of running away. Not until struck by that proverbial, hot fire shovel swung by Hannah Ashley in a fit of Dutch temper, did she take the words as personally as she took the arm-scar. She flew the coop and brought suit for freedom. It was a dramatic example of how the War for Independence sowed the seed for the Civil War.

Before the Revolution, freedom suits in Massachusetts had been too clouded by tangential issues to clarify the principle of emancipation. In this case, there was no cruelty charge nor defect of ownership. Ashley's bright, young neighbor and friend Theodore Sedgwick is said to have argued that slavery had never received specific legal sanction in Massachusetts and that the new constitution clearly outlawed it.

In August 1781, the case of *Brom and Bett v. Ashley* was decided for the plaintiffs before the Court of Common Pleas in Great Barrington. The first Massachusetts slaves appeared to be free on purely constitutional grounds.

But Ashley appealed to the Supreme Judicial Court; then, abruptly, in the following month dropped his appeal, assenting to the judgment of the lower court that Brom and Bett were not slaves.

Lawyers and historians have guessed variously at his reasons. It is a fact that the *Caldwell v. Jennison* case, concerning the runaway slave Quok Walker, was decided in September by the Supreme Court, but it was not clear whether the slave was freed by his master's promise or because slavery was in conflict with the new constitution. It is also a fact that the clerk of that court wrote fifteen years later that "the question of constitutionality of slavery has never come directly before our Supreme Court." Often, in the early stages of the American bench, decisions were ambiguous, unclear, not well recorded, and not quickly known.

By dropping his appeal, Hon. John Ashley became the first slaveholder in Massachusetts and in the new nation to recognize the abolition of slavery by court decision on constitutional grounds, whether in the high-court case, his own lower-court case, or both. Judging him on lifetime performance, historians might also credit him on moral grounds. One item: In his will he left bequests to three former slaves.

"I, John Ashley of Sheffield"

On May 21, 1799, Col. John Ashley, then eighty-nine years old, wrote: "being in full possession of my reason (blessed be God therefore) do make and publish this my last will and testament."

The substance is related here for an affluent society that lifts itself by bootstraps. John Ashley wore the boots. He must be considered Berkshire's first citizen, who as a lad helped his father lay out the first town in the wilderness and thirty-five years later was committeeman to establish the county.

The document continues: "I give and devise unto my well beloved son General John Ashley Junior" sixteen described parcels of land totaling about 2,260 acres. To his "well beloved daughter Jane and to the heirs male of her body" he left three tracts comprising 220 acres; and to his "beloved son-in-law, General John Fellows," 470 acres. To William Bull, beloved grandson, he left 117 acres, which would be forfeit if he caused any "cost, trouble, or expense, or any molestation whatsoever" to his mother.

This aggregated some 3,064 acres with seventeen dwelling houses, at least eight barns, and many outbuildings besides grist mill, cider mill, and iron works.

The next provision stated: "I give and devise to my son John Ashley Junior, Esquire, all my wearing apparel." This was followed by one-third divisions of his entire personal estate to son John Ashley Junior, to daughter Jane Dutcher, and to the heirs of John Fellows (his daughter Mary's husband). They also received money shares.

His housekeeper, the Widow Jane Steel, was to be paid $100 within sixty days of his death "in consideration of the many faithful and obliging services rendered to me." And the will ended: "I give and bequeath to the said Jane Steel one feather bed, on which she now sleeps, the ticking of which she has made since she has lived with me, together with all the bedding thereunto belonging, to be considered as no payment for her labor and services."

The old colonel survived four more years and indeed outlived his son the general, necessitating a codicil dated November 12, 1799. This transferred the general's one-third share to his wife Mary and upon her death to their children.

It also gave "to my great-granddaughter Elizabeth Sheldon, $150; to Alexander Gunn the 10-acre lot which I purchased from him; to Jane Steel the southwest room in my dwelling house and suitable furniture for said room and $150."

It also provided that "John, Zack and Harry, negro men, and for a great length of time my servants, be maintained and supported in a comfortable manner out of my personal estate during their natural lives when unable to support themselves."

Thereupon he divided the former bequest to the general of real and personal property into fifteen shares: "four to John Ashley; four to William Ashley; two to Hannah Ashley; two to Jane Ashley; two to Lydia Ashley; and one to Mary Lafargue, being my beloved grandchildren, and the children of my said deceased son."

The Indian fighter and father of a Revolutionary War general in his ninety-second year had occasion to write still one more codicil, dated May 15, 1801. There was a debt that he had almost forgotten.

He wrote: "As I have, on mature reflection, thought fit and proper to make the following alteration, I do therefore now make this second codicil to my last will and testament. I do give and bequeath equally unto my beloved grandsons, John Ashley and William Ashley, all the money which is, or may, at the time of my death, be due to me from the United States of America."

The old soldier never lost faith in his country.

Ethan Allen's Sheffield Years

Just how deep were Ethan Allen's roots in Sheffield, during his family's residence there from 1767 to 1777? In that period, one historian terms Ethan's whereabouts "mysterious," while another says he was "living around on the Wentworth Grants." Neither one dug very deep because the family genealogy compiled in 1909 makes it very clear that his home was in Sheffield.

This "Allen Memorial" also states that his sister Lucy, who married Dr. Lewis Beebe of Sheffield, was said to have lived and died there, and that his sister Lydia, who lived in Greenfield, often rode over on horseback to visit members of the family, and spent her last days there. Ethan's favorite brother, Herman, ran the general store

in nearby Salisbury, and brother Zimri ran the Sheffield farm during Ethan's frequent and extended absences.

Ethan was an impetuous twenty-eight when he brought Mary,
aged thirty-four, and their two children, Loraine and Joseph, to
Sheffield, after they were expelled from Northampton on account of
his wrangles with the town fathers. He was an individualist, an
avowed deist, a child of nature—self-schooled on John Locke and
Thomas Paine—a mixture of Robin Hood and Aristotle who swung
from stormy action to philosophic contemplation, with little
patience for anything in between.

Mary, on the other hand, was a pious Calvinist doomed by
plainness, nature, and training to dull mediocrity. The two could
hardly have been more opposite. While Ethan authored seven
books, she never learned to write her own name. Her constant
nagging may have driven him to heroism. Nevertheless, the
unhappy marriage endured for more than twenty years until
Mary's death in 1783.

Of their five children, the three youngest were born in Sheffield,
though no records have yet been found. These were Lucy Caroline,
born in 1768, and Mary Ann, and Pamelia in years soon after.

Without going into the details of Ethan's stormy career, let us
summarize his Sheffield sojourns recently revealed by Prof. Jellison,
realizing meanwhile that he must have been there many undiscov-
ered times as his activities demanded and his travels permitted.

His Vermont trips were at first hunting expeditions to secure
pelts for Herman's store, but he soon shifted to land speculation on
the grants that Governor Wentworth of New Hampshire had
allowed west of the Connecticut River. Ethan became the staunch-
est defender of settlers' rights on these grants, which were increasingly contested by New York claimants and their government in the
violent "Yankees vs. Yorkers" controversy that was ended only by the
unifying effect of the Revolution.

In mid-June of 1770, Ethan arrived in Sheffield, weary from a
horseback trip of 400 miles, largely through wilderness, to Portsmouth
to secure copies of the Wentworth titles, thence to New Haven to

get a lawyer to defend them. By the end of June, he was testifying stormily at the Albany trials. A year later, New York declared him an outlaw with a price of $100 on his head.

In the spring of 1772, Ethan spent several weeks with his family, much of it shut off in the front room of the Sheffield farmhouse composing angry tracts against Governor Tryon of New York and all of his "mercenary, intriguing, monopolizing men—an infamous fraternity of diabolical plotters." The *Connecticut Courant* in Hartford printed many of his diatribes which were signed "the Philosopher." His account of the New York vs. Connecticut and Massachusetts boundary disputes puts him in the select company of pre-Revolutionary Berkshire authors that includes Jonathan Edwards (though they will not be comfortable in the same sentence).

The next winter he was back in Sheffield to form a realty trust with his four brothers and cousin Remember Baker. The partnership was soon called the Onion River Co., and within two years it boasted over 100 square miles of choice settling land along the present Winooski River to Lake Champlain. Bought at ten cents an acre, this soon sold at $5 an acre, skyrocketing company assets to $300,000.

From the fall of 1774 to January 1775, Ethan remained in Sheffield waiting for a Hartford printer to clear his *Brief Narrative* of 200 pages in defense of the Wentworth Grants. By February, he was back on the Grants with his Green Mountain Boys.

After hearing of the "bloody attempt at Lexington," he determined to oppose the British tyrants by taking Ticonderoga and its precious cannons. Leading 130 Green Mountain Boys, he joined forces at Bennington with sixteen Connecticut regulars and Col. James Easton and Capt. John Brown of Pittsfield leading twenty-four recruits from Hancock and fifteen from Williamstown. With Benedict Arnold tagging along without followers, on May 10, 1775, they entered the fort without a fight. Ethan knocked down a guard with the flat of his sword, routed the commandant from his bed, and demanded surrender "in the name of the Great Jehovah and the Continental Congress," though he had no commission from either one. Thus did the mighty man from Sheffield carry out the first aggressive action of the American Revolution.

Having obtained the blessings of the Continental Congress in Philadelphia and an endorsement to Gen. Schuyler from the New York Provincial Assembly, in July Ethan made a last stopover with his family in Sheffield before undertaking the assault on the British Empire in Canada. He was captured at Montreal in September, imprisoned, and harshly treated for almost three years in England, Nova Scotia, and Long Island.

Ethan's release in 1778 came after long negotiations by Gen. Washington, whom he joined for three days at Valley Forge before setting out for Sheffield. He received the first official commission of his career as a reserve colonel in the Continental Army.

His arrival home May 25, 1778 was a sad one. Brother Herman had died only the week before from wounds suffered at the Battle of Bennington; Zimri was gone; and his eleven-year-old son Joseph (gravestone in Sheffield?), had succumbed to smallpox: "Mortality has frustrated my fond hopes, and with him my name expires—My only son the darling of my soul—who should have inherited my fortune, and maintained the honour of the family." Mary and the girls had removed to brother Ira's at Arlington on the Grants. The Sheffield years were over.

But evidently Ethan had some fond memories of South Berkshire, for the Great Barrington registry shows that the general purchased land, dwelling house, and shop from Moses Soul in New Marlborough October 25, 1782. Was this mere speculation, or did he for a time contemplate coming back?

Lafayette in Pittsfield

When Lafayette left Albany at 8 a.m. on June 13, 1825, his tour had become a race against time, for he had promised to be in Boston on the 15th preparatory to laying the cornerstone for the Bunker Hill Monument on the fiftieth anniversary of that battle. The long, strenuous trip had wearied the gallant Frenchman, who was approaching his sixty-ninth birthday. He slept in the jouncing barouche when he could, since every stop meant another celebration far into the night.

Preparations were hasty ahead of him now, because there had been less than a day's notice that he would take the middle way through Berkshire. The road through the little communities of Staats, Schodack, and Nassau was lined with cheering spectators. The *Pittsfield Sun* reported: "At Brainard's Bridge, there was a collation provided, of which the General partook."

At New Lebanon more praise was heaped upon him, after which he was introduced to more than a thousand ladies and gentlemen. The floor of Columbia Hall was shored up with extra timbers when it threatened to give way. After viewing the famous spring he was escorted to the Massachusetts border.

One Bay State lady had declared: "If Lafayette had kissed me, depend upon it, I would never have washed my face again as long as I lived!" A coachman had cautioned his horse: "Behave pretty now, Charley; you are going to carry the greatest man in the world." These were the sentiments of the 3,500 villagers of Pittsfield as the general arrived that afternoon about 4 o'clock in an "elegant coach tastefully festooned with flowers and drawn by four handsome greys." He was accompanied by the sheriff and other officials, the officers of the 7th Militia and a troop of cavalry. His approach was heralded by pealing church bells and booming cannon. The ladies of the village had that morning made an American flag forty-seven feet long with twenty-four stars. It billowed in the breeze and sunshine from the columnar trunk of the giant elm, known as the Pride of Pittsfield.

On the green beneath, Lafayette stood in an elaborate welcome arch of a kind that had framed him in a hundred cities. "He was greeted by a universal and irrepressible burst from the thousands present." Jonathan Allen welcomed him, and he replied "with much feeling." Thereupon, between files of school children and teachers, he proceeded to the platform of the Congregational meetinghouse overflowing with "the Ladies of Berkshire," whom he addressed "in a very affectionate and complimentary manner."

He was introduced to white-haired Revolutionary veterans, some of whom he remembered. It impressed him that they almost invariably asked, "What do you do for a living, or what was your father's business?" This attention to work and trade, the simplicity of life and the absence of accumulated capital distinguished America, but he thought much should be done toward prison reform and Negro emancipation.

The General was next escorted with music and a following crowd to Merrick's Coffee House. All who could endeavored "to touch the hem of his garment. Some of the leaders of our celebrated Shakers, contrary to their custom, approached the august personage with their hats in hand."

A sumptuous and splendid dinner had been prepared. "The Blessing was invoked by Rev. Dr. Griffin, president of Williams College, in his usual exalted stile." After a closing benediction "with a solemn allusion to the recent catastrophe on the Ohio," the customary thirteen toasts were given, and followed by six extras, Lafayette's, in a charming French accent, being: "to the citizens of Berkshire and the people of Pittsfield, may they continue to enjoy, more and more, the benefits of their industry and the fruits of their Republican institutions!"

Lafayette then pushed on in the June dusk, and may have slept here as he went. When he reached Dalton, it was pitch dark except for candles in every window, lanterns and torches in the streets. Nelson's

Coffee House was "brilliantly illuminated on the occasion, and a large number of Ladies and Gentlemen were introduced to him."

With the way lighted by scattered bonfires, the carriage rolled through the hills of Hinsdale and Peru to the usual change of escort at the county line, thence onward for a short night at the tavern at Worthington Corners.

It had been a long day for Lafayette, covering sixty miles. For thousands it was a vivid glimpse of history passing, but it would live long in the telling— 140 years now.

A Boy in the Hills

The Berkshire hills have nurtured many notable writers since the time of Jonathan Edwards, but, like him, few have been native.

By a four-mile stretch of the imagination, William Cullen Bryant is our one son of first magnitude that shines among American literary luminaries. He was born at Cummington, November 3, 1794, just outside the county boundary, and his first twenty-one years were spent in the hill towns east of Berkshire. But part of his education, part of his career, and a major part of his inspiration definitely belong to the county.

His country-doctor father had great ambitions for the sickly boy, who had learned the alphabet at sixteen months. He sought to harden him by a daily dip in an ice-cold spring, sometimes breaking a skim of ice for the purpose. Latin, Greek, farm chores, and the birch rod were other disciplines the youth came to know. But also there were cider and syrup parties, trout fishing, squirrel hunting, and just rambling in the woods and fields.

Reminiscing in autobiography, the octogenarian wrote: "In my ninth year I began to make verses, some of which were utter nonsense." At age ten he wrote a poem describing his school and it was

published in the *Hampshire Gazette*; it became a stock piece for reci-
tation. At thirteen he penned a political satire against Jefferson,
"The Embargo," which was published as a pamphlet in Boston.

Dr. Bryant realized that, of all his children, "Cullen" deserved as
much education as he could provide. Accordingly, for reasons of
economy, the sixteen-year old entered the sophomore class at nearby
seventeen-year-old Williams College. The college then comprised
two brick buildings and a smaller building or two of wood, which
the students used every two or three years for a bonfire. President
Fitch taught the senior class, Professor Chester Dewey, the juniors,
and two recent graduates, the lower classmen. Bryant enjoyed and
profited from his seven months in the "sea of mud" that was early
Williamstown, in spite of his undergraduate diatribe:

Where through the horrors breathing hall
The pale-faced, moping students crawl
Like spectral monuments of woe;
Or drooping, seek the unwholesome cell,
Where shade and dust and cobwebs dwell,
Dark, dirty, dank, and low.

He withdrew from Williams to prepare for Yale, but when the
time came, his father could not afford that. Cullen continued to
read and write poetry on the farm, but necessity pushed him into
study of the law in the office of a family friend in Worthington
and with his grandfather at Bridgewater. The lifelong conflict
between the dream and the reality was developing. He became an
attorney unable to afford a practice in Boston. Instead, he trudged
to nearby Plainfield to open an office. It was on that walk that he
saw a lone bird against a sunset sky, and felt a power that "in the
long way that I must tread alone, will lead my steps aright." A
native voice was beginning to speak for and from the New England
hills.

After eight months, the lawyer-poet walked through falling
maple leaves to Great Barrington to become the law partner of

George H. Ives, whom he soon bought out. His diligence built him a successful practice in the first years but left little time for writing, and few knew he was a poet at heart. It was a strange circumstance that revealed this to the world.

His father, rummaging through his desk in Cummington, came upon a few manuscript poems tucked away in a pigeonhole, among which was "Thanatopsis." The power and beauty startled him. He transcribed it in his own hand, since it was full of erasures and interlineations. On his next trip to the state Senate, he left the verses at the home of his friend Willard Phillips, an editor of the *North American Review*. They were shown to Richard H. Dana, who remarked: "Ah! Phillips, you have been imposed upon; no one on this side of the Atlantic is capable of writing such verses."

Phillips rushed to the Senate to see the supposed author, who was pointed out to him. "It is a good head, I said to myself, but I do not see 'Thanatopsis' in it." However, the poem was published in the *Review* as Dr. Bryant's, along with another by the son. The doctor revealed the mistaken identity, and the poetry was acclaimed as the very best that had been published in this country.

It was the work of a seventeen-year-old boy that had lain for six years in the dusty pigeonhole of the desk where it was written. Like the poem "Renascence" of nineteen-year-old Edna St. Vincent Millay, who lived on the western margin of Berkshire County a century later, the poem signaled an awakening. It came from the heart of the hills—the first authentic, articulate voice of the New World. Here are the first lines, and the last, from "Thanatopsis":

To him who in the love of Nature holds
Communion with her visible forms, she speaks
A various language; for his gayer hours
She has a voice of gladness, and a smile
And eloquence of beauty, and she glides
Into his darker musings, with a mild
And healing sympathy, that steals away
Their sharpness ere he is aware.

So live, that when thy summons comes to join
The innumerable caravan, which moves
To that mysterious realm, where each shall take
His chamber in the silent hall of death,
Thou go not, like the quarry-slave at night,
Scourged, to his dungeon, but, sustained and soothed
By an unfaltering trust, approach thy grave
Like one who wraps the drapery of his couch
About him, and lies down to pleasant dreams.

Bryant in Barrington

From October 1816 to May 1825, William Cullen Bryant lived in Great Barrington. He seems to have been a divided personality, torn between law and poetry, legal wrangles and the peace of woods and hills, petty neighbors and pretty Frances Fairchild. The conflict may have stimulated his writing, for this was the most poetically productive time of his career; certainly his love affair and the increasing requests of Boston editors spurred him on. From 1820 to 1825 he wrote some forty poems and hymns.

He boarded in at least five different homes and occupied three different places of business during these years. All three law offices are gone. The first was in General Ives' office just south of the Berkshire Inn; the second was in the Pattison house, which stood opposite St. James Church; and the last was an office on the site of that church. His first boarding place is unknown. Next he roomed with Ralph Taylor in a home on the site of the St. James parish house.

On January 11, 1921, he married Frances Fairchild, "Fairest of the rural maids." The wedding took place in her sister's home, the Henderson house, built in 1759, and now standing behind the Berkshire Inn. Bryant wrote his mother:

"We went in and took our seats; the little elderly gentleman with the hooked nose prayed, and we all stood up. When he had finished, most of us sat down. The gentleman with the hooked nose then muttered certain cabalistical expressions which I was too much frightened to remember, but I recollect that at the conclusion I was given to understand that I was married to a young lady of the name of Frances Fairchild, whom I perceived standing by my side."

The newlyweds resided in the Taylor house, now the Stevens Funeral Home, having the southeast parlor and bedroom, and use of the fireplace for cooking. Their eldest daughter was born there. An old account shows: $30 a year rent, 2 bu. potatoes 66 cents, 2 bu. ears of corn 56 cents, to pasture your cow 28 1/2 weeks at 17 cents, $4.85, 67 lbs. beef $2.01. Their last residence in Great Barrington was in the Russell house on Castle Street, now the Visiting Nurse Association building. It would seem a worthwhile civic project in this bicentennial year to place historical plaques on these three houses.

The poet-lawyer was twenty-two when he first trudged into Great Barrington, and so completely unknown that at a "sociable" two months after his arrival he was listed as "Bryant." When he left eight years and seven months later, he was a well-established lawyer and town officer and his poems were known on both sides of the Atlantic.

Book 3 of the town records contains sixty-four pages of his graceful, legible script beginning with election as town clerk, February 22, 1820. He polled eighty-one votes; his two opponents together, twenty. He carefully recorded the town warrants, election of officials, meetings, boundary disputes, and perambulations, and in 1821 such items as: "Voted to raise $400 for schools, $400 for highways (to be expended in labor at 6 cents per hour), and voted swine to go at large yoked and ringed according to law."

Almost the only blot in his records is where he registers his own marriage, and the only interlineation where, in giving the birth of his daughter, he had left out the name of the mother. He was also tithingman, justice of the peace, an overseer of accounts and of the poor, and a committeeman to examine schoolmasters, certainly enough to show that he had the respect of the community.

But more and more he disliked the contentions of his neighbors and the fence disputes that came to law. These may have inclined him more to rambling up Monument Mountain and writing "Green River," which he retrieved from the wastebasket to publish in Dana's *Idle Man*. His theme became the revelation of the beauty in nature. The Boston editors urged him to publish a book. It was only a small pamphlet of forty-four pages, containing eight poems. It appeared in 1821, the same year as his friend Catherine Sedgwick's *New England Tale*, Cooper's *Spy*, and Irving's *Sketch Book*. At long last there was an indigenous American literature.

Bryant wavered between the law, which grew increasingly distasteful to him, and literature, which he feared would not support him. In 1825 he secured a position as co-editor of the *New York Review*, and, except for visits and travels, his country days were at an end. From the magazine he shortly gravitated to the *New York Evening Post* to become its editor and a venerable poet and citizen of America.

Fifty-five years after his marriage in Great Barrington and ten years after his wife's death, he once more visited the Henderson house, walked about silently for a long time, and finally said: "There is not a spire of grass her foot has not touched," and his eyes filled with tears.

Holmes at Canoe Meadows

"Boston State House is the hub of the solar system," wrote Oliver Wendell Holmes. As dean and professor of anatomy and physiology at the Harvard Medical School, as a charter member of the illustrious Saturday Club, and as "occasional" poet, the young doctor himself was becoming an important spoke in the wheel. In 1843 his "Essay on Puerperal Fever," written before bacteria and asepsis were known, showed that the thirty-four-year-old man was well ahead of his times.

It was about this date that he revived the annual family pilgrimages to the ancestral lands in Pittsfield, to escape for a time the web of the hub. He had inherited 280 acres, a residue of the section of land six miles square, including a considerable portion of present Pittsfield, which his great-grandfather, Jacob Wendell, had bought from the Province of Massachusetts in 1736. He read a poem at the Berkshire Jubilee in 1844. The county was beginning to take hold of the doctor, who believed the old saw that "the best of all tonics is the Housatonic." In 1849 a $2,000 legacy to his wife enabled them to build "a perfectly plain shelter" on the property, which with their three children they enjoyed for "seven blessed summers, which stand in memory like the seven golden candlesticks in the beatific vision of the holy dreamer."

The doctor was often seen riding his little horse through the Berkshire Hills. An autobiographic fragment from *The Atlantic* says: "This gentleman warn't no great of a gentleman to look at. Being of a very moderate dimension—five foot five he said, but five foot four more likely, and I've heard him say he didn't weigh much over a hundred and twenty pounds. He was light-complected rather than darksome, and was one of them smooth-faced people that keep their baird and whiskers cut close, just as if they'd be very troublesome if they let 'em grow instead of layin' out their face in grass. ..."

The city doctor appeared as much at home on byways as on Beacon Street, for that first summer in his new home he was chairman of the committee for judging the plowing contest at the annual fair of the Berkshire Agricultural Society. He wrote and read *The Ploughman* for the occasion, poking fun at his own kind in his introductory remarks: "He no sooner establishes himself in the country than he begins a series of experiments. He tries to drain a marsh, but only succeeds in draining his own pockets. He builds a wire fence and paints it green, so that nobody can see it. But he forgets to order a pair of spectacles apiece for his cows, who taking offence at something else, take his fence in addition, and make an invisible one of it sure enough. ..."

But if his farming was not remunerative, it was profitable in other ways. It gave him needed relaxation from teaching and from the arduous Lyceum lecture circuit, where he delivered as many as eighty lectures in one season to eager audiences. It extended his field into rural subjects, which he used extensively in the writing that followed this Berkshire period. His *Autocrat of the Breakfast Table* and novel, *Elsie Venner*, show strong influences of his stay in Pittsfield, where the Housatonic meandered through his meadows and Greylock looked in at his study window.

This man of small stature took great interest in trees. He planted some 700 on his meadows. Giant specimens especially attracted him. "In my younger days, when I never traveled without a measuring tape in my pocket, it amused me to see how meek one of the great swaggering elms would look when it saw the fatal measure begin to unreel itself."

And in the *Autocrat*: "I call all trees mine that I have put my wedding ring on, and I have as many tree-wives as Brigham Young has human ones." When he reluctantly sold Canoe Meadows in 1856, a clause in the deed guaranteed that his favorite giant white pine would never be cut down as long as it lived. It is still standing. (Blew down 10-12-62.)

The congenial doctor made many friends during his Pittsfield years and furnished poems for such functions as graduation of the Young Ladies Institute, dedication of the Pittsfield cemetery, dinner at the Berkshire Horticultural Society and St. Stephen's Church fair. He must have seen a good deal of Herman Melville, farming just south of him on Holmes Road. By candlelight the two probed the foundation of the great chimney in Melville's cellar in search of a secret closet and the doctor later wrote his sometimes patient a letter on the chimney that reads like an allegory of Melville's dark mind. It could have been this neighbor to whom the frivolous doctor suggested his hay-fever cure: "Gravel is an effective remedy; it should be taken eight feet deep."

Nowadays, Holmes, who gave both anesthesia and the *Atlantic Monthly* their names at birth, seems strangely outdated. People on Holmes Road do not know where he lived. But there will always be some familiar with "Old Ironsides," "The Deacon's Masterpiece," "The Chambered Nautilus," and "The Last Leaf."

> And if I should live to be
> The lost leaf upon the tree
> In the spring,
> Let them smile, as I do now,
> At the old forsaken bough
> Where I cling.

A Stockbridge Bestseller

It is ironic that the passage of time should be a better appraiser of books than literary critics or bestseller lists. Impersonality thus winnows a field of personalities, and popular favorites fall by the way. Outside of Hemingway and Faulkner, what native novelists of today will be read after a hundred years have elapsed?

To probe this, let us go backward rather than forward, for it is easier to see into the past than into the future, except for Nostradamus, H. G. Wells, and the science-fiction writers. My youngest brother was in the habit of gazing out of the back window of the car to see what he had missed.

And gazing back a hundred years before Rachel Field's time, we find the town of Stockbridge boasting of another bestseller, Catharine Maria Sedgwick, member of a prolific and renowned family. Indeed, Longfellow remarked that "in Stockbridge even the crickets chirp, Sedgwick, Sedgwick, Sedgwick." So now when we search out reasons for neglect of her novels, let it be with respect for the talent that was there; and let us remember that her books were as much read as those of contemporaries Washington Irving and James Fenimore Cooper.

Catharine Sedgwick was thirty-three when her first novel, *A New England Tale*, was published in 1822. By this time she must have rejected a good many of the twenty-four suitors who sought to turn her from quill-pen career to housewife cares. She had broken from the hell fires of Calvinism into the gentler light of Unitarianism, after which an aunt had announced she would never see Catharine in heaven.

But Catharine was a crusader for righteousness and any good cause. So much so that it became the first reason her books are not read today. She was too moral for our time, as some of our novelists may be too immoral for the future. Her Lenox neighbor Hawthorne may have had her in mind when he prefaced *The House of the Seven Gables* with the remark that it was not worthwhile "to impale a story with its moral as with an iron rod, as though sticking a pin through a butterfly."

Her first book was an expansion of a tract she had written on the religious attitude toward life and the joys of freedom from Calvinism. As all her prefaces do, this one stated its didactic purpose: "to lend a helping hand to some of the humble and unnoticed virtues."

The novel's merit was in heroine Jane's moral fibre, which was Catharine's own; in the authentic Berkshire background; and in Crazy Bet, a local madwoman, simply and sympathetically presented. But for us the novel has stiffened on the pin.

Encouraged by the success of this first attempt, Catharine produced a succession of novels almost as regularly as Jonathan Edwards had produced sermons. *Redwood*, 1824, sparked a controversy in the Paris newspapers as to whether it was written by Cooper. *Hope Leslie*, 1827, her best work, crusaded for the Indian cause in the Puritan days. *Clarence*, 1830, the one novel of the New York City she visited, takes up the cause of the poor. *The Linwoods*, 1834, set in Dutch colonial New York, was written "to encourage in the young fidelity to the free institutions of our country." And so it went through six more books, one of which had the avowed purpose of lessening "the stigma placed on the term, old maid."

From the above it may be guessed that sentimentality is the second reason her books are not read today. This may have been her escape from a rigid New England environment, but it doomed her characters. No one wants to read the gushing, stilted ten-page letters that winged from hero to heroine. The modern reader cringes at the fragments of poetry dragged in for effect. Nowadays we like our valentines humorous.

A final reason her novels have no paperback editions is that she belonged to the vast school of omniscient authors. We find her stepping into the story with such pieties as, "God's image is never wholly effaced from the soul. No man or woman is irreclaimable." This may be true, but the reader wants to be shown, not told. Again we find her stepping in to divulge the dreams of sleeping characters, a neat feat to say the least.

But enough of faults. Despite this latter-day criticism, Catharine Sedgwick stands as the first American woman writer of note. Bryant wrote that it was "the first time the beautiful valleys of our country had been made 'the' scene of the well-devised adventures of imaginary persons." Can we not learn, from looking thus backward at a best-seller, how to test the last one we have read? If it rates A on all of the following, maybe it will be read a hundred years from now. Will the moral tone be valid in changing times? Is there sentiment or sentimentality? Is the author able and humble enough to let the characters live and discipline ego out?

Pittsfield's Prophet

Just 186 years ago today, in a hilltop farmhouse on the south side of West Street about a mile from Park Square, there was born to Captain William Miller and his wife, Paulina Phelps, their first of sixteen children. The midnight cry of this infant son on that frontier farm did not carry very far, but sixty years later the name of William Miller was on the tongue of every American, for it was he who interpreted the Bible as prophesying the second coming of Christ, along with the conflagration of the world, between the vernal equinoxes of 1843 and 1844.

William Miller's grandfather from Springfield was one of the first settlers in Pontoosuck in 1747, and his father was born there ten years later, before the name became Pittsfield. This restless Captain Miller, however, chose to move on from the hardscrabble farm. In 1786, when his son was four years old, he rented 100 acres of land for twenty bushels of wheat per year and built a log cabin, and later a frame house, for his family at Low Hampton, New York, almost on the Vermont line.

It might be assumed that young Miller's memories of his first home would be slight and of little influence. Yet, at that early age, in the manner of the day, his mother who taught him to read immersed him in Bible stories, that being the only book on most farms. Furthermore, upon revisiting the old homestead in 1827, he penned the accompanying acrostic which may be the first poem specifically written about Pittsfield.

At Low Hampton young Miller grew up as his father's unpaid farmhand. He showed unusual thirst for learning and often read until midnight on the hearthstone by the light of pine knots to save candles. Voltaire, Hume, Volney, Paine, and Ethan Allen led him into the paths of deism, that slough of negation from which it was but a short step into the Army. He was commissioned captain in 1812 and shared in the victory at Plattsburg, but he resigned from the Army four years later.

For him "Yankee Doodle" proved a weak substitute for "Onward Christian Soldiers," as Deism for Deity. He wrote: "I should prefer the heaven and hell of the Scriptures, and take my chance respecting them." Now, at a farm built by him still standing at Low Hampton, the Bible became his sole study. He pondered it, verse by verse, being affected most by its prophetic revelations. One night a vivid dream of a streak of blood along a rail fence seemed a very beckoning to him from the Savior.

By applying literal interpretation to verses of Daniel he became convinced that Christ's second coming and the millennium would occur sometime after 1843. For fourteen years he resisted the compulsive "Go out and tell it to the world," but his earnestness, sincerity, and scholarship began to be known anyway.

He covenanted to preach only if the Lord sent someone to ask him. That very day a young man arrived from nearby Dresden with a request that he speak to their people on the morrow on the second advent of Christ. Miller was distraught. He hurried to his woodland grove to pray for release. His little daughter returned to the house shouting: "Father's gone crazy." For several hours farmer Miller wrestled with the Lord. It was the turning point in his life. He returned to the house a devout preacher, and accompanied the young man on the first sixteen miles of what was to be a long, uphill journey.

Within four years the exponent of prophecy delivered 800 lectures. The doors of most denominations were thrown open to him. No one could hear him for more than five minutes without being convinced by his sincerity and instructed by his reasoning. His efforts built up the churches, though he was often discouraged in his personal mission. Scholarly divines argued against him. There were always the scoffers taunting with their "When do you go up?" The newspapers reported his every move, noting that he had refused to sell his farm and, indeed, was laying some stonewall for the future.

The humble Miller, who never pinpointed the exact day of the millennium, exhorted patience for the coming, repentance, and faith. Whittier, writing of a Millerite camp-meeting in western Massachusetts, told of a young woman who packed a complete new wardrobe in a trunk and strapped herself to it, so that both would enter the pearly gates simultaneously. Stories threatened to submerge the movement, especially when 1844 passed harmlessly. Pittsfield celebrated its Jubilee in spite of the prediction of its own son.

In the five years that remained of his life, William Miller often confessed his error of literal interpretation, but he continued to believe that the day of the Lord was near. The failure of one of his nineteen articles of faith did not discredit him. In fact, it was a blessing in disguise since it satiated the scoffers and purged the fanatics. He continued his crusade to a grand total of over 4,000 lectures in more than 500 towns and cities in America. At his death 200 other ministers were preaching his ideas to upwards of 50,000 believers in a thousand congregations.

After his death, in 1849, Millerism evolved into the present Seventh-day Adventist faith, which numbers some 1,700,000 souls worldwide. The farmboy's cry had been heard in the wilderness:

Why was I here the light brought to behold?
Inconstant life here first her pulses told;
Life's blood here through my veins began to flow;
Lo! here began my pilgrimage below;
I here first lisped with infant's prattling tongue,
And here heard mother's hush-a-baby song.
Murmuring, this pebbly brook taught me to play.

Meandering stream, by thee I used to stray;
In thee first saw the playful silvery fish;
Learnt here t'express the infant's simple wish,
Love, hope, and joy. I here my days began;
Even here the broomstick rode, the circle ran;
Rejoiced and prattled here to mimic man.

One-Woman Revolution

The arrival of songbirds will soon be followed by the arrival of summer people in Berkshire, one migratory wave following upon the other. Once there were simply birds and Indians, then settlers and natives. Then in 1835 arrived Fanny Kemble Butler to initiate a summer visitation that has grown ever since.

It was typical of this animated Shakespearean actress that she should be in the vanguard; she was never a complacent follower; her spirits were too high, her talents too numerous, and her individuality too positive for her to conform to the submissive feminine tradition.

That first summer, she came to Stockbridge to visit novelist Catharine Sedgwick, who found her "a captivating creature steeped to the very lips in genius." She came with her man-about-Philadelphia husband, who had assumed the name Butler as a condition of inheriting the wealth and plantations from his mother's side of the family. Blinded by love, she had abandoned a brilliant English and American stage career that began as Juliet in Covent Garden at age nineteen. This was an ill-starred love, doomed to founder on his weaknesses and her strengths, finally breaking up in divorce in 1849.

But the differences were deeper than that: There was a complete lack of intellectual companionship for this scintillating female who filled even Samuel Gray Ward with "a sense of his own inferiority"; there were the repeatedly rewritten conditions of obedience that Butler sought to impose on his wife, who was an ardent spokeswoman of women's rights, creator of the word "Womanifesto" and friend of Lucretia Mott; there was the Civil War between them over slavery, as may be seen in Fanny Kemble's recently republished journal of a residence on her husband's Georgian plantation.

The Berkshires came to be a happy summer refuge where she could exercise and exorcise her spirit among friends and nature. After that first visit, she returned to Lenox, sometimes with her two daughters, when she could have them, over a period of forty years. Usually it was to visit the Sedgwicks. Often it was for lengthy stays at the old redbrick Berkshire Coffee House that stood on the site of the Curtis Hotel. Thither young Curtis would drive her from the Hudson River steamboat, on one occasion charging her fifty cents extra for "sarce" when she told him he was hired to drive, not to explain the scenery.

Another driver, on being told dramatically that he had been conveying Fanny Kemble, replied laconically, "Madam, you have rid with John Smith." Once she informed a Yankee that gentlemen were in the habit of removing their hats in her presence, only to be told: "But I'm not a gentleman, ma'am; I'm a butcher."

These nasal banalities delighted and surprised her as much as her activities startled the local populace. Often she rode ten to twenty miles through the hills before breakfast astride a great black steed, stirring up a newspaper controversy as to whether it was side-saddle or not. She informed the admiring Judge Bishop that: "The great difference between you and me is that when you are on a horse's back, he knows you are afraid of him; when I am on his back, he knows he is afraid of me."

This original, alluring Amazon was known to the Alpine guides as *"la dame qui va chantant par les montagnes."* As Henry James put it, she went "flinging herself, in the joy of high places, on the pianos of mountain inns, joking, punning, botanizing, encouraging the lowly and abasing the proud, making stupidity everywhere gape (that was almost her mission in life), and startling infallibly all primness of propriety." She read *The Merry Wives of Windsor* to a staid Stock-bridge audience; she went fishing on Stockbridge Bowl and Laurel Lake dressed in trousers; she introduced archery to Lenox.

In the autumn of 1839 she accompanied some friends and a group of Mrs. Sedgwick's schoolgirls on an omnibus picnic to Bash Bish Falls. Such a bedlam of "eating, drinking, dancing, singing, tearing, climbing, and screaming" ensued that the emancipated ladies were pelted with rotten eggs by indignant farmers.

Her Elizabethan exuberance, acquired as it was directly from Shakespeare, was just the proper yeast to leaven soggy, Calvinist Berkshire. After first shocking, she gradually captivated all who knew her. By 1850, with proceeds from her public reading, she purchased "The Perch," a cottage overlooking Laurel Lake. She became the magnetic center of Lenox society in its literary heyday. Longfellow wrote in a sonnet: "How our hearts glowed and trembled as she read."

In 1876 she proudly walked Kemble Street one last summer before departing for residence in native England. The sunny meadow town was changed; it had grown with trees and with summer people who were enjoying a revolutionary freedom that she had begun in 1836.

In her own words, there was not by then so much "devotion to conformity in small things and great which pervades the American body social from the matter of churchgoing to the trimming of women's petticoats, this dread of singularity which has eaten up all individuality. ... The fact is that being politically the most free people on earth, the Americans are socially the least so, and it seems as though ever since that little affair of establishing their independence among nations, which they managed so successfully, every American mother's son of them has been doing his best to divest himself of his own private share of that great public blessing, liberty."

Melville and Balance Rock

In Berkshire a century ago, that is before Tanglewood and the parimutuel races, it was the custom of visitors and inhabitants alike to make frequent pilgrimages to places of natural and scenic wonder. Such affairs were usually gay all-day drives and picnics, whether made by some illustrious company of Mrs. Sarah Morewood's from Broadhall, such as ex-President John Tyler and friends, or by a farm family with a wagon full of children.

Balance Rock in Lanesboro was always a favorite destination for climbing boys and thoughtful men. On one visit there Oliver Wendell Holmes carved the word "Memnon" on a tree close by the rock, alluding to the ancient Memnon monument west of the Nile from which issued musical notes when the early morning sun arose.

In 1851 a party from Broadhall, including Pittsfield historian J. E. A. Smith and probably Herman Melville, was startled at hearing music emanating from the huge rock. The irrepressible Mrs. Morewood had smuggled along a music box, crawled under the overhang, and surprised the gathering with the sylvan notes of "Ave Maria."

That was the year Melville, at age thirty-two, had gone half-blind finishing *Moby-Dick*. Perhaps that temporary blindness turned him into the dark realm within himself, for before the next year was out he had finished *Pierre*, a dark, introverted novel, his spiritual autobiography, a pioneer exploration of his own mind foreshadowing the work of Freud and the psychological novels of Henry James and Proust.

The setting of the first half of the novel was Saddle Meadows, a name which Melville seems to have compounded from Saddle Mountain and Canoe Meadows; it represented the village of Pittsfield and its mountain-encircled farms. In this Garden-of-Eden setting the idealistic Pierre was swept from an Oedipus complex with his mother to a bucolic affair with Lucy, his good angel, then to flight from Eden with Isabel, his bad angel, and to a Narcissus complex that brought his doom in New York City.

The deeply philosophical Melville developed three ideas that fascinated him: one, that "in the minutest moment momentous things are irrevocably done"; two, that an idealistic, benevolent youth will be crushed by the practical, non-benevolent world; and three, that it is impossible for a man "to reconcile this world with his own soul," for he is condemned by the world on the one hand and by his conscience on the other.

In this novel of carefully balanced ambiguities, Balance Rock played a part in one dramatic episode of six pages so graphic that one feels sure the author himself crawled under the rock and risked his head in the balance.

Balance Rock "was shaped something like a lengthened egg." Beside the one obscure and minute point of contact, the whole enormous and most ponderous mass touched not another object in the wide terraqueous world. It was a breathtaking thing to see... beneath one part ... the vacancy was considerably larger, so as to make it not only possible, but convenient to admit a crawling man; yet no mortal being had ever been known to have the intrepid heart to crawl there.

"A flitting conceit had often crossed him, that he would like nothing better for a headstone. ... Sometimes, wrought to a mystic mood by contemplating its ponderous inscrutableness, Pierre had called it the Terror Stone. Few could be bribed to climb its giddy height, and crawl out upon its more hovering end. It seemed as if the dropping of one seed from the beak of the smallest flying bird would topple the immense mass over, crashing against the trees."

Melville hazarded Pierre beneath the stone. There, lying prone, Pierre flung his challenge of ifs at the universe.

They paraphrase thus: If my undisclosable miseries overcome me, if truth and virtue make a trembling, distrusted slave of me, if life proves an unbearable burden, if our actions are foreordained and we are serfs to fate, if evil laughs at our best efforts, if life be an empty dream and virtue meaningless, if my duty seems wrong to my Mother, and if all duty is purposeless, all things allowable and unpunishable, "then do thou, Mute Massiveness, fall on me! Ages thou hast waited; and if these things be thus, then wait no more; for whom better canst thou crush than him who now lies here invoking thee?"

Have any of the sightseeing, picnicking crowd ever looked at Balance Rock with like thoughts? Probably not, for agony is not the common property of the crowd; but it is often the private burden of genius.

A Whale in the Berkshires

The American whaling industry has gone the way of the whalebone corset, but it cannot be forgotten as long as men read the classic written by Herman Melville at Arrowhead on the south edge of Pittsfield. Against carpenter's advice, Melville built a narrow piazza on the north side of his house. Strange that this imaginative old salt did not build it shaped like a broad arrowhead and the foredeck of a whale ship, as Mark Twain had built his porch in Hartford like the deck of a Mississippi riverboat. At least he thought of it that way: "But even in December, this northern piazza does not repel—nipping cold and gusty though it be, and the north wind, like any miller, bolting by the snow in finest flour—for there, once more, with frosted beard, I pace the sleety deck, weathering Cape Horn." From that deck he viewed the vast snowy hulk of Greylock that could have suggested the great white whale to a mind so full of analogy.

The county is commonly said to have influenced Melville as little as he did it, but there were influences both ways. He came to Pittsfield first in 1833 as a fourteen-year-old boy to summer vacation at Maj. Thomas Melville's farm and hotel, Broadhall, now the Pittsfield Country Club. He liked it enough to return the next spring as a hired hand, staying almost a year. He helped his lame uncle switch the farm from cattle to sheep. Where golfers now swing their clubs, Melville swung the scythe; where they hook golf balls, he wielded a potato hook.

After working his way to Liverpool and back on a wretched trader, with no friends, for a final pay of $3, he was content to return to school teaching in Greenbush, and, in 1837, for a fall term at Pittsfield's Sikes District School in the morning shadow of Washington Mountain. He boarded around with the families of his thirty pupils, who were all sizes and ages up to his own eighteen. One day some of the bigger boys tried to lick him, but he overcame them, as he soon overcame New England clutches by sailing for the South Pacific. "A whale ship was my Yale College and my Harvard."

His wanderings over the seas and shingles of the world we skip to get him back in Berkshire County, now the famous author of *Typee, Omoo, Mardi, Redburn,* and *White Jacket.* Still, he remained largely in poverty and in debt to his publishers. With his great whale thrashing in his mind, he brought his wife and son in mid-July 1850 to Broadhall, now run by his cousin Robert. By the middle of September he had purchased Arrowhead, where for twelve years he toiled with plow and pen for a living.

The county served mainly as workshop for this mariner who had gathered his material elsewhere. Here he plowed the land by day, read Shakespeare, and wrote *Moby Dick* by night. That first year he was too busy to be very social, but did form a close friendship with Hawthorne that expanded them both at their most productive time of life.

His great work was dedicated to this friend with whom he hoped to "sit down in Paradise in some little shady corner by ourselves, and if we shall by any means be able to smuggle a basket of champagne there (I won't believe in a temperance heaven) and if we shall cross our celestial legs in the celestial grass that is forever tropical, and strike our glasses and our heads together till both ring musically in concert; then, O my dear fellow mortal, how we shall pleasantly discourse of all the things manifold which now so much distress us."

Traces of Berkshire began to increase in his work. In his portrait of Ahab is a graphic picture of the huge old elm that stood in Pittsfield's Park Square. His disastrous spiritual autobiography, *Pierre*, contained a description of Balance Rock, and was dedicated to "the majestic mountain, Greylock—my own more immediate sovereign lord and king hath now, for innumerable ages, been that one grand dedicatee of the earliest rays of all the Berkshire mornings. I know not how his Imperial Purple Majesty ... will receive the dedication of my own poor solitary ray."

Israel Potter and such magazine essays as "Cock-a-doodledoo," "I and My Chimney," and "October Mountain" belong to the county. Though Melville was "a gentleman of the old school" like his Uncle Thomas, who pulled a satinwood snuff box from his pocket in the hay field, many in Pittsfield considered him little better than a cannibal or beachcomber; and the bookseller who sold his books did not know that he lived nearby. As the golden age of whaling passed by, so Melville's literary reputation drifted into the doldrums. He became more introspective and metaphysical as he attempted to crack the nut of the universe.

Just 100 years ago his friends were trying to get him a diplomatic post. On March 22, in Washington, he met Lincoln. "Old Abe is much better looking than I expected and younger looking. He shook hands like a good fellow—working hard at it like a man sawing wood at so much per cord." A position in the New York Customs House was finally secured and, in October 1863, he moved his family from Pittsfield for good, and his literary career virtually ended.

His attachment to Berkshire had been as strong and deep as it could be to any land. "I have a sort of sea-feeling here in the country, now that the ground is all covered with snow. I look out of my window in the morning when I rise as I would out of a porthole of a ship in the Atlantic. My room seems a ship's cabin, and at night when I wake up and hear the wind shrieking, I almost fancy there is too much sail on the house, and I had better go on the roof and rig in the chimney."

Here was a man who could only live in the all. He had written Hawthorne: "You must often have felt it, lying in the grass on a warm summer's day. Your legs seem to send out shoots into the earth. Your hair feels like leaves upon your head. This is the *all* feeling."

Three Titans on a Mountain

In this Berkshire bicentennial year, local history is fresh with glimpses of past glory. We can travel in mind's eye (if not in a buckboard) over the bumpy dirt road the seven miles from Stockbridge Bowl to the village of Pittsfield. One hundred eleven years ago, in that small distance, lived Nathaniel Hawthorne writing *The House of the Seven Gables* in his "little red shanty" no bigger than one gable, looking, as he said, "like the Scarlet Letter."

Six miles north, Herman Melville in a white farmhouse called "Arrowhead" was writing *Moby Dick* while trying to wrest a living from the soil. At his nearby "Canoe Meadows" straddling the Housatonic, Dr. Oliver Wendell Holmes was summering and writing poems, and ten years later produced his own dark novel, *Elsie Venner*. In the milky way from Sheffield to Pittsfield were many lesser literary stars. Indeed, here was a literary county to rival the town of Concord.

The common bond in the three above-mentioned books is a black one seeming to stem by heritage from the old Puritan Calvinist doctrine of damnation, and by thought from the circles of

Dante's *Inferno*. *Moby Dick* has held its classic stature best. Its dark thread of mysticism hovers over Ahab like an innate curse compelling him to pursue the great white whale.

In Hawthorne's novel, it is Maule's curse upon the house of Pyncheon that makes the children suffer for the father's sins. In Holmes's novel, the prenatal bite of a Berkshire rattlesnake curses Elsie with aspish attributes all her life. It is almost as if the three writers had said: "When shall we three meet again, in thunder, lightning, or in rain?"

And that is just how they did meet August 5, 1850, at an all-day, mountain-climbing party planned by host David Dudley Field, the distinguished New York attorney who summered in Stockbridge. Melville brought two New York houseguests, Evert Duyckinck, editor, and Cornelius Mathews, author. James T. Fields, Boston publisher and editor, brought his new wife, "the violet of the season in Berkshire." Field's daughter, Jenny, with her ardent escort, Henry D. Sedgwick, Jr., added a further romantic touch.

Forty-five years later, Sedgwick recalled that he was the only male in the party who had not written a book. The account of the day is drawn from letters and reminiscences of the cast.

The day dawned brilliant. Melville and his guests came by the cars from Pittsfield and found Holmes, "a slight apparition ... with a glazed India-rubber bag in hand," at the station. David Dudley Field took them "to his Umbrage in a hollow in the skirts of Stockbridge—and just by way of a rehearsal, for the grand climb, we take a run to the top of Sacrifice Mount, not far off."

Meanwhile, Hawthorne drove down with the newlyweds from Lenox, publisher Fields in patent leathers and his bride in a delicate blue silk, scarcely prepared for Monument Mountain. Hawthorne and Melville were meeting for the first time, to begin a friendship that proved most fruitful for American letters.

The gay procession set out for the mountain some three miles distant. Pure prose flowed for conversation, and all spirits rose as they scaled the height that Fields fancied was 6,000 feet above Stockbridge. Mathews wrote: "Higher, higher up we go stealing glances through the trees at the country underneath; rambling, scrambling, climb-ing, rhyming—puns flying off in every direction like sparks among the bushes."

The three great spirits of the group strangely did not record the meeting, except for Hawthorne's brief listing of those present in his journal. Perhaps under the levity they probed each other's dark depths. Certainly the setting was right on that rocky top as a gather-ing storm "dragged its ragged skirts" over them. Lightning played about; thunder rolled; and a summer shower baptized the little cir-cle of elected friends.

The plump Fields sheltered his curly whiskers and patent leath-ers, his bride and her blue silk, under a convenient rock. The resourceful Holmes fashioned himself an umbrella of three cut branches, and opened some iced champagne, which the party drank from a silver mug, while Mathews read them Bryant's poem of the Indian maid who leaped for love from that same cliff: "It is a fearful thing—To stand upon the beetling verge, and see—Where storm and lightning, from that huge gray wall—Have tumbled down vast blocks."

Someone proposed Bryant's health and "a long life to the dear old poet." It took a considerable quantity of Heidseck to do this justice.

The rain ceased, and the party scattered over the rocks. Duyck-inck wrote his wife the next day: "While little Dr. Holmes peeped about the cliffs and protested it affected him like ipecac, Hawthorne looked mildly about for the great Carbuncle." Melville seemed most at home in the lofty setting, seating himself "astride a projecting bowsprit of rock" where he pulled and hauled imaginary ropes for the literary crew.

Was he furling the main topgallant of the whaler *Acushnet* on which he had shipped ten years before for the South Pacific? More likely he fancied himself Ishmael at the masthead of the *Pequod*, sighting for Moby Dick in the billows of Berkshire Hills where he was creating the voyage that still goes on in the minds of men.

Hawthorne
at Natural Bridge

Browsing through the registers kept by Edward Elder, the owner of that scenic and geologic wonder, Natural Bridge in North Adams, one immediately notices that Berkshire visitors are equaled if not outnumbered by sightseers from other counties, states, and countries. This columnist is probably fairly representative, having made his first visit after thirty years of residence in the county. Such neglect is inexcusable, and we can hardly wait until opening time next Memorial Day to further explore and report on this natural carving by Hudson's Brook through the far-flung Stockbridge limestone.

Here is a chance to probe the heart of rock laid down 500 million years ago in Cambrian seas. Here in an abandoned marble quarry, worked for a century, may be studied the rock of ages. Here in awesome grandeur the forces of compaction, metamorphosis, upheaval, and erosion are revealed. Here glacial clawmarks 20,000 years old occur upon scoured stone surfaces beside a man's recording: "Sept. 8, '89 Boston wrecked by volcano." Here Harvard's Prof. Billings may have identified the only fossil ever to be discovered in Berkshire County. In this grand setting, ancient and delicate calcite crystals keep company with rare, lacy lime-loving ferns. Here present meets past like brook water lapping upon marble.

Nathaniel Hawthorne was intrigued with the place. When he came in July of 1838 for a six-week sojourn at the new North Adams House, he was an anonymous Salem scribe who, for twelve years after Bowdoin, had been grinding out tales and sketches for periodicals and newspapers. Only the year before had his *Twice-Told Tales* caught the notice of classmate Longfellow, to whom he wrote: "I have seen so little of the world that I have nothing but thin air to concoct my stories of."

The Berkshire visit recorded in the first years of his *American Note Books* was deliberately undertaken to remedy this deficiency. Thereafter, one striking image that recurred frequently throughout his works was the simile between the human heart and the cavern that he observed at Natural Bridge, then known as Hudson's Cave or Hudson's Falls.

He wrote: "The cave makes a fresh impression upon me every time I visit it—so deep, so irregular, so gloomy, so stern. I stand and look into its depths at various points, and hear the roar of the stream re-echoing up. It is like a heart that has been rent asunder by a torrent of passion, which has raged and foamed, and left its ineffaceable traces; though now there is but a little rill of feeling at the bottom."

Nathaniel, the natator, liked swimming in this deep chasm. Of his eleven recorded Berkshire baths, at least those of July 31, August 11, 14, 21, and September 7 were in this wild, marble tub which did not always prove to be private: "A small stone tumbled down; and looking up towards the narrow strip of bright light, and the sunny verdure that peeped over the top, 'looking up thither from the deep, gloomy depth,' I saw two or three men; and, not liking to be to them the most curious part of the spectacle, I waded back and put on my clothes."

Even in 1838, Nathaniel the conservationist was concerned about the future of this wilderness abyss and the stream's voice "that has been the same for innumerable ages." Already men had dammed it for power and there were two mills for cutting the marble. "In process of time the whole of the crags will be quarried into tombstones, doorsteps, fronts of edifices, fireplaces, etc. That will be a pity. ... The marble is of very brilliant whiteness. It is rather a pity that the cave is not formed of some worthless stone."

Today Hawthorne would be pleased and surprised at the fortunate outcome at Natural Bridge. Its thirty-foot width and fifteen-foot thickness still arch majestically high above his tub. Nature's span may yet outlast all man's existent bridges.

Hawthorne at Tanglewood

Nathaniel Hawthorne first visited the Berkshires on a stage-coach tour during July 1838. He was thirty-four years old and little known, having written only an anonymous novel, *Fanshawe*, and a collection of magazine short stories entitled *Twice-Told Tales*. He was on the alert for new material which he might capture in his note-books for possible future use, and the six weeks in the Berkshires proved fruitful.

"Pittsfield is a large village, quite shut in by mountain walls. ..." He noted the churches and courthouse, and in the park "an elm of the loftiest and straightest stem that ever I beheld. ..." He recorded all kinds of people, their manners and jokes. Characteristically he noticed the gravestones and even peeped in at the crevices, and saw "the coffins" in the tomb of Pittsfield's first minister, Rev. Thomas Allen.

On July 26 he left by stage for North Adams. "Our driver was a slender, lathe-like, round-backed, rough-bearded, thin-visaged, middle-aged Yankee, who became very communicative during our drive.... He was the only man who had driven an ox team up Greylock."

The next day, walking in the scowl of that same mountain, Hawthorne met "an underwitted old man ... going to see a widow in the neighborhood. Finding that I was not provided with a wife, he recommended a certain maiden of forty years, who had three hundred acres of land." In his notebook he wrote: "Conceive something tragical to be talked about, and much might be made of this interview in a wild road among the hills, with Greylock, at a great distance, looking somber and angry, by reason of the gray, heavy mist upon his head." The short story that resulted was "Ethan Brand," one of the very best of the hundred that he wrote. The episode was pream-ble to his productive eighteen months in Lenox.

To Lenox he came in June of 1850 with Sophia and their two young children, riding the crest of *The Scarlet Letter*, completed only four months before. They had rented "the little red house" on the Tappan estate, overlooking Stockbridge Bowl to Monument Mountain, which in October foliage looked "like a headless sphinx, wrapped in a rich Persian shawl." The weary author called it "the very ugliest little bit of an old red farmhouse you ever saw, the most inconvenient and wretched house I ever put my head in." There was a large two-story chicken house adjoining, and little Julian reminisced years later that the inmates were "tamer than the pig in an Irish cabin."

Here Hawthorne and his wife regained health and vigor during a pleasant summer in which they made friends as various as Melville, Fanny Kemble, and the milkman next door. Yet the terribly shy author on his way to the Lenox Post Office jumped over a wall to avoid meeting some villagers, and once hid like a frightened schoolboy when callers appeared at his door. He seemed a moody mixture of opposites, as were the five books he wrote in Lenox.

The first book, conceived that summer and begun with the autumn frosts, was finished by the end of January. It was *The House of the Seven Gables*, his second major work, a period romance and picture of Salem with "the past weighing heavily on the present's back." The literary chickens in the story are drawn from his own housemates, as it were. Similarly, the change and decline in New England that he sensed and depicted hung over Lenox-like clouds of Jonathan Edwards's religious gloom masquerading in sunset ardor. The book was well received and, next to *The Scarlet Letter*, still outshines all American novels up to that time. Simultaneously, he prepared a new edition of *Twice-Told Tales*.

In May he wrote in his notebook: "I think the face of nature can never look more beautiful than now, with this so fresh and youthful green, the trees not being fully in leaf, yet enough so to give airy shade to the woods. The sunshine fills them with green light." Quite a change in tone from a December entry: "The print in blood of a naked foot to be traced through the street of a town." There was the same change from dark to light between two books written in

Lenox. A *Wonder-Book for Boys and Girls* was finished in July—a minor work, "but a clear tribute to the 'beautiful and comfortable world' in the hills where his mind was 'in a free and happy state, and took delight in its own activity, and scarcely required any impulse to set it at work.'"

This summer work culminated in *The Snow Image and Other Twice-Told Tales,* and meanwhile he had been conceiving *The Blithedale Romance.* Play with a snowman and with his children was scarcely enough to occupy him fully, though he loved his tight little family dearly. Into this breach rode "Mr. Omoo," and he records: "Melville and I had a talk about time and eternity, things of this world and of the next, and books, and publishers, and all possible and impossible matters, that lasted pretty deep into the night." There were many such visits. The two made an expedition to see the Shakers at Hancock and Hawthorne commented: "The sooner the sect is extinct, the better. ... They are certainly the most singular and bedeviled set of people that ever existed in a civilized land."

By November Hawthorne's spirits had fallen like the leaves. He wrote Longfellow: "My soul becomes troublous and bubblous with too much peace and rest. ... Here I feel remote and quite beyond companionship." In the privacy of his notebook so full of the joys of Tanglewood, and in the presence of the hills he had climbed, and loved, and praised, he wrote: "This is a horrible, horrible, most hor-ri-ble climate; one knows not; for ten minutes together whether he is too cool or too warm; but he is always one or the other. ... I detest it! I detest it! I detest it!!! I hate Berkshire with my whole soul, and would joyfully see its mountains laid flat... Here, where I hoped for perfect health, I have for the first time been made sensible that I cannot with impunity encounter nature in all her moods."

The man who could probe the depths of humanity and the universe could not fathom his own moods. "We left Lenox Friday morning, November 21, 1851, in a storm of snow and sleet, and took the cars at Pittsfield, and arrived at West Newton that evening." He was never to be so productive again, nor was he ever to feel at home.

The little red house was destroyed by fire in 1890. The National Federation of Music Clubs built a replica on the original foundation, which was presented to the Berkshire Music Center in 1948. Hawthorne originated the name Tanglewood, but he disliked music and could scarcely hum "Yankee Doodle."

Josh Billings Laughs

As the Josh Billings house in Lanesboro was burned to the ground last week, Henry Wheeler Shaw must have been in the wings laughing. Having out-witted death by humor, to some extent, he must have roared like the fire seeing Matt Reilly circumvent that other inexorable, taxes, to some extent, even though it cost Josh his birthplace. Although he always told his own jokes with a solemn face, he enjoyed a good laugh— "one that rushes out of a man's soul like the breaking up of a Sunday school."

Josh knew how to go at things by indirection. Perhaps taking a cue from those who had mined for gold on old Greylock and got laughed at, he chose to mine for laughter and got gold. For a small-town Berkshire farm boy, a coast-to-coast reputation was not as meaningful as a trout story, but one thing did lead to another.

Josh's Yankee dialect stories were so amusing that President Lincoln read some to his cabinet, and is reputed to have said: "Next to William Shakespeare, Josh Billings is the greatest judge of human nature the world has ever seen."

Joshing at his own discreet borrowings from Shakespeare, Josh wrote: "I and he often think through one quill." Behind his pseudonym he was variously guessed to be Horace Bigelow, Horace Greeley, and Abraham Lincoln; but Lincoln said that though his shoulders were broad enough to carry the burdens of state, they were hardly broad enough to carry the sins of the nation's wits and jesters.

Henry Shaw was born April 21, 1818, missing April Fool's Day by the figure 2 and missing the fire by seventy-seven years, but not missing much between. He was brought up on a farm further up Constitution Hill, known as the Hillcrest House. His grandpa, a Vermont surgeon, had been jailed for libeling John Adams, and was later sent to Congress for the same reason. His father ended a political career in the House by voting for the Missouri Compromise, unpopular in the Berkshires.

Josh mined his Puritan pedigree for all it was worth—in fun. One grandma "was smarter than chain lightning and cleaner than a ghost. Her hash didn't have any paving stones, nor cart wheels in it. You might as well hunt for the lost tribes of Israel on her premises as to hunt for a cockroach. She had red hair and was bony put together and could fry pork, tend bar, harness a horse, trade with a peddler, and make a gin sling that could almost talk."

His education, when he was not swimming in Pontoosuc or hooking apples or trapping muskrat, was in the district school, though he thought "learning was picked up oftener by running your head against a stone wall than by any other kind of mineralogy.—All the astronomy I ever got I learnt in spearing suckers by moonlight, and my geology culminated at the further end of a woodchuck's hole, especially if I got the woodchuck." He returned to this carefree Berkshire boyhood for subjects, smiles, and similes all his life, and once said he would gladly live his life over, if he could live it backwards, and at the last be a boy again.

Next at the Lenox Academy he picked up enough information to get into Hamilton College at age fourteen, but by mistake during his sophomore year, he shinnied up the lightening rod and stole the clapper from the bell. This accident resulted in prompt dismissal and return to the farm. The restless boy soon turned down the chance to be John Quincy Adams' private secretary and headed west with $10 and parental blessings. Ten years later and many wild oats later, without the $10, he returned to Lanesboro where everything always went right. He soon married Zilpha Bradford, his childhood sweetheart, the couple driving to Lebanon to escape the Massachusetts banns. They lived in a cottage overlooking Pontoosuc Lake and in due course had two daughters to cheer them.

In 1854 the family removed to Poughkeepsie for a real-estate and auctioneering business. Josh began sending his first humorous dialect sketches back to the *New Ashford Eagle*. Recognition came slowly but surely as his writings spread, and his lectures began, and his books were published. "The great desire of my life is to amuse somebody," he wrote. "But you can't tell a man when to laugh. He knows what pleases him, just as well as he knows what eats good. You can't play a burnt slapjack, or one that ain't well done onto him."

His kind, homespun humor and cracker-barrel philosophy took their strength largely from Berkshire farm roots. "This settling down and folding our arms and waiting for something to turn up, is about as rich a speculation as going out into a 400-acre lot, setting down on a sharp stone, with a pail between our knees, and waiting for a cow to back up and be milked." In his widely circulated *Farmer's Almanac*, of February he wrote: "This month is looked upon as unpleasant, and it is unpleasant for digging out woodchucks, but for setting in front of the fire, and skinning apples, and snapping the seeds at the gals, it can't be beat."

Wherever his travels took him, he always delighted in revisiting the boyhood hills. "The first thing I do in the morning, when I get up, is to go out and look at the mountain, and see if it is there. Yesterday I picked one quart of field strawberries, caught 27 trout, and gathered a whole parcel of wintergreen leaves—a big day's work. When I got home last night tired, no man could have bought them of me for $700, but I suppose, after all, that it was the *tired* that was worth the money. There is a great deal of raw bliss in getting tired."

His last trip home in 1885 was all the way from Monterey, California, to the little churchyard in Lanesboro. It was a big circle, and Josh had filled it with laughter.

Two Paths

Picture an Indian boy a hundred years ago crouched in a thicket beside the sky-blue waters of a Minnesota lake. What seemed like the root of a great tree floated in toward him, but he knew it for the head of a huge moose.

Thirty-five years after the incident, in his book *Indian Boyhood*, first published in 1902 and now reissued in a fine Dover paperback, Dr. Charles A. Eastman, a full-blooded Sioux Indian, goes on: "I was not more than 8 years old, yet I tested the strength of my bowstring and adjusted my sharpest and best arrow for immediate service. My heart leaped violently as the homely but imposing animal neared the shore. I gathered myself into a bunch, all ready to spring. The long-legged beast pulled himself out of the water and shook. I felt some of the water in my face and gave him my arrow with all the force I could muster, right among the floating ribs. Then I uttered my war whoop. The moose did not seem to mind the arrow, but he was much frightened by the yell and in a minute was gone."

This youth, Hakadah ("the pitiful last"), until he earned the better name of Ohiyesa, had been left five years in his grandmother's care after his mother died and his father was captured and presumed killed by white men at "the terrible Minnesota massacre." Then, for ten years, his uncle "Mysterious Medicine" schooled him in the ways of the nomadic Santee Sioux.

"What boy would not be an Indian for a while when he thinks of the freest life in the world? Every day there was a real hunt."

So began his account of his boyhood. The tale is an American classic of the Midwest in transition, of a last free-born Indian in complete harmony with nature while buffalo still roamed between the Assiniboine and Upper Missouri rivers.

Picture a little white girl about the same time on her father's remote potato farm in the Berkshire hill-town of Mount Washington, where "the child world was bounded by mountains and sky." Already, at age eight, Elaine Goodale was writing little verses for the "Sky Farm Daily," a family compilation that for many years was read aloud at suppertime.

Elaine was only twelve in 1875 when she and sister Dore published their first book, *Apple Blossoms*, which made the child poetesses household names in the land. With the naiveté of youth and Indian-like observation, they plucked verses like nosegays of wildflowers from field and wood.

In wildest fancy, who would ever guess that the Indian boy Ohiyesa would marry the farm girl Elaine? In fiction it could not have happened; in life it did!

President Lincoln unknowingly made this unlikely and incongruous match possible. After the Minnesota Massacre, among those under sentence of death he had pardoned Many Lightnings, the boy's father, because no direct evidence was found against him. Unbeknown to the tribe, when released from prison, the father became convinced that his new reservation life could lead only to physical and moral degradation, so he renounced all government assistance, adopted the white man's ways, and took land under the Homestead Act.

Ohiyesa, meanwhile, reached fifteen years of age and was considered ready for the warpath. With his first gun he had vowed to avenge his father's presumed death.

In his own account: "One day as I approached camp with game on my shoulder, my face burned with the unusual excitement caused by the sight of a man wearing the Big Knives' clothing coming toward me with my uncle. "'My boy, this is your father, my brother, whom we mourned as dead. He has come for you.' In a few days we started for the States. At first, I disliked very much to wear garments made by the people I had hated so bitterly. I felt as if I were dead and traveling to the Spirit Land."

The journey was from the Stone Age to civilization, from war to peace, from veneration of the Great Mystery to Christian worship, from earth love to love of mankind.

The path led to a little schoolhouse in Flandreau, South Dakota, to Dartmouth College (1887), to the Boston University School of Medicine (1890). The next year the paths of those so-different eight-year-olds, each a poet in his own way, became one.

Dr. Eastman was made Indian secretary of the YMCA and served as government physician at the Pine Ridge Agency, then as attorney for the Santee Sioux in Washington, D.C. Finally he came full circle back to some of his own people as physician at Crow Creek, South Dakota.

October Mountain

Men cannot move mountains, but mountains have often been known to move men. Mountains figure repeatedly in song and story, poem and novel, legend and journal. The names of men have frequently and easily become attached to mountains; there is an upright affinity between the two.

Even when mountains have not assumed the names of men, they have adopted certain sons in their lineage, so to speak, as Emerson, Thoreau, and Melville will forever be associated with Greylock; Bryant, Hawthorne, and Melville with Monument Mountain.

October Mountain has two favorite sons: Herman Melville, who never ceased admiring in all seasons from his Arrowhead farm, and William C. Whitney, who actually bought the mountain and lived there.

Melville may have given the mountain its name, for the earliest printed reference seems to be in his 1853 essay, "Cock-A-Doodle-Doo!" in which he mentions "a densely-wooded mountain, which I call October Mountain, on account of its bannered aspect in that month."

J. E. A. Smith in his *History of Pittsfield* (1876) attributed an essay to his friend Melville which remains dubious because no one has ever found it in print or in manuscript. He stated that among tales written on the piazza was "October Mountain," a sketch of mingled philosophy and word-painted landscape, which found its inspiration in the massy and brilliant autumnal tints presented by a prominent and thickly-wooded spur of the Hoosac mountains, as seen from the southeastern windows, at Arrowhead, on a fine day after the early frosts. But whether Melville named it or specifically wrote about it is relatively unimportant when we know from constant allusions that this tartan-clad highland was for years in his view, in his mind's eye, or in his "mad poet's afternoons."

William C. Whitney, secretary of the Navy under Grover Cleveland, was the other with wide-ranging sea interests who fell under the magic spell of October Mountain, which he came to know when summering in Lenox. In 1896 he began acquiring old hill farms and parcels of woodland on the mountain for $5 an acre. His estate soon aggregated 14,000 acres, twenty-four houses and thirty barns, primeval forest, immense boulders, steep precipices, beaver swamps, tangled underbrush, and wilderness into which few had ever penetrated. It spread to include one-third the township of Washington and remote sections of Lenox, Lee, and Becket. Elevation, never less than 1,200 feet, reached 2,290 feet on one rocky top.

On this sequestered highland, Whitney built a honeymoon cottage, a rustic home, and a stone sentinel tower. A thousand acres were enclosed by a wire fence nine-feet high to confine his assorted menagerie of 180 elk, thirteen buffalo from Wyoming, ten rare black-tailed deer, several moose, and some other deer species. At one time he employed fifty-five men, including a corps of mounted game wardens. He maintained twenty miles of bridle paths and practiced his hobby of road-building extensively.

His wife's death in 1907 brought an end to his happy days and eccentric experiments on October Mountain. Now a forlorn road sign reading "Whitney Place Road" is all that attaches his name to the mountain. Gaping stone entrances may be found, leading into the brush and toward tumbled, overgrown foundations. Tall spruces, planted as seedlings by CCC boys in the 1930s, hold sway over all.

Take advice from one who has at heart your getting lost in the natural world. Go up October Mountain in October. The roads are not marked except by asters. They will let your heavenly lostness overwhelm you. Steer simply by the sun or by south-drifting hawks. Go where you will how you will: by car, on horseback, with bicycle, or by shank's mare.

Excellent and endless dirt roads invite and wander through falling red and yellow leaves. Here everyone is equal in copper and gold. Grassy roads marked by lost apple trees beckon with gentians. Wood roads are luminous with the sun trapped in sugar maples. In steep places, logging and charcoaling ways are indelibly pressed into the forest floor. Swamp roads with corduroy long since swallowed in sedge may be traced by parallel lines of red maples. Deer runs make natural paths; wandering stone walls offer a direction, if not a passage.

Threading this October maze, one may, in the midst of nowhere, come upon fifteen rusted remnants of fence wire embedded in and distorting some woodland tree that once marked the perimeter of the Whitney compound. Or glancing off through October branches, one may see, like Melville, "a golden mountain-window, dazzling like a deep-sea dolphin."

A Lenox Luminary

When Ethan Frome pushed through the snow onto Berkshire television screens recently, he was coming home, even into the parlors of unpainted old farmhouses where he had arisen fifty years before. His creator, Edith Wharton, in search of a more genuine life, had built a home in Lenox at the turn of the century. At the Mount, as she called it, she and her husband spent ten summers, some extended to six or seven months.

She had wished to escape the elaborate social life of her New York City upbringing, the frivolous emptiness of summers at New-port, and the footless insecurity of European travels. At this, her "first real home," overlooking Laurel Lake, she wrote and gardened contentedly, feeling "the deep joy of communion with the earth." She said she would doubtless have ended her days there but for the grave neurasthenia that crept upon her husband.

She arrived in Lenox along with the first "motors" of the day and has pictured the duster and claxon excitement of these first flights over the hills which were so carefully charted as to heights. The Whartons delighted in showing off the Berkshire countryside to vis-iting friends from New York or Boston, England or France. Some days they motored as much as eighty miles.

The American expatriate author Henry James was a frequent house guest, and could be seen in the noisy, showy Wharton car chugging over the hills, exploring remote villages with his hostess, whom he called "the pendulum woman" because she crossed the Atlantic every year. The cars, for all their brassy brilliance, often broke down on the hills and horse-drawn travelers would pass, laughing unmercifully. Once James and his devoted disciple sat by the road until four in the morning while the chauffeur tinkered with the car.

Fortunately for American literature, Edith Wharton had a photographic mind and memory. While at Lenox, she wrote chiefly of Italian architecture, villas, and gardens, and of travels in France and England. It was from this expatriate life that her first short stories and novels grew. Her first long novel, *The Valley of Decision*, though set in Italy at the time of the French Revolution, was partly written in Lenox.

But to get back to *Ethan Frome*, the first part of this New England book was written in Paris and in French as exercises to satisfy a French tutor. These early chapters were thrown away, but a few years later "at the Mount, a distant glimpse of Bear Mountain brought Ethan back to my memory, and the following winter in Paris I wrote the tale as it now stands."

Similarly her second New England novel, *Summer*, was written in Paris during the war turmoil in 1917, six years after she had reluctantly sold the Mount. Her memory of the Berkshires was still fresh and green. In her autobiography, *A Backward Glance*, she tells how the rector of the Lenox church had once told her of the colony of drunken outlaws on Bear Mountain twelve miles from her home; and these she wove into her story.

These two novels are close to her best, although her two Pulitzer prizes came from *The Age of Innocence*, concerned with "old New York" society, and a drama entitled *The Old Maid*, drawn from her New York childhood era.

One wonders what might have resulted if her husband's infirmities and social bent had not forced them to leave the Berkshires. Or what might have happened if she had been raised in a New England farmhouse (or at least Boston) instead of seeing the villagers from an Italian villa of her own design and decoration intruded on the scene. What if she had not spread her great talents so widely over the world, but had grown them deeper? What if she had square danced and run the town library, like her heroine, Charity, instead of driving through in a showy car?

Perhaps a deeper participation along with her exceptional perception might have placed her among those of first rank in American Literature, might have produced other *Scarlet Letters*. Her two spare, stark New England novels, each whittled to a bare three characters, good as they are, fall just short in power and revelation. Understanding and compassion seem too much replaced by observation.

Yet as Ethan Frome faded from the television screen, we rose to put out the dog and put out the light. A blinding, swirling storm was sweeping the mountain. The dog barked out into it as though he sensed some scarred, limping man leaning into the storm. Ethan Frome was still alive.

Joseph Choate's Briefcase I

In colonial beginnings every American was perforce a Jack and master of all trades; but also from the beginning, specialization set in, gradually sapping self-sufficiency, until we find ourselves in a time when each man is a small cog instead of a big wheel. For example, doctors specialize in a left nostril instead of in the whole patient; even thieves have narrowed down to car radios or some other specialty item.

Now that we are reducing ourselves by looking through the wrong end of the telescope, it may be broadening to glance back 100 years upon the career of some general practitioner, such as Joseph H. Choate of Salem, New York, and Stockbridge, who knew his subject in its entirety.

Soon after graduating from Harvard Law School in 1854, the young barrister became an apprentice at $500 a year in the New York law firm of Butler, Evarts, and Southmayd. Thus, began his forty-year association with the brilliant, philosophical William M. Evarts, whose lack of specialization later elevated him to senator, attorney general, and secretary of state.

With Evarts mapping out case strategy and waging the battles, the young Choate found himself assigned details of such diverse cases as the impeachment of President Johnson and the defense of Henry Ward Beecher's morality. Within four years, the firm name read "Evarts, Southmayd, and Choate."

One of the first cases the senior partners assigned their junior was a life-insurance suit that both agreed could not possibly be won. The policy was void if the insured died by his own hand, and he had been found dead, pistol in hand, with a bullet hole through the roof of the mouth. Making himself the thirteenth man in the jury box, as became his habit, the young lawyer convinced the others that the insured was blowing down the barrel when the weapon discharged by no act of his. Choate won the case. Joseph Choate's law cases read like the history of the times. They were tried in local, state, and federal courts, and many times in the Supreme Court (before Justices Field, Brewer, and Brown of Stockbridge) or before international tribunals. Often they commanded national attention. It was said that Choate could make even a mechanic's lien interesting. He was equal to any occasion.

Once, before the Supreme Court his opponent charged: "Mr. Choate, you are arguing directly contrary to what is stated in your brief." "Oh, well," he replied nonchalantly, "I have learned a great deal about this case since the brief was prepared."

Somehow he always succeeded in commanding respect, although not infrequently he demolished an adversary with a quip or convulsed the courtroom with laughter. He seemed to regard every case as a huge joke. Once a judge admonished him: "You are late, Mr. Choate, and this court sits to do business." Instantly he replied: "I thought, your Honor, that it sat to do justice, and I should like to be heard;" and heard he was.

A briefcase of some of his important litigations hints at the versatility and competence that place him among the great American advocates.

Early in his career, Choate defended the interests of the Metropolitan and the Natural History museums, being an incorporator of both. At the same time, he was prosecutor for the Committee of Seventy that ended the Tammany scandals and the Boss Tweed Ring that had appropriated $45 million in direct spoils and caused a tax loss of $200 million. Meanwhile, he handled railroad suits all over the country. Once he conducted a defense of milk farmers' freight rights against all the railroads centering in New York, and the very next week represented the same railroads, defending them against government regulation before the same commission.

Major cases running concurrently in various tribunals did not ruffle him at all; between courts he prepared in many a sleeping car. In the public interest and for no fee, at martial law he overturned the court martial of Gen. Fitz-John Porter of sixteen years' standing, while at the same time in probate court he was contesting the Vanderbilt will case. Some of his other will cases of fabulous amount and legal complexity were the Cruger, A.T. Stewart, Samuel J. Tilden, Hoyt, Drake, Vassar, and Vanderpoel legacies.

One of his will cases that stirred considerable Berkshire interest was that of Mrs. Hopkins-Searles, whose fortune approached $40 million. It was she who built the French chateau in Great Barrington, then married the boss-carpenter thirty years her junior. Soon after, when she died in her seventies, the entire fortune was left to this new husband. Choate wrote his wife: "Certainly a good investment in matrimony for only three years." To which we can only add: "Why specialize?"

Joseph Choate's Briefcase II

It may be *reductio ad absurdum* to try to contain Joseph Choate's sixty-year law career in two briefcases, but to an age of overspecialization his example speaks volumes for the virtues of diversity.

While advising the Turkish government on replevin action to recover rifles, and with an election-fraud case pending, he was preparing for the trial of the greatest action of deceit ever brought in New York: the controversy between the Banque-Franco-Egyptienne of Paris and leading New York bankers over an international bond sale. He represented Canada in the Bering Sea seal-fishery disputes and the New York Indians in land claims, both against his own government.

The New York Aqueduct case coincided with the Tilden will and the Vanderbilt divorce cases, preventing Choate from joining his family in Stockbridge, as so often happened. Then came the extraordinary trial of Laidlaw vs. Russell Sage, involving dynamiting, assault, and trespass. He handled interminable suits for the New York Elevated Railway embodying completely new light, air, and access rights, yet reverting to titles as old as the Dutch streets.

In all parts of the country, he dealt with the quite novel questions of the anti-trust law for the Standard Oil Co. and other large corporations, with attendant congressional investigations.

Landlord and tenant cases for the Astor estates were followed by Canadian Railway and Brooklyn Bridge cases tested in the Supreme Court. In the same court, he recovered $15 million for the Stanford endowment fund, thus guaranteeing the future of a great university. It was he who preserved entire the Bell Telephone patent.

In his briefcase also were the Pullman Car leases, Southern Pacific land grants comprising vast areas of western territory, the Chinese Exclusion Acts, the alcohol-in-the-arts case involving rebates in the millions under tariff law, the Massachusetts fisheries case, the controversial cup race between *Defender* and *Valkyrie* III, and an admiralty law collision suit hinging on abstruse problems of hydraulics and suction.

In swift order there were cases of insurance-company taxation, the Kansas Prohibition Law cases, and California irrigation settlements. A knotty legal problem was the law itself in the Smythe *vs.* Goff case, where Choate triumphantly vindicated the rights of the bar against aggressions of the bench; and in the murder attempt by Judge Terry in California upon Mr. Justice Field, which raised the astonishing question of the Supreme Court's ability to protect itself within a state.

Many of his cases, such as Hutchinson *vs.* the New York Stock Exchange, were legal pioneering; or precedent-making, such as the great building contract case initiating the law of arbitration. Many cases such as the Berdan arms case, the Alabama Awards, the Spanish treaty case, and certain revenue cases, dragged on for years. After an intricate partnership-accounting matter, Choate undertook a long jury case in which he represented the Western Union Telegraph Co. and Jay Gould; in one particularly hot June session, his voice became husky for the only time recorded in his long career.

Choate's greatest feat of jurisprudence was the 1894 income-tax case involving every American and his way of life. Like the boy with his thumb in the dike, he held back for nearly two decades the inevitable, graduated taxation introduced by the 16th Amendment. With Southmayd's brief in his pocket, he accomplished this almost impossible task by overthrowing on constitutional grounds the entire scheme of the income tax enacted by Congress, and by persuading that august court to reverse a previous decision that allowed "the biggest fish to get out through the rent that your Honors have made in the meshes of the tax."

In this case involving billions of dollars, Choate's fee was $34,000; when he secured $6 million for the Interboro Street Railway, the client had paid him $150,000.

On ability like his rested the brief age when men still controlled events. His versatility at law impelled him into ambassadorship to England, where his diverse talents effected the Open Door Policy toward China, solved the Alaskan boundary dispute with Canada, and secured broader U.S. jurisdiction over the Panama Canal. From this national service, he stepped on to world service as head of the American delegation to the Peace Conference at The Hague, where it was said: "Mr. Choate holds the whole conference under his hat."

Less and less do we find his kind as men are trained to specialize. When all men are specialists, who will the leaders be?

The Naumkeag Gardens

Ten years ago, shortly before her eighty-ninth birthday, Miss Mabel Choate, the younger of Ambassador Joseph Choate's two daughters, died in New York City. But these hills where she reposes are the lovelier for her being.

It was she who moved and transformed the old Stockbridge Casino into the present Berkshire Playhouse and art gallery. She then moved the 1739 John Sergeant Mission House to the Casino site, restored and furnished it in memory of her parents, and endowed it in 1948 to the Trustees of Reservations.

She engaged the distinguished Boston landscape architect Fletcher Steele to extend Nathaniel Barrett's original ground plans at the family summer home, Naumkeag. This Steele accomplished gradually over a period of thirty years, having his own room in residence. The two agreed that, in sharp contrast to the Colonial austerity and ancestral hardships displayed at the Mission House, "the aura of grand times and gracious living" that lingered within Naumkeag just as the family always knew it, must be maintained outside, but with the design clarified and modern ideas of fitness inaugurated. The composition in landscape that resulted gives lift to the human spirit and ranks the garden among the loveliest in America.

To the south the Outdoor Room and Afternoon Garden were established. Oak pilings dredged from a seventy-five-year rest at the bottom of Boston Harbor were carved and colored to resemble Venetian posts, which, with their garlands of woodbine, secure intimacy and at the same time frame vistas of distant Berkshire Hills. The elm canopy dapples marble-chip paths outlined in boxwood where four small fountains flow into a Claude Lorraine, blackmirror pool so shallow that "little dogs can walk upon the water." At the corner a wren uses the MacMonnies' heron-bill to toboggan into its nest in the bronze gullet. Silvery-leaved olives suggest memories of Moorish gardens. Ironwork benches, yellow-tile tables, and pink Roman thrones supplement the colors of lily and lobelia in sunken beds.

Below this garden a gentle slope was graded to the Chinese Pagoda across a carpet lawn limned on the uphill with a double hemlock hedge and overlooking a grassy glade centered by a monarch white oak, the largest tree on the property. A fan of red Japanese maples backs up the red-roofed pagoda which enshrines on a Ming pedestal the sacred fingered rock brought by Mabel Choate from the Summer Palace at Peking, where it had reposed for 300 years. The pagoda was fashioned from a cast-iron veranda support from an old home in Washington, D.C., and its grapevine relief was painted and gilded by Miss Choate herself.

The Linden-walk archway of some sixty trees planted by her mother beckons invitingly into the ferny woods. Back toward the terraces west of the house, through a shimmering grove of snow-white birches, climbs a broad stairway, trickling down the middle with four successive founts. Below the lower terrace are orchard, picking garden, greenhouse, vegetable garden, and the hidden farm buildings with level hayfields basking in the sun. Above are the pebbled steps of tree peonies that cascade showy blossoms in late May, where once laughing children rolled down a grassy steep.

Northward this terrace leads to marble-chip pathways curving among small beds of summer roses. Steps wind upward to a formal topiary promenade between great, dark ovals of arbor vitae. Globe locust trees like glorified lollipops on sticks cast pleasant shade. The walkway suddenly opens on a reflecting pool that in August doubles its siege of Spanish bayonets and their creamy white sprays.

Uphill is the brick-walled Chinese Garden created to unify the stone Buddhas, lions, dogs, figures, and carvings brought back from the Orient in 1935 by Mabel Choate. This mossy cloister shaded by a mystic nine ginkgo trees is entered by a twist designed to thwart the devil. A runnel of cool water trickles through marble channels across the floor. In one corner a marble table circled by marble-cushioned stools suggests a chopstick feast or a game of mahjongg.

Over all presides the tile-roofed temple approached by the Spirit Walk past a tablet carved with the Imperial Dragon over which only the emperor could be carried for purification. From bamboo chairs one gazes past pots of living bamboo 10,000 miles across Berkshire Hills to the inscrutable Orient.

The round Moon Gate through the Chinese Garden wall returns the visitor, perhaps somewhat humbled, to the upper terrace. This west threshold of the house once fell away so steeply from the library door that no chair could rest on four legs. It is now a level mingling of lawn and stone walk, of floribunda rose gardens and ivy-draped or apple-espaliered walls. It looks equally outward to views of the permanent hills, or inward to period rooms where the very walls whisper to those with a sense of history.

This singular heritage bequeathed to the Trustees of Reservations has been open to the public since 1959.

Angling Artist

Berkshire streams and ponds have spun the reels and filled the creels of many an ardent fisherman. Some have been illustrious like Presidents Garfield and Hoover; others have been literary like Matthew Arnold, Henry Van Dyke, and Bliss Perry; still others have been barefoot boys like Josh Billings. But one thing is as certain as high water in the spring: They all looked alike to the trout, that is, all except George M. L. LaBranche. Trout rarely saw him at all, unless it was through the slit in his creel.

He pursued his avocation in the streams of the Eastern states,

in Canada and England and in the Berkshire Hills where he summered at Green River. He was as deft with a thought and a pen as
with a trout and a rod, which happy combination produced the
angler's classic *The Dry Fly and Fast Water*, published in 1914 and
reprinted in 1951 with his subsequent *The Salmon and the Dry Fly*.
The book is a veritable running brook of 252 shimmering pools or
pages of delight. Perusal will lift the fisherman by his waders to
new insights.

Isaak Walton wrote: "As no man is born an artist so no man is
born an angler." George LaBranche, who died at the age of eighty-
six, attained his mastery of angling, as he took his trout, with infinite patience, observation, and perseverance, believing that "the
man who hurries through a trout stream defeats himself." He
learned to see things from the fishes' point of view, often crawling
along the banks making on-the-scene notes in his diary to help
plan future campaigns. In every encounter he considered the fish
an admirable confrere rather than an ignorant adversary. "The
actual taking of trout constitutes but a very small part of the joy of
fly fishing."

His particular innovation in the ancient sport was the use of the
dry fly under all conditions. Previous to 1900 it had been employed
in England and there mainly on quiet waters. American fishing usually consisted of worm dragging or flogging the streams with a wet
fly. George LaBranche brought the new dry-fly technique to such
perfection that he was able to take fine fish at low water in sultry
weather when the local experts agreed that it was impossible. By the
finesse of his casting and his writing he shows how "the fly, shorn of
impulse, remains suspended for an instant above the water and falls
thereon as lightly as the proverbial feather," more often than not in
a natural upright position inviting the most diffident trout.

No dandiprats for him. There were always big fish if one read the
streams right. It was a matter of studying the lurking places besides
boulders, under banks, beneath snaggy tangles, or in the white swifts
or dark eddies. Then, after forethought, came the etiquette of presen-
tation. Often he succeeded in raising surfeited giants from the pebbly

bottom through many feet of clear water to accept his artfully proffered lure. Occasionally this required fifty to a hundred casts, any one of which, if flawed, might have put the fish down for good.

His patience secured for him the big fish that got away from others, but his modesty (strange fisherman's virtue) rarely permitted him to tell of the conquests that illustrated his techniques.

A story or not in his book: One day in 1919 in four hours' fishing of a quarter mile of the Konkapot at Mill River, he took nearly a hundred trout, releasing all but six browns that weighed more than twelve pounds when presented to the Berkshire Inn. If the big trout escaped him, it was usually in this way: "Although he proved to be a fine brown trout, his manner of taking the fly appealed to us more than his quality, and he was returned to the stream."

Expert as he was with reluctant fish, he confessed there were times to try men's souls: "The thermometer recording 94 degrees in the shade, the stream at its lowest point, and the temperature of the water very high —I really believe that the only chance he (the angler) might have would have been with a very 'wet' mint julep. Under the circumstances it would have required considerable self-denial to have offered that."

The virtues of *The Dry Fly and Fast Water* are the inherent virtues of a brook. There is nothing artificial about it, in the sense that good art is never artificial; there is no basic truth in it. The book hints at the fish ladder of the angler's art up which anyone may ascend. The first few pages give a glimpse of the bottom and top rungs when, in 1900, George LaBranche bribed a worm-dredging lad from a coveted pool by means of a chocolate bar; thereupon he cast the first dry fly of his career and within half an hour had four solid fish.

He had gladly hooked himself, for he concludes the book: "Even as a knowledge of the better forms of music leads, eventually, to a distaste for the poorer sorts; and as a familiarity with the work of great painters leads to disgust with the dauber, so, too, does a knowledge of the higher and more refined sorts of angling lead just as surely to the ultimate abandonment of the grosser methods."

The Forest Seer

When fellow columnist Hal Borland wrote about Charley Fuller last week, he sent us to the attic to dig out some journals, a picture and a verse of twenty-five years ago. Charley was no legend to us; we had tramped mountain and slogged bog with him. He was more than an extraordinary fisherman, hunter, and trapper. He belonged somewhere between a non-writing Thoreau and Amos the woodchopper. He had the six senses and the woodlore of an Indian. All outdoors was his province, and even in his late eighties it was difficult to catch him at home in that sidehill house that rises above the Schenob Brook alders as naturally as a muskrat house.

All thirty-two Berkshire towns have had and still have able woodsmen. Some have lived in caves to escape the law; Charley could have lived in a cave simply to escape the house. The first time we met him was on a wood road beneath the ledges of Race Mountain on an April day. His rubber boots were printing the mud where a deer had trod, and he pointed out the fresh heart-shaped tracks with his fishpole. He wore a weather-beaten brown jacket and faded corduroy cap. His face was like well-tanned leather. He had the air and earthy ease of a woodchuck. Long, grizzled hair poked from under his cap. It nettled him to go out of his way for a barber when formerly any neighbor would cut his hair for the visit.

One day we sat on the side hill watching his bees bring in apple nectar and pollen. The day before he had climbed a tamarack to recover a swarm. From a half-bushel basket he had poured them into a homemade hive "like corn out of a pail, but they skedaddled." The range of mountains from Mount Everett to Bear spread panoramic before us. Charley pointed to a promontory or gully as another might to some passage in a book and related past natural history: how he had seen four wildcats chasing a deer below Race Mountain; he found the kill and trapped five cats there. To a skeptic who scoffed at his bear tracks on Mount Everett he brought a positive basket of droppings—all blueberries.

Shortly before World War I, a cougar haunted Schenob Brook Swamp and made several deer kills. Its track was twice the size of the hundred-pound black and tans used unsuccessfully to trail it. Charley with rifle pursued this elusive creature in the snow and sometimes found it had followed him. He prepared a special large trap with spikes in the jaws and caught it momentarily in Sage's Ravine, but it tore the trap all to pieces in escaping. Charley smiled. He liked his freedom, too.

Mr. Birdsong

The redwings gurgle spring along the flooded bottoms, and the song sparrows voice it in the melting hills. More than 150 bird species and millions of individuals will gradually swell the awakening season's chorus.

No one in these hills will be more aware of it than Aretas A. Saunders in Canaan, Connecticut. He, who once traveled the country listening to, noting, and diagramming over 200 different voices, now hears the songs come as they will to the lilac bush at his window.

What more pleasant than to be a collector of birdsong, to make nature's finest utterance the avocation of a lifetime? Mr. Saunders was a pioneer in this field, one of the first ornithologists in the country to bring to book the momentary notes of wood and field in a systematic way useful to bird students for all time. In the Roaring Twenties when ears jangled to the "Black Bottom," this naturalist was attending the more delicate music of the blackpoll warbler and the plaintive whistle of the black-bellied plover. As

Audubon did with pencil and brush, so did Mr. Saunders with pitchpipe and stopwatch garner his material from Maine to Montana, from Florida to Oklahoma.

Recording sound as various and fleeting as birdsong before the tape recorder was invented demanded some wholly new approach. Musical and kilocycle notation were both less than adequate in capturing the five complex components of song: time, pitch, intensity, quality and phonetics.

By 1929, Mr. Saunders, whose bird observations had begun along the Connecticut shore before the turn of the century, had developed a highly original system of diagramming which he called "musical shorthand." In a little book published that year called *Bird Song* he treated the subject more fully than had been attempted in one volume, discussing such little explored subjects as variation in songs, seasonal and daily cycles of song, singing habits, ventriloquism and mimicry, learning and heredity of the young, best singers, purposes and origin of song, and finally presenting his notation system. The book was a synthesis of the study of many other naturalists plus the author's own published articles and his years of field work.

This was predecessor to his major work, *A Guide to Bird Songs*, published in 1935 and now in a new expanded edition. The guide sets forth in unique, easily understandable diagrams the songs and calls of 201 species of birds so that they can be learned and with practice recognized and remembered in the field.

The careful, cumulative field work that went into this guide should stagger an age that prides itself on distinguishing among car models. Mr. Saunders counts in his collection variations in the songs of the common species numbering anywhere from forty to 1,040, the latter being the varied renditions of the Eastern meadowlark. In some birds he has detected regional dialects, as when comparing ruby-crowned kinglets in the east with the same species in the Rocky Mountains. Once, camping on a small island in Long Island Sound, he discovered song sparrows singing a curious ending that seemed as distinct a localism as Yankee twang.

Mr. Saunders moved to the Berkshires in 1950. Promptly he discovered a worm-eating warbler's nest at Point o' Rocks below Canaan for an extreme northern site; later he spotted a rare northern grass on the top of Greylock at an extreme southern site. Once near Canaan, his car struck a butterfly, knocking an underwing askew. As he carefully reset the wing, he realized this was a Western *Chlorippe* species new to the state. Joyfully he watched it flutter off in search of a mate and a hackberry tree.

Of such stuff the naturalist dreams. Waldo Bailey liked to tell how once in New England there was extricated from the clutter of a closet shelf an old shoebox labeled "string too short to save." His naturalist friend Mr. Saunders might chuckle thinking of his own collection of 800 song-sparrow songs.

Washington from Berkshire

The sculptor and his wife stood on the steps of the Red Lion Inn looking up and down Stockbridge's Main Street. The year was 1896. Mrs. Daniel Chester French recorded it this way: "It was a long, flat, restful street—the quiet old houses, the big trees, and such a convenient opening at the far end for the sun to set. ... I said decidedly: "I don't know what you're going to do, but I am going to live here."

A few days later the Frenches owned the Warner Farm three miles toward sunset, "and there we settled down to live for the rest of our lives, at least in the summertime." It was a location remembered by Matthew Arnold in a letter from England: "I wish I could go with you to the Warner place, and stand where we stood with my arms upon the bars, and gaze upon that beautiful and soul-satisfying view."

The sculptor's first need was for a commodious studio, even before the cramped farmhouse could be supplemented by a new residence. He had just been commissioned by the Washington Memorial Association, Women of America, to do an equestrian statue of George Washington to mount in the Place d'Iéna in Paris.

Where the old barn had stood, a splendid studio was designed and erected by Henry Bacon. It was by no means the first collaboration of architect and sculptor, who a quarter-century later were to complete the Lincoln Memorial. The gray stucco building arose as a perfect thirty-foot cube with peaked and skylit ceiling to accommodate tall monuments. Two giant cottonwoods guarded the east, and two thirty-foot doors opened to the west, so that the largest works in progress could be wheeled out on broad-gauge tracks for daylight inspection.

Daniel French, with his flare for landscape gardening, blended the studio into its environs with gardens, walks, trellises, pergolas, columns, benches, and fountain as they are today.

That July, while stucco was still being applied to the exterior, Edward Clark Potter set up his plaster creation of Washington's horse, and Augustus Lukeman and an assistant named Biemer erected upon it the framework for the general's figure, while French was modeling the likeness from the costumed torso of a powerful neighbor farm lad who posed astride a barrel. When the youth had to be about his haying, Anne French, hooted in army style, sat in for Washington's legs.

In the art world, such a motley fusion of hopes had not transpired since Washington raised his sword in supplication to heaven as he took command of the tatterdemalion troops on Cambridge Heights.

On an August day in 1898 the first statue entirely completed at Chesterwood was ready in its plaster form. The entire family and many friends were on hand to see the preview. The great doors swung open. Impelled on the track by Lukeman and Biemer, slowly the Commander in Chief rode forth, sword raised against the back-drop of Monument Mountain.

French went below into the meadow to see the sun upon his work and to visualize the final bronze that would be unveiled two years later in the public square at the Paris Exposition. The sword arm needed some attention, and the coat front a few creases to break up reflection, but on the whole the General passed muster.

The two years flew by with press of other works, developing and farming of Chesterwood, and a first trip to see the marvels of Greece and Rome. At last French and his wife arrived in Paris the very week of the unveiling. The foundation had been sunk thirty feet to the bottom of the Catacombs, and the pedestal was in place —*but there was no statue!* Officials were frantic.

The sculptor finally found it on a Seine riverboat, but customs delays and hoisting of horse and mounting of rider occupied additional hectic days. On the final morning, the sculptor found himself straightening the sword and beating down the base about the horse's forefoot.

In the afternoon, to the tunes of Sousa's band, the flag drapery was dropped. Throngs of Americans and French broke into cheers. French himself learned that he had earned the Medal of Honor.

Lincoln from Berkshire

When Daniel Chester French came to Stockbridge in 1896, he was forty-six years old. His reputation was solid; it had been instantaneous with the unveiling of "The Minute Man" in his hometown Concord in 1875. Of his eventual 200 sculptures, comprising some 400 figures, about sixty were behind him.

Now he was in search of a summer workshop a little nearer to his New York City studio. The Marshall Warner farm in Glendale with its intimate view of Monument Mountain seemed perfect. After all, monuments were his business, though he could hardly know that the greatest were yet to come while this natural, white marble monument peeked in at his studio window.

In 1910 he was commissioned to do a Lincoln statue to be placed before the Statehouse in Lincoln, Nebraska. For that purpose he built a special little studio among the meadow daisies below Chesterwood. After much study of all the pictorial and written material he could collect, he settled on a standing Lincoln, hands clasped, head bowed in thought.

He worked on it for two summers before it was rolled out into the sunshine for approval. His wife wrote: "We gave a tea in its honor, and people came, as they always come to see Lincoln anywhere, from all over the country. I remember how picturesque it was, on a perfectly beautiful afternoon, to see the groups of people, women in bright clothes, wandering down across the field to see 'Lincoln's Shrine,' as they called it."

Today an eight-foot replica of that noble bronze stands, sometimes with snowy cap and mantle, against the dark trees of a Chesterwood that is now and forever a national shrine. Yet this work, for all its Gettysburg greatness, was but preamble. The challenge of a lifetime came a few years later. In 1911 Congress had appropriated nearly $3 million for a site, a building, and a statue for a Lincoln memorial. The experienced Henry Bacon was chosen building architect, and finally, on his recommendation, Daniel French was named sculptor. The two had been friends and collaborators for years.

French renewed his study of Lincoln. He took casts of the hands and life mask at the Smithsonian. He pored over the Brady and Gardner photographs. He devoured Lincolniana. He poured himself into the character until the molder became the mold. Then, about Lincoln's birthday in 1915, with hope and trepidation he put his fingers to the clay seeking the president, the statesman, the preserver of the Union.

It was a long task involving preliminary small sketch models, three-foot models, eight-foot models, and the plaster casting of each, uncounted trips to Washington, trials of giant solar prints *in situ*, and ultimately the realization as the building progressed that the final would be a nineteen-foot statue on an eleven-foot pedestal. So integral was the artist with the creation that he cast his own right hand for the desired grip on the arm of the curule chair. Half the work was done at Chesterwood and half at the New York studio since the precise sculptor had evolved a routine of coming to the Berkshires May 15 and departing November 1.

As the supreme Lincoln arose from the Civil War years, so America's greatest memorial arose from the World War years. It was dedicated on Memorial Day 1922, with 200,000 people present, including some who had known Lincoln. Standing against a column, the sculptor overheard his colleague Henry Bacon explaining to friends that French's work could never be taken for anything but American. His was the vision, and he had realized the dream.

Perhaps the tribute that French liked best came from a five-year-old boy whose mother had taken him into the deserted memorial. Standing in the hallowed light, he pulled at her skirt, saying in a loud whisper: "Mother, shall I take off my hat?" She agreed and turned to admire the frescoes, inscriptions, and columns. Presently she noticed the boy on the pedestal fumbling at the great statue. She lifted him down reprovingly as he explained: "I was only going to climb up in his lap, Mother, he looked so lonely!"

The last time French saw his statue was on a spring night in 1929. Margaret French Cresson tells it this way in her biography, *Journey into Fame*. "They stood, he and Penn and Mary and Margaret at the foot of those great flights of steps that come down like rushing water. They looked up at the huge white temple, all shimmering in the moonlight, with its backdrop of purple sky and, inside, the pearly light falling on the head and shoulders of the great War President. For a long time none of them spoke. Finally Dan turned to his daughter and very softly said: 'I'd like to see what this is going to look like a thousand years from now.'"

Ellery Sedgwick (1872-1960)

When a family procession of Sedgwicks walked down Stockbridge Main Street behind a horse-drawn casket two weeks ago, Ellery Sedgwick was coming home. He had completed a world-wide circle in eighty-eight years back to the scenes of boyhood.

His book, *The Happy Profession*, tells what a circle it had been, encompassing much of the world and many of its persons and personages. It is scarcely an autobiography; rather it tells about others, and in so doing remarkably reveals the author. In his boundless enthusiasm the story runs away with him, delightfully, one anecdote upon another. Any one would have furnished his Great-Aunt Catharine grist for a whole novel, but to him understatement is all. The reader wishes he had expanded into novels, but the role of editor never gave him the time.

As a boy in Stockbridge he fraternized as much with the fishmonger as with Joseph Choate, ambassador to England. This quality of congeniality remained with him always. In one sense he never left the Berkshires; he took them with him. "To this day my yardstick of height is Monument Mountain. Besides, it is convenient to have fixed standards like Stockbridge Bowl or Hatch's Pond when you are called on to appraise the loveliness of Lucerne or Lake Louise!" Armed with the memories of youth, he went forth to become cosmopolitan.

Armed further with a Groton and Harvard education, he was not deterred when his father was swindled at retirement. He took only the price of a railroad ticket when he left Stockbridge for a year's teaching at Groton. From there he began his editorial career by joining *Leslie's Monthly* in New York City. He helped pull this rickety publication from red ink to black, only to see it swindled, and the whole thing to do over. It was his joy to encourage Dorothy

Canfield Fisher and Ellis Parker Butler, whose *Pigs Is Pigs* appeared in his pages. However, these were exceptional writers, and it was from the ordinary that he pried his stories. He even mingled with the big-city underworld in search of fresh material.

After five years he moved on to *McClure's*, in whose stable were Stevenson, Meredith, Kipling, and Conan Doyle. Willa Cather was a fellow office worker. But under the stormy personality of muck-raking McClure, few could stay for long. Sedgwick frankly told him the truth was not in him and left after a year for another year with the book publishing firm of Appleton & Co. Here he dealt with Theodore Dreiser, Robert Chambers, David Philips, and Joseph Lincoln.

All this New York experience was sound preparation for what followed. In Harvard he had told a friend he intended to edit *The Atlantic*.

Fifteen years later the magazine with its fifty years of tradition, its circulation of 15,000 copies, and its annual deficit of $5,000 was his. For $50,000 he bought it from the Houghton Mifflin Co. that had run it respectably as a literary sideline under seven editors from James Russell Lowell to Bliss Perry. But Ellery Sedgwick was the most dedicated. In a year *The Atlantic* had profited $4,000. In his thirty-years' guidance it became a national institution.

The emphasis of the magazine had been literary and its techniques clearness, force, and elegance. It had had the quality of a glorified Harvard house organ. Sedgwick added the ingredient of interest and extended the search for material from Boston to the corners of the earth. "What I wanted was an unpremeditated record of interesting happenings by an interesting person."

Many of the contributions he secured were from the great, such as Woodrow Wilson; many he made great, such as James Hilton, Walter Edmonds, Nordoff and Hall; many were ordinary, but interesting people, such as a Wyoming woman homesteader, a Negro housekeeper, a South African adventurer, a hobo or jailbird, a refugee from the Russian ghetto, or a young girl brought up in nineteen Pacific lumber camps.

It was his belief that every individual had his story. It was his genius to extract it, meanwhile making himself a host of devoted, lifelong friends.

The book is expectedly a story of the editor's successes. It might have achieved a higher level if it had told of failures that must have been. A doctor's mistakes are all in the graveyard, but an editor's often come back to haunt him in his own magazine.

Robert Frost submitted poems annually to *The Atlantic* before his recognition in England, and just as regularly Sedgwick rejected them. In 1915 the two met in a Boston street, and Sedgwick begged for some poems. Frost mischievously gave him "Birches," "The Road Not Taken," and "The Sound of the Trees," which he had previously refused to print.

The Happy Profession is an entertaining, happy book that might equally well be entitled *The Profession of Happiness*. Ellery Sedgwick knew his niche, pointed to it, gained it, and adorned it. Contentedly must he rest in the family ground at Stockbridge, "Sedgwick Pie."

Norman Rockwell, Painter of Presidents

Norman Rockwell modestly calls himself an illustrator; everyone else calls him an artist, and we believe he can be called a painter of Presidents. This title he would disclaim, since his relatively few formal portraits are far outnumbered by the friends and neighbors who have told graphic stories on some 325 *Saturday Evening Post* covers since May 1916—that first was the baseball-minded boy having to push the baby carriage. But the last two covers were Senator Kennedy and Vice-President Nixon, and thereby rests our case.

In 1934 the *Post* arranged a sitting with President Franklin D. Roosevelt, the pictures to illustrate an article called "So You Want to See the President." Mr.Rockwell spent four days sketching White House scenes and had a half hour with the President at his desk. All this work was lost along with much else (including irreplaceable favorite pipes) when his Vermont studio burned.

But two days later he was invited back. The White House staff, secretaries, and Secret Service men welcomed him warmly. After the sketching, the President said: "Will you have lunch with me?" The nonplused artist, knowing there was a war to be run, stammered: "Yes, sir," to the Commander in Chief, and discovered that one of the secrets of political genius lay in forgetting for a moment that there was anything else to be done.

His second presidential portrait was of Harry S. Truman at Independence, Missouri, in full regalia, painted for the Masonic Lodge.

Since the late 1930s Mr. Rockwell has used photography in his work, and still feels some guilt about it. But he uses it creatively, being master over it, not slave to it. He may make use of more than fifty photographs for one painting. This has been an indispensable aid in capturing busy notables who can only spare time for a "color sketch."

He likes his presidents and candidates to pose well, and asks them to think of something they like, such as ice cream or grandchildren, to effect the desired expression. Delegate Henry Cabot Lodge at the U.N. was difficult. When asked to look more pleasant, he snapped: "No, I can't do that. You take it like this." Perhaps a bad day with the Russians.

Cover illustrations must be prepared well in advance, which sometimes means sketching possible candidates even before nomination, such as Dewey, Stevenson, Harriman, and Kefauver. Stevenson was anxious to destroy the egghead label, when Mr. Rockwell met him on his unpretentious New England farm near Chicago. He was posing for *Look* photographers, wearing a big straw hat, under an apple tree, and leaning on a fence with a straw in his mouth. When Mr. Rockwell asked him to think of something pleasant, he chose his grandfather, vice-president under Cleveland, who narrowly missed nomination for the Presidency.

Eisenhower chose his grandchildren, and his face lighted up like a diamond. He said, laughing, "Don't show this gold tooth. Mamie doesn't like it." Mr. Rockwell painted him in 1952 just after his first nomination and again in the White House in 1956. "He has the most expressive face I've ever painted, all the mobility of an actor; when he smiles it is like the sun coming out. He is the most lovable man I ever met."

Two days ago at the polls perhaps no citizen was in more of a dilemma than artist Rockwell. He had been charmed by both candidates. His November 5 cover on Vice-President Nixon was started last February in rooms of the new Senate Office Building. Nixon came in after opening the Senate. He was a good subject. He made Mr. Rockwell feel like the only man that mattered. He had acquired the politician's grace of selling himself all of the time.

Senator Kennedy was sketched in June at his Hyannis Port home a month before nomination. At the time there was much talk of his being too young to run. He told Mr. Rockwell to make him look at least his age. Between sittings the two strolled to the dock to see Kennedy's boat. It was a splendid two hours.

At his Stockbridge studio, Norman Rockwell worked on these two portraits side by side, avoiding all partisanship by carefully making collars, coats, ties, and backgrounds identical. Care was taken that one showed no trace more smile than the other. The artist noted well the wide, determined jaws of both candidates. Meanwhile, through it all, he was making himself absolutely impartial. So much so that a few days before election he still said, "I don't honestly know how I'll vote."

The Cobble Warden Retires

Aſter eleven years as a warden-naturalist for the Trustees of Reservations at Bartholomew's Cobble in Ashley Falls, Howard T. Bain of Mill River, the genial genie of Cobble boulders and cedars, will retire at the close of this October season.

It will be no more than Pan retiring among New England asters, because the many who have come to know him know also that he will never neglect the ferny flowery places, the bird nooks and the arrowhead fields, those outdoor places where a friend invites and a child questions.

Howard is a self-taught naturalist whose twig was bent by a country upbringing in Millerton, New York. The same twig was well leaved out with field observation and reading. Business interests occupied his middle years, but he finally outflanked the establishment by submitting his work from the country.

He formed a close friendship with S. Waldo Bailey, who was Cobble warden from 1946-63, and learned a respect for the Cobble bordering on veneration, perhaps from one incident.

After driving the warden on a very successful all-day arrowhead hunt, Howard parked one wheel slightly on Cobble grass, eliciting from Waldo: "I'll tell you just like anybody else, never to park on the grass; park in the road!"

In the spring of 1963, the warden's staff passed from one to the other. The chickadees knew it and come as readily to Howard's hand for the seed. The only Scott's spleenwort in the county appreciated it as it was nursed through bare or snowy winters, wet or drought summers, past insect chewing or animal scratching, and from disappearance to a fragment back to a lovely four-leaved compass rosette this autumn.

Over the years, Howard's visitors have come from every state in the union and many foreign countries. They have included experienced scientists to whom he has revealed new wonders like the white gentian. At least half the attendance has been children, many awakened by him to lifetime outdoor interests by their fearsome glimpse of an ant lion or the tickle of a wild bird on the hand.

What tickled Howard was the man who brought a pair of boots to be cobbled. What exasperates him most, indeed even more than the occasional purloiner of a nesting box, is the typical worldly visitor who wants to know how long it will take to go around. Howard is well aware that one could spend a lifetime at it, as Thoreau did in Concord. A former director of Harvard's Gray Herbarium spent several summers at the Cobble cataloguing 740 growing plants.

The best tribute to Howard was a remark penned in the register representing the feelings of innumerable visitors to this National Natural Landmark: "Very friendly and knowledgeable ranger."

This personal courteous guidance of the public combined with conscientious management of the property has directly made possible the successful preservation, improvement, and expansion of this sanctuary within Howard's regime.

To be specific, attendance has tripled to 8,000 per year. Acreage has grown nearly six-fold from the original thirty to 168. The memorial Bailey Museum was built, and it displays next to Waldo's forty-one orchids of Massachusetts, a gallery of fifty-two color photographs by Howard of favorite, showy, Cobble wildflowers. His other exhibits range from ancient arrowheads down to a white-faced hornet queen just recently pinned out beside her first-stage, golf-ball-sized nest.

Increasing public support of this reservation is primarily attributable to Howard's constant labors of love around the paths of this unique outdoor natural-history museum. With this rock-solid base, the fund-raising committee has now come within $5,000 of achieving the needed goal of $167,000 to complete and protect the reservation and the newly acquired Col. Ashley House.

Howard has built better than he knew. It has been in a series of small steps culminating in a National Landmark. Each step was probably memorable to someone, whether it was a pteridologist seeing his first adder's-tongue fern hidden in the grass or a small boy discovering the Indian profile on the boulder against the sky. Or, for that matter, Howard finding his first western moonseed vine during his last weeks of tenure. For him, teaching will always be synonymous with learning.

PART 5
Conserving the Berkshires

A New Reservation

Tyringham Cobble is the most recent scenic and historical addition to the thirty-seven properties of the Massachusetts Trustees of Reservations, which in the Berkshires include Monument Mountain (since 1899), Bartholomew's Cobble (1946), Stockbridge Mission House (1948), and Naumkeag (1959).

This cobble or rocky-topped knoll, upthrust like Edinburgh Castle in the middle of the Tyringham Valley, presides over Hop Brook and the town on the east and Fernside on the west. For ages, like a lofty parapet it has caught the first and last rays of the rising and setting sun in this Shangri-la valley. For generations it has been a rampart for the young to explore and a haven where their elders might picnic. Now as a 200-acre reservation, it will remain so.

In 1762 the first white settler in the valley, Deacon Thomas Orton, built his cabin safely high at Fernside, west of the Cobble. The whole valley bottom was an abysmal, swampy tangle of hops, ivy, and hemlock yet to be cleared. Another early pioneer, Solomon Heath, and his father, are said to have built their cabin against the huge boulder high on the south face of the Cobble. They and their descendants cleared and farmed the Cobble, and their stone walls are still there. Tradition has it that Chief Konkapot's son also lived in a cabin on the Cobble. In 1792 the Clark farm embracing the east side became the Shaker Community that grew to over 100 souls and lasted eighty-two years. Where the Cobble sloped to Hop Brook stood their huge garden-seed packaging house, great red kiln, and other buildings. Then the once-forested Cobble became upland pasture as pioneer families slipped from its lap into the drained and domesticated valley.

Through the 1800s the Cobble remained a grassy landmark clipped by sheep and cattle, a great somnolent presence overlooking industrialized Tyringham busy about its rake and paper manufacture.

Each spring the children looking up saw a sizable letter J marked by the last lingering snows of winter. They called it "Job's Folly" after an impatient Yankee who, seeking quick riches, had mined a quartz vein no more productive than the snow, as he sought to outstrip in one strike the slow labor below.

Toward the turn of the century, Richard Watson Gilder, poet, editor of the *Century* magazine, and intimate friend of Grover Cleveland, who visited him there, took up residence at Four Brooks Farm facing the north side of the Cobble. Often he sat in his pastures, the brooks and cowbells tinkling about him as he watched shadows steal up the Cobble to extinguish the last rosy rays of the sun. Little wonder that his farm produced more poems than milk.

In one Gilder poem the Cobble is graced by a fancied visit from John Muir, naturalist, runner of mountaintops and lover of glaciers:

"See his path," said John Muir,
"Here it held
Northwest to southeast;
Slow and sure,
Like a king at a feast
Eating down through the list,
Inch by inch, crunch by crunch;
Yonder hollow his lunch,
Of the valley one gobble,
Then he supped light on Cobble!

Where the quartz glistens white
Smooth as ice
In the clear slanting light
The fine striae show,
Like arrows they go
Northwest to southeast..."

Our first visit to the Tyringham Cobble was in the middle of August. It sprawled and slept in the hot sun like a huge, lazy bear while two of us made our way up the pasture flanks toward the rocky crown. Tyringham fell away below as we passed glacier-strewn boulders, huge wheels of juniper, and tumbled walls fringed with sweet hay-scented fern. Goldfinches undulated overhead, eyeing clumps of magenta thistles knowingly. Underfoot sounded the dreamy saw of the grasshopper and the crickets' chirp on sun-warmed schist or quartz hearthstones.

Lavender blankets of thyme spread everywhere. This low-growing ground cover, which probably escaped from Shaker herb gardens in post-Revolutionary days, filled the air with aromatic pungency. Honeybees worked with a passion in the multiflowered fragrance, raising a buzzy din about our knees. We looked forth out of a heathery sea into the deep field bottoms of the Tyringham Valley like Rob Roy in the Scotch Highlands, surveying Berkshire's latest reservation.

One Mountain to Another

At a time when the country as a whole by the Wilderness Bill shows a desire to preserve valuable wild areas for posterity and when, at the other extreme, a small urban community like Darien, Connecticut, begins to acquire woods and fields in its very midst to preserve its character, we find Berkshire, through commissioners appointed "to care for, protect, and maintain" Greylock for the Commonwealth, about ready to hand over half of their public trust to private commercial interests, and with the approval of the governor. Perhaps Berkshire, so wealthy in woods and hills, can still afford to be profligate. Or perhaps, cut off by these same hills, Berkshire is behind the times in conservation. At any rate, it seems a singularly shortsighted betrayal of the state's loftiest eminence.

Of the several excuses used to cover the blunder, we find the old cliché, "for the greatest good of the greatest number," as quoted by one of the commissioners, to be the most fatuous. If a reservation were for the greatest number, Greylock could be converted into a populous anthill by leveling the top for a heliport and hotels, by ringing the mountain at several levels with racetracks for horses, autos, and motorcycles, and by making a football stadium of the Hopper, a baseball field of Wilbur's Clearing, and a roller coaster of Jones Nose. To be fair with public property, all sorts of commercial interests besides a tramway should be invited. Additional memorials, radio and TV transmitting towers, relay towers, and beacons could top every ridge. If a tramway is to be the salvation of Adams, complete use of the mountain might well support the whole county. The mind boggles.

Meanwhile, Mount Everett, commissioners preserve her, will remain a sanctuary where refugees from Greylock can take a laurel walk to restore their souls. The road there does not scar the summit, where the low, gnarled pitch pines give an unobstructed view northward to Greylock, eastward over the Housatonic valley to Talcott Mountain and Mount Tom, southward over Twin Lakes to Canaan Mountain and the Litchfield Hills and westward over the Hudson valley to blue lines of Catskills.

Too bad the battle to hold pristine pinnacles must always be a defensive one. The Mount Everett commissioners, as they look northward at the siege of big sister, would do well to contemplate some preventive and protective legislation. At a time when the nation and many of its communities are more conservation-conscious than they have been since the two Roosevelts, it should be possible to pass legislation banning from Mount Everett all commercial interests, operations, and installations, public and private, at least until the time when Berkshire schist shall become precious. Furthermore, there should be required a public hearing period before any intrusions such as memorials or additional roads were constructed. One former commissioner, Walter Prichard Eaton, did not favor replacing the present road when it washed out. To get more commissioners like that, it should be stipulated that they be residents of Berkshire County, which they have not always been.

The paradox about reservations is that they are good for the greatest number by being the refuge for the few. Like churches, they are there for those who want them. They need no billboards or fireworks; they already have their trillium trinities and thrush choirs.

And lest anyone think that so much acreage is wasted in per capita terms, we would balance a John Muir on a Sierra Nevada peak against the whole Los Angeles sprawl, or a solitary Thoreau on Greylock against the whole host who would play pinball or politics with the mountain. Theirs was a loftier perspective.

A hundred years ago, before the need was obvious, Thoreau wrote: "As in many countries precious metals belong to the crown, so here more precious natural objects of rare beauty should belong to the public. ... Think of a mountaintop in the township, even to the minds of the Indians a sacred place—I think that the top of a mountain should not be private property; it should be left unappropriated for modesty and reverence's sake, or if only to suggest that earth has higher uses than we put her to."

Holding the Status Quo

Holding a wild piece of land in trust for the public entails a never-ending fight. Commercial interests and population expansion everywhere increasingly press in upon places long deemed inviolate. At the north of the county we see the battle joined over Greylock in court and legislature because close to 1,000 far-sighted citizens have chosen to stand up against the immediate self-interest of a few small pressure groups.

In contrast, at the south of the county in the much smaller reservation at Bartholomew's Cobble, the battle is of a more pleasant nature. Rather than threatened encroachment of a tramway and attendant impertinences, there is the threat of the expanding woods and the trampling of an occasional escaped cow.

The problem then becomes a struggle to hold things as they are, to keep some climax forest, some transition woods, some sproutland, some scrubby pasture, some goldenrod, and some mowed fields in order to insure the maximum variety of flora and fauna in the forty-four acres.

Voltaire once said that nothing is so permanent as change. One who attempts to hold back forest progression can fully savor that saying. The march of any forest is like Birnam Wood overrunning Dunsinane. From raised arms the woodland army fires explosive bullets of seeds, nuts, berries, samaras, and catkins in all directions as it advances.

When some visitor, recalling a youthful picnic, asks: "Why don't you keep the Cobble as it always was?" we are tempted to counterquery: "When do you mean? Back in the Cambrian when it lay for eons deep beneath the ocean? Or in the Taconic or the Appalachian Revolutions when it was heaved among the world's loftiest peaks? Or in the Pleistocene when it was repeatedly overridden by thousands of feet of ice? Or in pre-Colonial times when it was needle-carpeted and shaded by a climax forest of towering hemlocks?"

Since it is impossible in any lifetime to resist such slow forces or to duplicate them, the problem then becomes one of preserving things as they are, not as they were or will be.

Accordingly, our little group of four, including two nationally known naturalist ecologists, patrolled the Cobble paths with the purpose of maintaining the status quo. It was like Canute attempting to hold back the sea. We could mark some trees to be cut, some lusty, wild grape vines to be removed, and some sproutlings that threatened to undo the work of other years; but we could not stop growth or decay. Here it was a problem of keeping a vista of Bear Mountain, Race, or the Dome, blue in the west; there it was holding a view of burnished Housatonic oxbows reflecting wine-glass elms on the east.

Everywhere it meant making compromises between a wild jungle tangle and a park-like overneatness. Windfalls would be removed only where they interfered with trails. Dead trees would be left standing for fungus, beetle, and woodpecker to demolish. Rampant grapevines furnishing plentiful bird food, but strangling desirable old, red cedars, would be cut back like vineyard grapes to a single stem. Many of the ancient cedars were themselves loaded with bird food, a crop of blue-gray berries, the heaviest we had ever seen, that whitened the dark forms like hoar frost. This plethora of seed on the shallow soil of the north cobble probably resulted from four drought years. Distressed plants often bear seed in a frenzy.

The hardest line we had to hold was the transition woods circling Craggy Knoll. The heavy forest of hemlock, pine, oak, and other trees were prisoned by the moat of the Housatonic on the east and by cliffs and ledges on the south. Consequently it seemed to double efforts to expand north and west. Young seedling trees of many sizes and kinds vied for sunshine against an imaginary lean-to roof that sloped from the mother forest down to the meadow grasses.

One example of the carnage and mayhem taking place among the graduated offspring in this no-man's land was the contest between a Goliath of a pine six inches through and a slim David of a hemlock half that in diameter. In its effort to escape the shade of the slower-growing hemlock, the pine had twice sacrificed its central, terminal shoot, and each time a lateral branch, away from the hemlock, had taken over growth. The trunk, as long as it survived, would always bear those two staggered steps toward sunshine. Nevertheless, the patient hemlock had already killed five tiers of pine branches with shade and someday would surmount the whole tree.

Here and there we marked a tree for cutting, in our man-sized attempt to hold and slow that transition forest, but plainly we were dealing with a timeless force as irresistible as oceans, upheavals, and glaciers.

Cougar Again

Cougars and rumors of cougars—may they always be with us! We need some wilderness in our lives to keep us from becoming synthetic.

Lately we received a letter from a representative writing from the Vermont Statehouse. He was watching a doe in the woods while he wrote. It was a refreshing letter, and included clippings about the latest cougar.

The large animal, yellowish brown in color and with a long body, round head, and long tail, was seen three separate times within the first ten days of January by three different sets of people, each time at night by car headlights, near Chittenden, Sherburne, and Pittsfield, Vermont. This was no apparition, for every time large, round tracks bore witness in the snow.

The once-common cougar began disappearing from the northeast about 1860, along with its natural prey, the deer. By 1900 unlimited shooting had virtually exterminated both animals.

With present deer repopulation, it is actually beneficial to the fitness of the deer herd to encourage natural predators that keep numbers to what the range can support. In most states the gun fails by a wide margin to control the annual 35 to 40 percent increase of deer, which then becomes surplus subject to malnutrition and disease. Western states, heeding biologists, have removed bounties, and many have no predator controls at all. New England should have no bounties on wildcats, and paradoxically we would have better rabbit hunting. Cougars should be protected everywhere except in the occasional rare act of killing livestock. When they were common from southern Canada to Florida and British Columbia to Mexico, the hunting was far better. But hunting by the bye, the real importance of cougars is wildness. What need do we have for African safaris or trips to India when we have mountain lions in our own woods? Early settlers wrote of killing lions near Boston. That probably reminded them that they had left complacency behind.

The journals and lore of America treat this fierce, shy animal with great respect, calling it cougar, mountain lion, panther, painter, puma, catamount, brown tiger, red tiger, purple panther, silver lion, American lion, deer killer, Indian devil, sneak cat, king cat, and just plain varmint. This was the common people paying respect to royalty. Think of deserving all those names.

In his travels Audubon once stayed in the hut of a swamp pioneer on the Yazoo River in Mississippi. He went on a cougar hunt with his humble host who had left Connecticut because, "The people are grow-ing too numerous now to thrive in New England." That was in 1820. Conversely now, cougars are too few for people to thrive in New England.

One writer saw a fine specimen of a cougar killed in northwestern Connecticut about 1840. The last kill in Rhode Island seems to have been in 1856 and New Hampshire's in 1860. In 1856 Thoreau saw the skin and skull of one killed in Brattleboro measuring eight feet in extreme length: "I was surprised at its great size and apparent strength. It gave one a new idea of our American forests and the vigor of nature here. It was evident that it could level a platoon of men with a stroke of its paw ... the inhabitants regarded it as common; they only kicked it aside in the road, remarking that was a large one."

The last Vermont kill in 1881 may be seen in the Historical Society Museum at Montpelier. It measured seven feet six inches from nose to tip of tail and weighed 182 pounds. After that record came a gap of nearly 40 years in the Northeast with few sightings before the winter day in 1929 when Waldo Bailey and a comrade saw one on Greylock and were too incredulous to tell about it. From that time on, sight records have occurred increasingly all the way from Quebec to Washington, D.C.

In 1938, Bruce Wright, director of the Northeastern Wildlife Sta-tion at Fredericton, New Brunswick, secured a specimen trapped on the Maine side of Little St. John Lake. He has since been compiling valid sight records on the eastern panther and believes there may be as many as 100 roaming the forests of the Northeast. The noble creatures have been seen on Cape Breton Island, in Quebec, Ontario, Maine, Massachusetts, and within thirty-two miles of New York City and in New Jersey. Two years ago a friend of ours made casts of the footprints of one lurking in the Waterbury area of Connecticut.

The tracks of this "big, slinking, unicolored cat" so admired by Teddy Roosevelt measure a full four inches across. Unfortunately, they are enough to lure forth hoards of hunters armed with rifles and shot-guns and accompanied by dogs, traps, and poison. In the West, when they can be had, the spotted kits sell for pets at $150 apiece.

We intend to get two and put them on Greylock. For the future, that would be a better investment than a tramway.

A Garland for Greylock

Mayor Del Gallo's suggestion to the Department of Natural Resources for placing a natural history museum atop Greylock deserves the strong support of all Massachusetts citizens. Already a unique outdoor museum, Greylock, the ancient cornerstone of the Commonwealth, merits something better than to be crowned by a tombstone for war dead. It should be graced by a living memorial—serviceable, educational, and beautiful for the living.

Veterans' organizations with their stake in the present, decrepit, medieval cenotaph, which has proven to be a waste of money and a break in faith with those who died, should realize this most of all. Now they have the opportunity to pass the torch to the living by moving their plaque and supporting a meaningful museum.

DNR sponsorship of a summit museum would be a welcome and natural extension of its services to the public. By lively collections, charts, and exhibits, it could present forestry practices, wildlife management, state rock and mineral resources, land and water uses, and the newest conservation ideas, as well as the story of the mountain itself.

Over a year ago, in its March leaflet on development of the reservation, the Mount Greylock Protective Association put forth the original of this idea, proposing, among other good ideas: "the building of a Greylock nature museum to contain exhibits, illustrations, and reference materials dealing with the plant, animal, and bird life and geology of Greylock, with special emphasis on specimens that are rare or unique in Massachusetts. It might also serve as general headquarters for the reservation, with administrative offices and a center for information."

The Massachusetts Audubon society has long realized the outdoor-museum values of Greylock, as evidenced by annual campouts to observe such rarities as breeding Bicknell's thrush, olive-sided fly-catcher, mourning warbler, and saw-whet owl. A supplementary indoor museum might engage its active participation.

The Appalachian Trail Conference, whose 2,000-mile footpath from Maine to Georgia might pass through one museum door and out the other, would certainly endorse the idea and could display its own interesting story. The Massachusetts Forest and Park Association and other outdoor-oriented groups should approve of such a facility designed to harmonize with the mountaintop.

Neighboring schools and colleges would appreciate and use the educational features that would inevitably spring from such a museum. Indeed, more than 125 years ago Williams College had its own observatory on the mountaintop, an offshoot of its 1836 astronomy laboratory, the oldest in the country and a worthy precedent that could be carried on by telescope for the public and rooftop promenade.

A natural history museum on Greylock would be no duplication of those already existing in Berkshire County; it would balance and supplement them. Now the Bailey Museum at Bartholomew's Cobble serves south county; the Pleasant Valley and Berkshire Museums serve the central section; but north Berkshire remains in need of one, the uneven Williams College collections being generally unavailable to the public.

A good part of the DNR million-dollar appropriation for reservation development, perhaps augmented by war veterans' memorial funds, could create a high-quality museum worthy of the state's loftiest eminence. Taxpayers, veterans and the 140,000 visitors per year to the summit would benefit in perpetuity.

Besides presenting the natural history and geology of the region, such a museum could tell the illustrious story of men and the mountain, using pictures and quotes. A few hints:

Early settler Jeremiah Wilbur cleared and farmed a large part of Greylock and sowed foxtail grass to the very top for his grazing cattle.

1799—Rev. Ebenezer Fitch, president of Williams College, and Rev. Timothy Dwight, president of Yale, in the second party ever to ascend Greylock, climbed wind-twisted trees to view "Williamstown shrunk to the size of a farm, its houses, churches, and colleges like the habitations of martins and wrens."

1820—Susan B. Anthony, born at Bowen's Corners, South Adams, looked to the mountain or helped her mother in its shadow, as she later helped all women achieve the right to vote.

Born on the sunny side, Josh Billings said: "The first thing I do in the morning, when I get up, is to go out and look at the mountain and see if it is there."

1830—Dr. Edward Hitchcock, first state geologist and later president of Amherst, was first to measure Greylock, first to suggest and carry out a geological and natural history survey to catalog the state's resources— the first such government-sponsored project of its kind in the world.

1838—On a six-week stay in North Adams, Nathaniel Hawthorne penetrated a cloud in ascending to the Notch on Greylock and wrote in his notebook: "The students ought to be day-dreamers, all of them when cloudland is one and the same thing with substantial earth."

1844—In his first book Thoreau devoted eleven pages to his Greylock visit. He reached the top at sunset, dug a two-foot well for water, cooked his rice, having already whittled a wooden spoon to eat it with, and read by firelight newspaper scrap from sandwich wrappings. After sleeping the night encased in some boards, he awoke to find himself "a dweller in the dazzling halls of Aurora."

1849—For "seven blessed summers" Oliver Wendell Holmes wrote with Greylock "peeping in" at his study window.

1850 —Melville built a north piazza on his farmhouse, the better to view "Greylock's Most Excellent Majesty," to which, with three impassioned paragraphs, he dedicated his spiritual autobiography, *Pierre*.

The dramatic Fanny Kemble declaimed *Romeo and Juliet* for a picnic audience on the summit.

1865—Sixty-two-year-old Emerson, staying a week with Williams College students, climbed Greylock with them and mused that many would remember the mountain more than the college. As an undergraduate, Washington Gladden had written "The Mountain" for the alma-mater song.

1898—Professor Bascom: "One is lost in admiration where one has the whole side of Greylock clothed in forest directly before him."

Francis W. Rockwell on the first commission: "A passion for high mountains involves fine things for their own sake."

1944—Sinclair Lewis, looking on Greylock's October gold from the Taconic Trail: "If this beauty were in Europe, it would be known all over the world in song and story, in poetry and legend; here like true Americans we let it go to waste."

Development without despoilment could cure that.

At Long Last Onota

Pittsfield at long last is beginning to realize the many beauties and values of Onota Lake for the public. We say "at long last" because it has been 231 years since surveyors laying out the original six-square-mile plat of the town added a sixty-rod strip westward "to compensate for the waste ponds comprised in the township." No one then had the foresight to see that water would be as valuable as land. From the start, water and water rights belonged to the abutter.

In 1754, when choosing a site for a blockhouse "for ye protection of Stockbridge," Col. Israel Williams recommended a hill on the southwest shore of "Ashley's Pond," as Onota was then called after David Ashley, who had lived there since 1749.

A 1759 plat of the township employs the name West Pond, which seems to have been used commonly until at least 1800. The deep, spring-fed lake was then two ponds divided by the long, narrow, east-west moraine which still shows well at low water. The larger, south part of 486 acres was one and three-quarters miles long and three quarters of a mile wide; the north part was a thirty-four-acre beaver pond impounded by a giant dam across Onota Brook, which the industrious creatures enlarged year after year.

In 1752, one of Col. Jacob Wendell's proprietary lots of 1,275 acres contained the whole of Onota Lake. He probably considered it a lovely loss, but all the farmers who shared in the subdivision must have counted the pure water, crystal ice, and plentiful fish as sheer gain. Before and after 1800, two iron forges were using the water power: Aaron Hicocks's just below the beaver dam, and John U. Seymour's further downstream.

In 1844 Elijah Peck and William Barnard purchased the water-privilege formerly occupied by Seymour's forge and erected a batting mill. This was continued by Jabez Peck, who manufactured balmoral skirts during the Civil War. In 1864, at the upper forge site, he enlarged the dam, flooding out the beavers and unifying the lake into 617 shimmering acres.

For years, the upper mill turned out flannel; the lower mill, cotton. In 1890 the J. L. and T. D. Peck Manufacturing Co. added cotton warps, cassimeres, and thread. And in that same year a town meeting, using a park fund bequeathed by Abraham Burbank, appropriated the first public land on the shores of Onota. In 1910 the Berkshire Woolen & Worsted Co. improved the upper mill and dam with expenditure of $150,000, and five years later, 450 employees were turning out fancy cassimeres and World War I cloth.

By the next World War, the Berkshire Woolen Co. was rolling out millions of yards of cloth for military uniforms, coats and blankets. Men's fabrics carried the name "Berkshire" and the women's wear, "Cerey," an acrostic of the last letters of fabric, style, color, vogue and quality.

After two drought years, waters from Onota in 1909 were first pumped into city mains. In 1945 this auxiliary source was pumped steadily for nine months, and it has been much used since.

Great Pond legislation in 1923 opened to the people the boating and fishing that they were enjoying anyway, even before Burbank Park.

After its eras of aborigine and Ashley, of iron and ice, of farm and fishing, of cassimere and cottager, of water supply and water skier, Onota seems about to realize its full potential as park for the people.

In 1963 some shore acres of land at the west end of the causeway were acquired by the Conservation Commission, which has lately been promised 100-foot easements for hiking and fishing all the way from Burbank Park to the south shore. Just last week the City Council appropriated funds to purchase the dam and water rights, which really meant some 480 acres of mud that will be flooded by repairing the dam.

This necessary accomplishment of buying land and getting water, years ago had a strange parallel at Pontoosuc Lake, which was long known as "Joe Keiler's Farm." A clever Yankee of that name deeded it to a gullible New Yorker who mistook it, when covered with ice and snow, for very scenic and desirable meadow. But that was when ponds were "waste."

Now the precious, oval, green common in Park Square is a souvenir of the cleared land that was once so valuable. And the sparkling blue "waste" of Onota, reflecting the purple hills, at long last becomes the jewel of the day.

Our One Carolinian Swamp

This week we learn that a pumped-storage hydroelectric installation is economically feasible in a south Berkshire location. Economically feasible, mind you—not necessarily environmentally desirable. Practical for the populous areas that need extra-peaking power—not necessarily sensible for rural Berkshire.

Crying for the wilderness that will be necessary for future souls, we would like to point out to the Federal Power Commission, which is more interested in electrical gadgets, that such a project (to which there are many alternatives) would mean the destruction of Berkshire's only Carolinian swamp. This portion of the Housatonic watershed is ecologically just as unique in a southerly way as the summit of Greylock is in being our sole Hudsonian Zone, therefore just as worthy to be saved from power projects as the latter from tramways.

For something like $200 million men can now transform Schenob Brook Swamp into electrical energy. How mighty that makes man seem until we consider that for 100 times that amount he could not recreate the Carolinian swamp community that is already there. Only nature accomplished that, working through eons of time with the powerful forces of glaciation, erosion, and evolution. By comparison, engineers are meddling midgets.

Over the years, many naturalists have realized this swamp's unique quality, which is demonstrated prominently in both floral and fauna. The first Massachusetts state ornithologist, Edward Howe Forbush, in his work published in 1927 by the Commonwealth, deemed the area of sufficient import to show the odd Carolinian intrusion on his map of New England life zones. He made clear that Massachusetts is almost entirely Alleghanian with some Canadian Zone at higher elevations. To find Carolinian traces similar to those of Schenob Brook Swamp, one had to travel directly south or proceed east into the tobacco country of the Connecticut Valley or go all the way to the Bay coast and Cape Cod.

A century before that, in the first (1829) history of the county, the Rev. David D. Field saw fit to include Prof. Chester Dewey's list of nearly 800 Berkshire plants, many of them unique to Sheffield, the scientist's native town. One of the plants, the southern cat brier, was not found again until discovered in Schenob Brook Swamp ninety years later by Mr. F. Walters, who added many new plants from that region, not previously known to the county.

From thirty years of collecting experience, Ralph Hoffmann, in his *Flora of Berkshire County*, published by the Boston Society of Natural History, listed forty-two species of plants indigenous to Berkshire that do not grow further northward, twenty-eight that do not extend southward into Connecticut, and fifty-six ranging westward that have never been found east of the Connecticut River. Of these 126 trees, shrubs, ferns, grasses, and flowers that reach their limit in Berkshire County, all but a few mountaintop species can be found in the 6,000 acres of Schenob Brook Swamp, *and many of them only there*, in company with most of Hoffmann's total 1,656 species for the entire county.

If a major part of that swamp is to be wiped out by electric power interests, there is one consolation: Because of Ralph Hoffmann's indefatigable efforts, Berkshire posterity can travel to Cambridge to study in the herbarium of the New England Botanical Society the pressed and faded forms of rare plants that now flourish in our only Carolinian swamp.

The same rich documentation over the years can be provided on the unusual buds of the swamp. Obviously, we are talking about far more than checklist trophies and Berkshire records.

Rather it is a matter of a choice, fragile, irreplaceable ecology and all its human impacts.

Walter Prichard Eaton, a predecessor in this column and a Yale professor who chose to live his last forty years on the margin of this marsh that he called "the great swamp," writing a preface fifty years ago for his book *In Berkshire Fields*, penned what this week seems clairvoyant: "One who is not a scientist does not deliberately toy with a 40,000-volt high-potential current. But you or I may, I trust, explore for the *Cypripedium spectabile* in its swamp, or track a weasel over its snowy rocks in a spirit of pure adventure, in the quest, let us say, for the essential flavor of the wilderness."

This January and this June those quests in that same swamp may be possible for very nearly the last time. From his Carolinian Zone outpost, facing the ozone of up to two million kilowatts of power, Walter Eaton today might have stepped up his own voltage and agreed, with Loren Eiseley, who, in his latest book, *The Invisible Pyramid*, says: "If inventions of power outrun understanding, as they now threaten to do, man may well sink into a night more abysmal than any he has yet experienced."

Schenob Birds and Birders

Since altitude affects climate as much as latitude, elevation becomes an important influence upon wildlife. In fact, topographical contour lines become, to a considerable degree, control limits for flora and fauna.

This is dramatically illustrated by comparing the two Berkshire extremes: the summit of Greylock at 3,491 feet and the Housatonic bottomland and Schenob Brook Swamp in Sheffield at elevations from 648 to 700 feet. The almost 3,000-foot differential puts Canadian and Carolinian Zones only forty miles apart, a singularity within the state and a fact that has intrigued and attracted many naturalists over the years.

William Brewster, the eminent ornithologist, was one of these. Bringing his tin bathtub with him, he often stayed with Daniel Chester French at Chesterwood, whence he made study tours to Greylock and the Sheffield swamps.

For thirty-nine years before the turn of the century, Hoffmann and Faxon were cataloguing the same extremities. They listed 197 birds, but noted: "The absence of swamps has a marked effect on the bird population of Berkshire." Recognizing then the richness of Schenob Brook Swamp and environs, they wrote, "The flora has a more southerly aspect. There is a strong admixture of so-called Carolinian birds which are common from southern Connecticut southward, but rarely found north of that region. The Louisiana waterthrush and orchard oriole are two Carolinian birds present in small numbers. The hooded warbler should be looked for." Twice they found white-eyed vireos resident, and among other observations: long-eared owl—not very rare; yellow-breasted chat—not rare, summer resident; grasshopper sparrow—a good many; Henslow's sparrow—considerable numbers; Lincoln's sparrow—fairly common in autumn.

Now most of these birds are scarcely to be found anywhere in the county unless in or near Schenob Brook Swamp. How long since anyone has seen a screech owl? In 1919 Walter Eaton told in a book of counting twoscore screech owls hunting mice among corn shocks beside the swamp: "It was strangely unreal, almost as if you stood with Dante on a brink where the lost souls fluttered past." Forbush in his *Birds of Massachusetts* showed that the rarer short-eared owls also hunted that swamp.

Many other naturalists, professional and professorial, have found it worthwhile to visit Schenob Brook Swamp; to name twenty: Brewster, Hoffmann, Faxon, Eaton, Griscom, Eliot, Bagg, Snyder, Wallace, Hagar, Bailey, Hendricks, Sanborn, Parker, Bowen, Kleber, Borland, Conant, Storer, and Peterson. The last-named world-renowned authority traveled back roads in the swamp area sketching wildflowers for his popular field guide. Ten of the others have traveled repeatedly from the eastern part of the state, just to observe the birds, some for twenty-five years and more.

Published sources, records of these men, of Hoffmann Bird Club members and other observers show the following fifty species have been seen in the swamp region, in addition to some 190 more usual kinds.

Carolinian birds (most having nested): turkey vulture; bobwhite; king, clapper, Virginia and sora rails; Florida gallinule; redheaded woodpecker: rough-winged swallow; tufted titmouse; Carolina, long-billed and short-billed marsh wrens; mockingbird; blue-gray gnatcatcher; white-eyed vireo; prothonotary, worm-eating, goldenwinged, Brewster's, Lawrence's and hooded warblers; Louisiana waterthrush; yellow-breasted chat; orchard oriole, grasshopper and Henslow's sparrows.

More northern birds (those starred included for having nested): great blue heron*; merganser; goshawk; rough-legged hawk; golden eagle; marsh hawk*; duck hawk; Wilson's snipe; screech, snowy, long-eared, and short-eared owls; Canada jay; red-breasted nuthatch*; brown creeper*; hermit thrush*; northern shrike; Philadelphia vireo; pine and Canada* warblers; vesper*; white-throated* and Lincoln's sparrows.

These birds bear witness to the exceptional ecology of Schenob Brook Swamp, which is far from saying the swamp is for the birds. The area, even if never actually preserved for the public, already constitutes a priceless public sanctuary, because it is surrounded by delightful public roads: Undermountain, Bow Wow, Barnum, Scoville, and Beaverdam. Furthermore, it is transfixed north and south by lovely Giberson and Foley roads, and crossed by scenic Curtiss, Berkshire School, Salisbury, Kelsey, Ravinehurst, and Hammertown roads. Driving, biking, or, better yet, walking these byways, the public already has access to this unspoiled 6,000-acre lowland wilderness.

Plainly these values do not suggest just the simple question: Do we want blue-gray gnatcatchers or electric backscratchers? We can have both. When electricity can be generated in less-visited places, in less-valuable environment, and in less-wasteful ways, does it make sense to squander our one Carolinian swamp that has been recognized for a century by the most competent naturalists as singular in Western Massachusetts?

A Secret Swamp

Out of the haze of twenty-five years ago shines a sunny June day when we happened in to see Walter Prichard Eaton, a predecessor in this column. He was the proud squire of Twin Fires, the old brick farmhouse that appears to have rolled off the side of Mount Everett. He took pride in what flat land and pasture the beetling mountain left him, and even farmed it a little. His cow had provided the cold milk on the kitchen table where we sat. The sweet scent of new hay drifted in at the window.

He was spreading six or eight manuscript pages of Thoreau's *Journal* on the unfinished wooden table before us. The somewhat yellowed pages in a hand difficult to read were plainly cherished possessions. We read through the original sentences of America's best nature painter in words, sentences written a hundred years before, yet still as fresh as new hay. The old pages drove us outdoors to see June for ourselves.

Prompted by the rarity of the June day, the green power of the pages, or the fraternity of common interests, at length Mr. Eaton allowed, in an air of confidence, that he had a certain swamp we might visit to see the showy lady's slipper. The swamp was some ten miles distant. But it was true he had it, since none got into it without his guidance.

We were soon lurching over dirt roads to the mysterious destination; nor did he blindfold me, and the reasons soon became apparent. They were mud and mosquitoes. His pipe maintained some control over the latter, and we immediately abandoned ourselves to the former, often plunging in up to our knees. But the dark water and muck were refreshingly cool. By the sun he piloted as straight a line to the heart of the bog as treacherous tussocks would permit. It was a shaded swamp with sunlight filtering through small ash, red maple, basswood, and ironwood. Presently we found ourselves waist deep in the water-loving royal fern (*Osmunda regalis*). The sensitive fern had grown gigantic from the rich muck. It appeared we had reached the inner sanctum.

And here the swamp queen held court. In any direction could be seen the lovely white lady's slippers with their splash of wine-red at the lip. The rare orchid was no rarity here; we must have seen a scattered two hundred: *Cypripedium reginae*, or *spectabile* of Gray, who with scientific precision called it the most beautiful of the genus. Many have called it the most beautiful wild flower of all.

Between pipe puffs Mr. Eaton told of another such swamp that had been ruined overnight by a lumbering operation. He felt this flower was especially sensitive to conditions of sunlight and shadow, and that even this host of plants might be extinguished by the increasing shade of the natural growth overhead.

A recent trip seems to confirm his speculation. Led by memory and the song of a swamp sparrow, we investigated the marsh for the first time since the original visit. No sooner had we gotten feet wet in the oozy edges and sedges than we spotted a pair of showy lady's-slippers in an open swale of wet grass. Like two white-bonneted Dutch maids, they stood out in full sunlight to be admired. They were only a foot tall, indicating they had strayed beyond optimum conditions. Some of those of yesteryear had been close to three feet, being our largest orchid.

We followed a deer run into the trees of the deeper swamp. The shade was dense, the trees bigger than we remembered. Blue flag and fall meadow rue were in blossom. There was a full acre of lush, broad skunk cabbage leaves affording background for the delicate fern fronds, rue, and horsetail. After much circling through the swamp, we discovered only a few clumps of osmunda fern and a dozen showy lady's slippers, all beyond blossom stage. They were clearly being shaded out. We returned by the two Dutch maids who were evidently fleeing swamp and shadow for their very lives.

So it appeared that the refuge of a swamp, perhaps not visited for twenty-five years, was only temporary sanctuary for this rare and beautiful flower. But its own mobility could save it.

Earth-Song

W ashed by April showers and the melt of winter snows, ancient arrowheads now lie revealed in Berkshire fields. White quartz, black flint, sparkling argillite, red jasper, they are cradled in the lap of earth as once in the skillful hand of their maker. Bathed by spring sunshine, their cleansed shapes repose in the earth whence they came, like so many Amerind hearts.

About the edges of the same fields, in fencerows, along roadsides, gleam the coarser artifacts of the newcomers: their pop bottles, beer cans, hubcaps, paper trash, and plastic litter. During the spring ritual of Earth Week a few crusaders make some overtures toward earth, then the super-sophisticated civilization slumps back into its old ways of polluting, dumping, slashing, stripping, blasting, bulldozing, paving, smudging, damming, silting, billboarding, wiring, overcropping, overgrazing, overcrowding, deafening, poisoning, and exterminating.

Is it not time for the makers of the atomic bomb to heed the makers of the arrowhead?

Too long the original American was falsely regarded as either a soulless savage or as a simple child of nature. He had no written language; he had no boundaries; he had no luxuries. In fact, about all he had, before he was corrupted by civilization, was a way of life in harmony with nature that had worked for 10,000 years.

His profound spiritual legacy, evolved through the ages, has been neglected, or misunderstood, by the newcomers because it was never engraved in tablets nor printed on any page. It was simply lived.

Almost universally, the various tribes believed in body, soul, and spirit; or gross, subtle, and pure. This made man intermediary between earth and sky, a synthesis of both. What need had he for cathedrals, temples, and shrines who lived all his days within the greatest temple of all?

Nor was this a naive pantheism. In the words of an aged Dakota Sioux, Black Elk: "We regard all created beings as sacred and important, for everything has a *wochangi*, or influence, which can be given to us, through which we may gain a little more understanding if we are attentive. We should understand well that all things are the works of the Great Spirit. We should know that He is within all things: the trees, the grasses, the rivers, the mountains, and all the four-legged animals, and the winged peoples; and even more important, we should understand that He is also above all these things and peoples."

An old Omaha has said: "When I was a youth the country was very beautiful. Along the rivers were belts of timberland, cottonwood, maple, elm, ash, hickory, and walnut trees, and many shrubs. Under these grew many good herbs and beautiful flowering plants. In both the woodland and the prairies I could see the trails of many kinds of animals and could hear the cheerful songs of many kinds of birds. When I walked abroad I could see many forms of life, beautiful living creatures, which *Wakanda* had placed here, walking, flying, leaping,

running, playing all about. But now the face of all the land is changed
and sad. The living creatures are gone. I see the land desolate, and I
suffer an unspeakable sadness."

In the words of these old Indian sachems, one senses something far
more troubling than sadness. It is the failure of the *nouveaux riches* to
realize the difference between stewardship and ownership; between reverence for the land and exploitation of it; between values and profits.

Our wisest sages, like the Indian sachems, have always seen that difference. It was what Emerson was thinking about 125 years ago when
he wrote "Hamatreya" and "Earth-Song," which could as well have
been written for Earth Week:

Bulkeley, Hunt, Willard,
Hosmer, Meriam, Flint
Possessed the land which
rendered to their toil
Hay, corn, roots, hemp, flax,
apples, wool and wood.
Each of these landlords
walked amidst his farm,
Saying: 'Tis mine, my
children's and my name's.

Where are these men?
Asleep beneath their grounds:
And strangers, fond as they,
their furrows plough.
Earth laughs in flowers,
to see her boastful boys
Earth-proud, proud of
the earth which is not theirs.

Earth Week—as we look across our abused land, befouled waters,
and laden airs, we are beginning to understand that the Indian had
more to teach us than we him. Nor is it necessary to return to primi-
tivism to practice stewardship and earth love.

Farewell, Wilderness

In the remote hills along the south border of Berkshire County, miles from the nearest house, lies a black spruce swamp, one of the few outposts of Hudsonian tundra south of the Vermont line. It is an acid peat bog formed by some fifteen millennia of leaf-fall since the last surly glacier withdrew. Up to now, the greatest change in that wild Eden has been the quiet accumulation of an additional inch of peat each 100 years.

Till now, this natural sanctuary, protected by bastions of laurel and tangles of scrub oak, has scarcely known the tread of man. For a century, botanists have made their occasional pilgrimages there for a first glimpse of some rarity like the dwarf mistletoe, the white-fringed orchid, or the fragrant white azalea.

Within resisting thickets of mountain holly, some have encountered their first creeping snowberry, white pearls upon velvet cushions of green moss. Near the quaking pond-edge where teeters the solitary sandpiper, under the Labrador-tea bushes, others have photographed insect tragedies within the maws of carnivorous pitcher plants.

In August, blueberry pickers in the know wend thither to harvest clusters by the handfuls from bushes so tall and sturdy that one climbs up into them to pick. In autumn, a few duck hunters creep through dim spruce aisles to the margin of the half-mile pond where, crouched in Andromeda and Cassandra, they may bring down a ringneck, shoveler or some other species they have seldom seen. In winter, the snowy sanctum knew only the crisscrossing of animal tracks sometimes overlaid by the snowshoe imprint of a venturesome wildcat hunter.

So has it been: silent, timeless, changeless, a place apart, always peaceful and quiet through all the vicissitudes of man, from stone-age savage through woodland Indian to civilized 1972.

But no longer. The snowmobiles have found it out. The narrow path winding through the laurel is a crushed and matted wrack and ruin of dead and broken branches, straighter and wider, as if a bulldozer had driven through. The inviolate surface of the pond where once otter and snowshoe rabbit cavorted is transformed into an oval racetrack by a helmeted pack of Martians that appears mysteriously on weekends, numbering up to a dozen at a time.

The desultory tapping of the pileated woodpecker among the tall spruce poles has given way to an angry and spasmodic snarl that reverberates through woodlands and hills formerly enjoyed by hikers on the Appalachian Trail, snowshoers, and cross-country skiers.

This is but one and an isolated instance of a new breed of Americans that is rapidly changing our environment in its misguided pursuit of sedentary recreation. Off-road recreational vehicles (ORVs) have reached four million in ten years with six million more expected in the next five years. They presently include 2.5 million motorized trail bikes, 1.4 million snowmobiles, 200,000 dune buggies, 50,000 all-terrain vehicles, and a new mushrooming of hovercraft. In other words, we are arming to damage all types of environment.

Lest the cited numbers of riders and drivers equipped for mechanized mayhem (much of it innocent but no less damaging) believe that their might makes right, let it be remembered that they constitute a mere 2% of the 200 million that they can annoy in one way or another.

Before public and private wilderness are hopelessly overrun, eroded, violated with racket, and otherwise denatured, is it not time to initiate and enforce strong controls over those who run rampant beyond the bounds of their own property? Not just regulations and restrictions, but prohibitions from entire districts. Is it not as logical to zone ORVs from the woods as cows and roosters from residential suburbs?

It would probably be considered discriminatory, un-American, and illegal for a Berkshire township to ban snowmobiles as Norway has done, even if it could be sledded through a town meeting. We would also need an entire revamping of property laws to shift the burden of trespass to the trespasser and away from landowners, who should not really be obliged to post their land in the country against anything, any more than their town brethren.

Under present law and increasing population pressures, the ORV problem can only get worse. If you know a wild nook like the black-spruce swamp, take a last look so you can tell your grandchildren how it was when men walked; and grieve for a nation that more and more substitutes the pursuit of luxuries for the pursuit of happiness.

What Price Wild Plants?

Somewhere Oscar Wilde wrote of a character who knew the price of everything and the value of noth-ing. Sometimes it seems the American twig has inclined that way too far in its competitive pursuit of commercialism.

Even the sacrosanct kingdom of ferns and wild flowers has been debased to coinage of the realm. How does one put a price upon the rare Hartford fern or the showy lady's-slipper plants, which few have seen growing in their natural haunts? Beside these, emeralds and rubies are commonplace.

Yet in wild-flower catalogs like that of the Putney Nursery in Ver-mont, and at various wildflower gardens in New England, these and other rare species are for sale, Hartford ferns at $2 and three kinds of lady's slipper, including the showy, at $1.25 per plant.

Although born in Hartford and long familiar with its disappearing woods and fields, this columnist never found the twining, palmate-leaved Hartford fern, because it had been picked so recklessly for deco-rative use in the previous century that it was virtually exterminated. In 1869, the Connecticut legislature passed what may have been the first wild-plant protective law in the country in an effort to save this fern so prized for its beauty.

The author of an 1899 field guide How To Know the Ferns remem-bered from childhood how her New York home was "abundantly decorated with the pressed fronds which had been brought from Hartford for the purpose." Aretas Saunders, the late naturalist of Canaan, Connecticut, knew this rare fern only from the pine-barrens of New Jersey, where some natural stands still flourish today.

The only place this columnist has seen it growing is at the Norcross Wildlife Sanctuary in Monson, where it was planted after removal from a proposed highway route in New Jersey.

In the Putney nursery catalog, the handsome, rare, Goldie's fern, tallest of the evergreen woodferns, may be had for a two-dollar bill, if you can find one, but "only one to a customer." How much more satisfying to come upon its four-foot-high and foot-wide fronds in the golden twilight of a deep Berkshire woodland!

These remarks are not to deprecate the value of nurseries and wildflower gardens in their important function of perpetuating and increasing vanishing wild plants. Rather they are to emphasize what landscape architect H. Lincoln Foster of Falls Village, Connecticut, has pointed out: namely, that "certain wild plants are rare because they do not multiply quickly in nature and therefore every effort should be made to conserve them in those places that furnish the kind of special conditions they require; it means also that these conditions are difficult to produce in most gardens."

Nor are these thoughts intended to discourage amateur wildflower gardening, which can be thoroughly enjoyable and educational. Most common plants move readily, and many multiply. Some of the most robust wildflowers we have ever seen have been in amateur gardens where natural competition was reduced.

What we do mean to stress is that rarities are best left in the nooks that they have selected. This does not necessarily mean that they are forbidden to the proper wild-flower garden. Indeed, you might help save a few species by removing them from the path of a planned highway development or landfill project. Permission can usually be obtained from the owner or superintendent.

We see many lists of extinct and endangered species in the animal kingdom, but almost none in regard to threatened plants. The British on their tight little island have faced up to this problem much sooner than profligate America. The Botanical Society of the British Isles has formulated the following "Code of Conduct" which is widely respected:

1. For conservation of our wild plants the first essential is to preserve the habitat, the sort of place and conditions they can grow in. This people can easily and unwittingly damage—and the more people there are, the greater the chance of damage—by, for example, compacting the soil and so preventing seedling establishment, treading on young shoots unawares, or damaging cliff surfaces.

2. When going to see a rare plant, avoid doing anything which would expose it to unwelcome attention, such as making an obvious path to it or trampling on the vegetation around it.

3. "Gardening" before taking photographs may also have this effect. Bear in mind, too, how readily nearby plants can be crushed by the toes of kneeling photographers.

4. Remember that photographs themselves can give clues to the localities of rare plants, quite apart from the information accompanying them.

5. Avoid telling people about the site of a plant you believe to be rare. Your local nature conservation trust should, however, be informed, to help safeguard it.

6. Respect requests from conservation bodies or land owners not to visit particular sites at certain times.

7. The uprooting of wild plants is to be strongly discouraged, except, with discrimination, weeds. Most local authorities have bylaws against this, so it may well be illegal.

8. If living plants are needed for cultivation, take seed or cuttings sparingly, and not from those that are rare.

9. Pick only flowers known to be common or plentiful in the locality, but whenever you can, leave them for others to enjoy. If you wish to identify a plant, take the smallest adequate bit; often a photograph may serve the purpose.

10. No specimens should be taken from any nature reserve or trail, National Trust property, or a designated Site of Special Scientific Interest.

11. In particular, teachers, organizers of wild-flower competitions, and leaders of outings and field meetings should bear these points in mind.

River Report I

Whe mountaineers descend to the river bottoms, it is not with any high expectations. It might be called condescending, for they are accustomed to clear, clean springs that supply water even in mid-summer. We know one New Yorker who visits one of these fern-draped springs like Ponce de León, to take some jugs back to the city with him. The mountain brooks, like the springs, run clear and sparkling over polished quartz and granite pebbles and between boulders of porphyry as gayly speckled as the small trout darting under them. The lofty fields are never flooded, but are continually brushed and cleansed by low clouds sweeping the mountain.

Accordingly, when two of us set out by canoe during the first week in August for a two-day junket from Pittsfield to Sheffield, it was not with the poetic thoughts of observers 100 years before. Had not Holmes called the Housatonic the best of all tonic? In a prose paroxysm he found it a "dark stream but clear, like lucid orbs that shine between the lids of auburn-haired, sherry-wine-eyed demi-blondes. ..." Longfellow called his favorite oxbow at Stockbridge "this silver Dian's bow of the Housatonic." Fanny Kemble thought it so pure that "it should be used only for baptism."

We did not find it thus as we launched our canoe at the bridge on Holmes Road. A fall on the greasy bank was our baptism. We shoved off into the miasmal morning mists as though down the river Styx. The three headwaters of the Housatonic had picked up their complement of civilization; the water was a dirty gray-brown, slithering between slimy banks strewn with assorted rubbish. We were aware of the 6-million-dollar Dalton-Pittsfield sewage disposal program now underway and the Crane & Co. and Byron Weston Co. industrial waste disposal plan 40 percent completed. The trip could be more pleasant in the future; we wished to see the before and after.

As the sun broke through over Canoe Meadows, the former Holmes property where Indian hunting parties once pulled out their birchbarks, it revealed an iridescent oil shimmer on the water. In many places the banks were graced by extensive beds of ostrich fern; great ten-foot plumes hung over into the river looking lush and tropical.

But the tips were oil-blackened. Indeed, any vegetation at water level was coated with oil. The oil slick, sewage, and waste obviously repelled all wildlife in the river all the way down to Woods Pond at Lenox Station. There were no water insects, no mosquitoes, no deer-flies. If suckers and carp were present, they could not be seen in the discolored water. There were no animal tracks on the fouled banks. Even birds seemed to shun the river.

The first frogs appeared on new fill supporting the experimental high-tension line of the General Electric Co. The gravel was still fairly clean, and the amphibians could live in the backwaters, if not in mid-stream. We paddled along several miles under the highest transmitted voltage on earth; the six heavy wires snapped and crackled while our paddles splashed.

The confining banks lowered here, and cattail marshes began to appear, wood ducks and blacks flew up, two or three at a time. The river was trying to cleanse itself. There were no houses dumping over the banks as yet. The water-loving buttonbush was a mass of white blossom; showy steeples of firewood were reflected in long patches at the river's brink. The water began to clear enough to reveal a few large goldfish whose progenitors had probably escaped down some-one's drain. But the clearing did not fool us; this was only a settling-out stretch of the river a few miles below the Pittsfield sewage beds.

October Mountain clad in sunny greenery rose above us on the east; some large hawks wheeled lazily over it. Lagoons covered with lily pads led invitingly to the west, teeming with prodigious perch, pickerel, and bass that some caught but none dared to eat. A rickety bridge, pieced of drift scraps, spanned one inlet with a sign saying: "Food, Guests, Pool," nailed on for bracing, reminding us that at least the canoeist escapes advertising.

We slid quietly through watery islands of white arrowhead blossoms and blue pickerel weed into the long expanse of Woods Pond, created by the first dam of the Smith Paper Co. This was portage number one of ten major dams to be bypassed, plus "carries" around the skeleton of an old timber dam, a washed-out cement dam, and 100 yards of tree jam in Sheffield. We learned to damn all dams. Most had mills completely blocking one bank and nettles, poison ivy, thick brush, and steep slippery banks blocking the other.

Finally, somehow, the canoe was on the shoulder of this first dam, and off of ours. We could look back toward Woods Pond and up the valley past October Mountain. It was five-and-a-half crow-flight miles and eleven meandering canoe miles back to the starting point. It was probably the easiest canoeing of the trip, being free of rocks, shallows, snags, and fallen trees. Few houses could be seen from the stream, so it might have been the wildest part of the trip —except that there was little wildlife. With the ostrich fern, the overhanging trees, and mountain vistas, it might have been the most beautiful part of the trip—but that was 100 years ago.

River Report II

Within the county the Housatonic, like Gaul, is divided in *partes tres*. The part above Lenox Station and the part below the Great Barrington dam are easily navigable. A canvas-covered canoe can safely run the few riffles at low water by following the smooth vees that point between rocks or snags.

Not so the middle section between Lenox and Great Barrington, which measures eleven-and-a-half crow-flight miles and twenty-five canoe miles. At low water a canvas canoe would be useless and an aluminum one would be badly dented, if not ripped open. We used an old canoe purchased for $12, re-covered with two layers of fiberglass cloth, well painted with plastic filler. Being keelless, this presented a smooth bottom as hard as bone and practically indestructible. It slid and bounced easily over and off countless boulders, shallows, and snags without cracking a single rib.

The river traveler is in for surprises at every bend. He has taken to an abandoned highway at the world's back door. The paddle pace is conducive to observation and reflection. There are constant reminders that the watery artery was once the heart of the county's traffic and industry. We glided smoothly over one large millstone showing like a moon in the dark waters. We saw a potbellied stove and a buggy chassis with wheels half out of the water. Antique collectors might help clean up the river.

Below the first portage opposite a derelict paper mill, we were surprised by the Lenox frog crouched in a patch of boneset; this is a giant, shapely boulder painted green and yellow with saucer-like eyes forever regarding the river. Passengers on the New Haven Railroad were once amused by this local wonder that now sees only one freight a day or tracks that may soon be as rusty as the river.

When we brushed with civilization at some bridge or mill, we were reminded of our archaic mode of travel, usually by Indian war whoops. One woman, through whose yard we portaged, had seen but one other canoe pass by in years. Another startled individual, trying to rationalize, asked if we were surveyors. Lewis and Clark perhaps!

We were brought up to date rather suddenly below Lenox Dale by some fast water that spun the canoe sidewise against a rock having a stranded pole and a six-by-six timber astraddle to catch us under the arms. The canoe tipped toward the current and rapidly swamped. We improved these circumstances by dumping the canoe and crawling out on the rock to eat soggy sandwiches. The river was clean for a mile or two here, from the filtering effect of Woods Pond. We glided on, led by sandpipers, kingfishers, occasional ducks and herons, all indicators of clean banks and clear water. The sun began to dry us.

Then a thundershower blew up, and the Lee sewage corrupted the river. Gaunt skeletons killed by Dutch elm disease loomed along the banks clad to the waist in poison ivy. The twisted torso of a windowless car stared over the waters like a skull. We sought shelter from the downpour under a railroad bridge but were forced to shove our bow into the bank sewage for the better protection of a silver maple.

The rain lessened, and we resumed our watery way to where the Massachusetts Turnpike crossed our shunpike at Lee. A steady stream of traffic roared over the high cement bridge, under which was a weird symbol: a spindle-backed chair firmly planted midstream, lacking only the policeman to direct an occasional canoe around the westward swing to Stockbridge.

Early next morning we were on our way through the lovely Stockbridge oxbows where Longfellow owned property but built only castles in the air. A sleepy owl flushed from a tree over the river and was soon the center of a mob of angry crows. The river again was trying to clean itself here. Washed gravel bars showed in the lazy meanders, but unfortunately some estates dumped refuse over the banks, and any tree reaching out into the current collected a floating mess of cans, bottles, and modern tinsel. It appeared that cleaning up the river was everyone's affair, not just a problem for the cities and mills. Below the old mill dam at Glendale we slid the canoe down a long incline through banks of maidenhair fern into a portion of the river more stone than water. It was necessary in this dry summer to rope the canoe nearly a mile through these rocks while we slipped and waded after it, startling trout. There was sporty canoeing from where Monument Mountain crowded the river to where we shot into the quiet pond at Housatonic.

Below the Rising Paper Co. dam once more the river wound gently through meadow and pasture to the final dam in Great Barrington. The ten dams with their settling ponds and the aerating rapids of this rambunctious section of the river obviously had a cleansing effect on the waters, giving us high hopes for the final run to the Connecticut line.

River Report III

In August of 1676, Major John Talcott was the first English man to see the "Ausotunnoog River" within Berkshire County. In an aftermath of King Philip's War, he pursued 200 Indian fugitives from the Connecticut Valley over the Indian trail to the ford at the Great Wigwam, now the approximate site of Great Barrington. The name Housatonuk, meaning "place-beyond-the mountains," was first applied to this site, then to the Indians, and finally to the entire river. Talcott's massacre of twenty-five Indians "dabbled the bushes with blood and reddened the river." White men have been staining it ever since.

Into these dark waters at the ford we launched the canoe for the final tortuous course through the Sheffield Plain to the county line below Bartholomew's Cobble, a distance of eleven-and-a-third crow-flight miles and twenty-two canoe miles. As June Mountain fell back on the east, the broader, deeper river slithered its serpentine way through the wide plain dominated by Mt. Everett on the west. One twist after another showed the truth of Thoreau's observation: "There is a male and female shore to the river, one abrupt, the other flat and meadowy—on the one hand eating into the bank, on the other depositing sediment." Large trees were often toppled into the river on the eroded side, creating a temporary impasse for us and convenient shelter for wood ducks.

Around one bend we surprised a paddling of these shy ducks in midstream. The young, not yet able to fly, skittered over the surface to the protection of a snag beside the bank, while the parent birds floundered downriver barely ahead of us, peeping anxiously, one along each shore, using wings laboriously and splashingly like broken paddle wheels. When their stratagem had led us far enough downstream, they arose effortlessly, if not derisively, and circled back through the woods.

The water cleared progressively as we rode the lazy current out onto the Sheffield Plain. The steep banks became sandy, offering easy excavating to bank swallow, kingfisher, and muskrat. The latter often slid quietly into the river ahead of us, leaving fresh diggings, caches of clamshells, or simply a favored sunning spot. Painted turtles slipped silently from logs ahead of us.

Around one bend we surprised a gaggle of two dozen Canada geese on a gravel promontory, handsome birds, yet inconspicuous with body feathering blending into the pebbly background and a camouflage pattern of black and white breaking up the head and neck forms. The canoe drifted by like a lifeless log, and the geese stalked off with stately gait into the tall grass.

The river, having learned of pollution at its origin, after a flirtation with Route 7 recoiled east below the covered bridges, avoiding Sheffield, and by twisting west skirted Ashley Falls, thereby preserving a brown clarity that must have been its color when Major Talcott first saw it.

Life in all forms was increasingly abundant. The water surface was teeming in places with a new hatch of some ephemeras. The empty sarcophagi of dragonflies clung to the sedges. Fish now and again broke the surface, beneath which could be seen green water plants. A great blue heron arose lazily from a sand bar ahead, and we measured his huge footprints with our hands that were smaller. We came upon two boys catching rock bass while their grandfather dozed on the grassy bank.

Below Bartholomew's Cobble, approximately on the state line, as if for a grace note at the end of our trip, an American egret sprang from the water's edge and lifted into the sunshine against a cumulus cloud rendered dingy by comparison. His pure white was somehow symbolic of a clean river.

Our two-day trip totaling fifty-eight canoe miles from Pittsfield to Weatogue showed the river at its worst and at its best. There was certainly a measure of hope in the fact that the down-county section seemed wild and clean in spite of man's abuse upstream. This was no passing languishing creature, but a sinuous beautiful snake ready to slough off a scarred skin with the assistance of the communities close to the bank. Here was a living entity not irreparably damaged by past misuse. In fact it seemed that one roaring spring flood would be sufficient to purge it, if all defilement could be stopped in the future.

Time for a Change

Fourteen years ago, when we began writing this "Our Berkshires" column, we were snug by a cozy chunk stove that, along with a wood-burning cook-stove, heated the entire house in Mount Washington.

Now that men have walked on the moon, we are writing this last column in a Pittsfield house with the thermostat turned down to 65 degrees (58 at night) to save oil for the next space shot or for other questionable, deferrable, or superfluous uses. Is that fourteen years of progress? Yes, if we realize the implications.

In the first instance, we were president and sole employee of an ax-and-saw corporation that was a vertical monopoly from the seedling ash in the woodlot to the final ashes in the chunk stove which, incidentally, went into the garden to grow beets which fueled the family again.

In the second instance, we are the victim of government restrictions and a vertical oil monopoly which in turn is victim of its own Arab exploitation, insufficient development at home, and price rigging. Even a little stock in that monopoly is cold comfort.

The energy crisis is the best thing that has happened to the United States since land grants ran out on the western frontier. It has shocked the country from youthful *nouveau riche* into a wiser husbandry and sager responsibility.

We needed forceful reminding that resources are limited and, consequently, so also are growth and "progress." "Spaceship Earth" can no more tolerate one nation going hog-wild in luxury than it can withstand a confrontation of nuclear bulls in a china shop.

We presently consume one-third of the world's resources and 30 percent of its energy; yet we comprise but 6 percent of its population.

Of available petroleum, we burn double our share or one-eighth of the world supply. The morphological Midas was given ass's ears; Croesus lost his Persian empire; and more recently the British Empire was dismantled for like overindulgence; now it is impoverished.

We have come to regard as necessities such absurdities and frivolities as hermetically sealed glass skyscrapers, passenger planes with empty seats, air conditioning, pleasure craft for all seasons, color TV, electric can-openers, toothbrushes and card shufflers, and all the other "as advertised" items that help some individual but cheat civilization.

What can we expect next, if not electric canes that take walks for us? We who are freest in the world to choose simplicity have instead elected complication.

On food the story is the same: Americans go whole hog. Lester Brown, U.S. Department of Agriculture expert, has pointed out that, historically, there was only one important source of growth in world demand for food; there are now two. Affluence makes people want to eat better. The very poor, eating products made directly from grain, consume at subsistence levels about 400 pounds of grain per person a year. But as incomes rise, people start to consume grain indirectly in the form of meat, milk, and eggs, which take much larger amounts of grain to produce.

Each American now eats almost a ton of grain a year, only 150 pounds of it directly in the form of breads, pastries, and breakfast cereals. In that light, the Russian wheat deal is seen to be a conspiracy of selfishness marking off the world's "haves" from the "have-nots." How stable can such a world be?

The great danger is that the energy crisis will not be long enough nor severe enough to teach us ways of moderation. All the talk is of solving the problem so as to go on as before. But remember what that "before" was. Even in this affluent land, 90 percent of the people live on 10 per cent of the land. We have not had the wit to solve that problem-causing imbalance. Do we have the wisdom to change our life style? One should have his feet on the rail of a chunk stove to ponder that.

GREEN BERKSHIRES

The author has asked that royalties from the sale of this book be donated to Green Berkshires, Inc. Based in Great Barrington, Massachusetts, its primary purpose is to protect the open spaces and wilderness character of the Taconic mountains and Berkshire hills of western Massachusetts, known collectively as "the Berkshires."

Green Berkshires, Inc.'s main focus is sponsoring research of the mountain landscape and wildlife and educating the public about the results in order to enlist broad support for protection of these disappearing resources. Recent studies have covered ridgetop dwarf pitch-pine communities, rare lichens and mosses, and old-growth forests.

Please visit our website: www.GreenBerkshires.org.

Donations may be sent to:

GREEN BERKSHIRES, INC.
P.O. BOX 342
GREAT BARRINGTON, MA 01230